Venezuelan Stick Fighting

Venezuelan Stick Fighting

The Civilizing Process in Martial Arts

Michael J. Ryan

LEXINGTON BOOKS
Lanham • Boulder • New York • London

Published by Lexington Books
An imprint of The Rowman & Littlefield Publishing Group, Inc.
4501 Forbes Boulevard, Suite 200, Lanham, Maryland 20706
www.rowman.com

Unit A, Whitacre Mews, 26-34 Stannary Street, London SE11 4AB

British Library Cataloguing in Publication Information Available

Library of Congress Cataloging-in-Publication Data

Names: Ryan, Michael J., 1960- author.
Title: Venezuelan stick fighting : the civilizing process in martial arts / by Michael J. Ryan ; foreword
    by Thomas A. Green.
Description: Lanham : Lexington Books, 2016. | Includes bibliographical references and index.
Identifiers: LCCN 2016033987 | ISBN 9781498533201 (cloth : alk. paper) | ISBN 9781498533218
    (electronic)
Subjects: LCSH: Stick fighting--Venezuela--History. | Martial arts--Venezuela--History. | Self-de-
    fense--Venezuela--History.
Classification: LCC GV1141 .R93 2016 | DDC 796.855--dc23 LC record available at https://
    lccn.loc.gov/2016033987

∞™ The paper used in this publication meets the minimum requirements of American
National Standard for Information Sciences Permanence of Paper for Printed Library
Materials, ANSI/NISO Z39.48-1992.
Printed in the United States of America

To the late José-Felipe Alvarado, Labor-organizer, freedom fighter, garrotero and his late beloved wife Clementina Alvarado.

Contents

Foreword

In *Venezuelan Stick Fighting*, Michael Ryan does not break new ground. He does, however, sow seeds whose plants yield a rich harvest. The discipline of hoplology (the ways and means of combative behavior) was announced by Sir Richard Burton in 1883 and revisited in the mid-twentieth century by Donn Draeger and his disciples, but the fields demarcated by these pioneer lay fallow for most of the twentieth century. As a general rule, martial arts remained a topic that was the domain of "popular" overviews and "how-to" manuals. Authors rarely looked beyond East Asia for their subject matter. Notable exceptions exist. Anthropologist William Lessa published a monograph on Bwang, a Micronesian fighting system, in 1978. The book went relatively unnoticed except for an article in the popular media *Black Belt* magazine. Historian Elliot Gorn's 1985 journal article on the social significance of clashes that resulted in the brutal maiming of combatants in the southern United States during the eighteenth century is another separate treatment. As an analysis of a vernacular style of fighting, Gorn's article is an obvious precursor of Ryan's book.

Until recently, similar discussions of truly vernacular martial culture—those localized traditions open to the idiosyncrasies of combative individuals and unfettered by formal bureaucracies—were relegated to passing comments such as Richard Dorson's on the folk traditions of the Upper Michigan Peninsula in which brawling lumbermen stomped the faces of fallen foes with their spiked boots in order to leave scars called "logger's pox" and ethnic Finns settled quarrels with knives. As confirmed by other studies in the emerging literature on vernacular martial arts, modes of transmission are often relatively unstructured and harsh. Mentors give up their knowledge reluctantly and even incompletely as a precaution against a student returning at a later date to defeat the teacher. Rather than styles or systems in the conventional sense, these ways of fighting are, as Ryan notes, idiosyncratic collections of successful techniques and tactics, like the "rough and tumble" described by Gorn, prison fighting styles (Jacktown, Comstock, and the like), "knockin' and kickin'" alluded to in the American South from the plantation period to the 1970s, and African-descended fifty-two hand blocks in the urban northeastern United States. Though violent, juego do palo is, like the other vernacular arts just listed, not mere physical anarchy. On the contrary, such ways of fighting are highly cultural. At the corporeal level, they incorporate motor behaviors from other movement traditions such as dance and games. Just as Ryan notes the correlation between martial versions of juego de palo and the choreographed play preserved as an element of local festival, the "Fifty-twos" is kinesiologically and historically related to breakdancing and hip-hop, and stick fighting attends Carnival in much of the Caribbean. At the technological level, while the garrote (itself a sartorial accessory and tool) is the core weapon of the juego, the attributes developed thereby provide "stepping stones" to the use of other weapons and the physiological modification of tools into weapons—as was the case with Wisconsin loggers and as continues to be the case with the adaptation of sticks, or herding tools, into weapons by pastoralists globally. Socially, juego de palo provides the means of contesting community status and obtaining justice through symbolic violence that usually stops short of mortal injury. Again, this is consistent with the general features of vernacular martial arts. For example, a characteristic diss (from "disrespect") tactic used by practitioners of the fifty-two hand blocks consists of catching an opponent's punch, kissing the fist, and throwing it back in the puncher's face. Physically, the move is useless; as a means of publicly humiliating an adversary and increasing one's own street status, it is worth its weight in gold, or more accurately worth its weight in social capital. Similarly, although the garroteros prefer more private arenas to establish hierarchy and reestablish honor, the adherence to principles, codes of behavior, and even aesthetics carries more weight than sheer physical dominance. Clearly, although localized folk systems of civilian combat do not have rules of engagement exemplified by Broughton's Rules or similar codes duello, each bears the stamp of its context not only historically and physiologically, but ethically and aesthetically.

The twenty-first century has seen a legitimization of martial studies as a discipline, the rise of international, interdisciplinary academic societies (such as International Martial Arts and Combat Sports Scientific Society) and networks (e.g., the Martial Arts Studies Research Network), journals (*Ido Movement for Culture: Journal of Martial Arts Anthropology*, the *Martial Arts Studies Journal*, *Revísta de Artes Marciáles Asiáticas*), and regular academic conferences in Italy, Poland, Portugal, and the United Kingdom designed to support martial arts scholarship. European scholars and institutions have taken a leadership role in this movement. The current volume by a North American author examining indigenous South American martial culture is a welcome addition to this dialogue.

Beyond adding to the existing literature on vernacular martial culture outside Asia, this book explores, from the perspective of the juego de palo, the dynamic that often emerges between folk arts and external entities. Nations, ethnic factions, and other larger than local associations turn to traditional forms of expressions to create rallying points internally, and externally, to develop stages on which to display politically crafted identities. In the wake of UNESCO's enfranchisement of the notion of intangible cultural heritage, the promotion of tourism comes to play as well. Folk arts, in turn, appeal to these larger entities for validation and more tangible forms of support, such as grants and performance venues. The trade-off, however, tends to be a homogenization and domestication of the public facade of the original vernacular form.

Capoeira, as it came to be offered for public consumption, can serve as an example of the compromises that develop. As the Brazilian art went through a transformation from a criminalized street system at the turn of the twentieth century to a "whitening" and upward mobility via the efforts of Mestre Bimba (Manoel dos Reis Machado, 1899–1974), from the late 1930s to the 1950s, Capoeira Regional—as Bimba's reformed version came to be called—became standardized and lost the individuality that characterizes a vernacular art. Ryan offers us cases of garroteros and their disciples at various points along a spectrum from conservative embedded cultural practice to potentially globalized commodification, thus adding to the store of knowledge of the "gentrification" of vernacular martial arts—and folk arts in general.

The volume that follows warrants a close reading as a first-rate example of the work produced by the current generation of martial arts scholars and of the preoccupations and methods of the discipline of martial arts studies as it develops in the early decades of the twenty-first century. From a more general perspective, I commend it to those readers who want a clearly focused view of the results of one encounter when modernity and nationalism encounter tradition and localization. Approached from either the particular or general, time devoted to reading Ryan's insights into the culture and practice of the Venezuelan vernacular martial art of the juego de palo will be time well spent.

Thomas A. Green
Texas A&M University
February 8, 2016

Preface

Venezuelan Stick Fighting: The Civilizing Process in Martial Arts is an ethnographic study of the practice of stick, machete, and knife fighting, or *garrote*, as it currently practiced in rural Venezuela. First and foremost, garrote has been seen and practiced as an art of self-defense originating from the needs of the rural laborers, independent farmers, and merchants of rural Venezuela. Well into the twentieth century, men regularly carried a hardwood walking stick with them when appearing in public to defend themselves against any possible attacks, while serving a powerful symbol of one's manhood and his ability to defend his property or honor against all threats. As such, the study and practice of garrote has been a semi-secretive art form not readily disclosed to outsiders, the curious, or potential opponents. Over the last seventy years, garrote has been popularly associated with a ritual performance known as the Tamunangue where, as a performance oriented mock duel, it precedes the number of other dances that make up the ritual. The array of instruments backing these performances and the diverse nature of these dances, each which purportedly have their own origins in indigenous, African, and European cultures, have been held up as an example by elites of how Venezuela has always assimilated different peoples and their cultures into a greater Venezuelan nation where race and ethnicity is irrelevant. What was once a local festival, the Tamunangue has been raised to the level of a national icon, serving as a microcosm of the Venezuelan people as a whole who, while living far apart with separate histories, are all citizens of the greater nation of Venezuela.

At the same time that a performance-oriented version of garrote was celebrated by Venezuelan nationalists and deconstructed by folklorists and anthropologists, the art of garrote as a local form of self-defense continued its shadowy, practically oriented existence in the rural towns and working-class neighborhoods of Venezuela, where it persists today. Early in the twentieth century, in what I see as a "Civilizing Process," Venezuela underwent a number of profound changes, transforming the nation from a primarily rural agricultural country fought over by competing warlords into a modern urban democracy, and then into a socialist state. Despite these profound changes, a number of character traits and values that can serve one in good stead in an often harsh and unfair world, such as determination, fortitude, and cunning, are best felt to be cultivated and instilled through a rough apprenticeship with a hardwood walking stick, a garrote. The diverse ways garroteros have organized a pedagogical ladder to hone and perfect their bodies and minds for the stress of combat and then turn around and become a caring and respected member of a community is what I call the "warrior's habitus." I find this a useful concept to explore how practioners of different combative systems over time and through space have wrestled with and tried different solutions to deal with the realities of violence facing young men. Faced with various modalities of combat ranging from the battlefield melees or raids to civilian oriented self-defense needs, ritual male hierarchical dueling contests, or recreational agonistic contests, a number of culturally specific physiological skills, affective structures, ethical guidelines, in association with material technologies, have been developed and continue to be refined today by people who face violence in their everyday life and train to meet and successfully dominate any combative encounter while instilling a sense for the sanctity of the life of their opponent and that of their community.

Chapter 1 begins with the most common venue most people continue to be exposed to garrote, the Tamunangue ritual. Here I briefly look at the ongoing contestations regarding the history, status, and representation of garrote among those who feel they have a stake in the way the Tamunangue is represented and performed. Following the claim by Tocuyano garroteros who have repeatedly told me "garrote came to the area first and was later added into the Tamunangue," I suggest garrote is best treated predominantly as a unique local manifestation of a much older Western Pan-European form of fighting with single-edged bladed weapons, which was eventually transferred to the Americas where it took on different manifestations to meet the needs of practioners as it blended with stick and blade tactics from the Canary and Azores Islands, West and Central African traditions. To this end, I survey the migration patterns of African and Europeans into Venezuela over the centuries and take note of the combative practices they brought with them to discover possible avenues for the transmission and emergence of garrote in Venezuela. Treating garrote as a modular embodied knowledge passed down at a single point in time in history within one area, as it is often treated, distorts its history. Instead, garrote should be seen as arising independently and repeatedly at different times and places in response to the way combative acts took shape in the civil sphere during the nineteenth and twentieth centuries. In the case of the Segovia Highlands where the majority of my fieldwork was done, the growth and development of garrote seems tied in with the struggles of local indigenous and mixed-blood populations to resist and or negotiate some form of coexistence with the exploitative practices of a series of conquistadores, hacenderos, caudillos, and then a centralized modern state seeking to control their land and labor. In other areas of Venezuela, indigenous, African, and African-indigenous communities developed their own forms of garrote or other combative traditions for many of the same reasons. As a result of these differences, the local histories of migration, colonization, resistance, and accommodation calls for sensitivity to the historical forces that shaped both communities and the unique developments of garrote throughout Venezuela.

Chapter 2 looks back at the historical social and political-economic developments that led Venezuela from a minor possession of the Spanish crown to one of the first Latin American countries to declare itself an independent nation. One common theme that runs through this story is that the reliance on an extractive economy subjected the nation to the unpredictable cycles of global markets alternately strengthening or destabilizing efforts to create a stable nation-state. The eventual emergence of a federalist form of governing led local politicians to gather an enormous amount of power in their hands, which they guarded jealously and used to attack other politicans holdings to augment their power. Finally, in the early twentieth century, one local warlord was able to defeat all others and impose a centralized modern state that has continued until the present. Within these historical conditions, the once widespread popularity and subsequent decline of the use of garrotes, machetes, and knives in civil combative contexts can best be explained by drawing on Norbert Elias's idea of a "Civilizing Process." Simply stated as it relates to the subject of this work, the formation of a strong central state in the early twentieth century resulted in increasingly powerful constraints against the legitimacy of self-help strategies of violence. One effect of these greater macro-forces was the curtailing and reconfiguring of the ways garrote is taught, transmitted, and enacted today.

Chapter 3 narrows its focus to examining a number of sites where garrote was taught and practiced. Looking over accounts of those who trained to prepare themselves to fight, one element that stands out is the wide variety of training sites and methods both in the past and continuing up through the present. Numerous people I interviewed stressed how garrote is only taught to relatives or close friends. Nevertheless, there is also a tradition of more formal, semi-restricted schools of garrote in the area pointing to a more diffuse and fragmented genealogy reflected in the diversity of the art today. As a student progressed in his understanding of how to hold and move the garrote, he would often be introduced to the use of other agricultural tools or weapons. In this way, the student could gain a feeling how each different type of weapon shapes the way their body should move in order to take full advantage of its inherent properties. Through handling a palo and other weapons and the way it changes the way a practioner looks at, feels about, and moves through the world that one can detect the reorganization of the habitus operates through an intimate connection with material technology.

Chapter 4 examines the social and cultural fields of everyday life among garroteros. The importance placed on managing the flow of information is a major factor in the practice and transmission of garrote that continues to shape how it is experienced through the present. Chapter 5 looks at how local forms of disciplined training is designed to reconfigure the way a student moves through and feels about the world. A training where learning how to hold and move like one's teacher acts to anchor an individual to a place, a lineage, or a local tradition. In a type of environment where men relations were governed by the idea of honor as a limited and valued commodity, the knowledge and use of the garrote plays a much diminished but important role in the creating and maintaining respect from one's peers. Chapter 6 turns to the ways students are taught to evoke the proper emotional frame and psychological intent to close-in and dominate a combative encounter. The pleasure that comes with the dispatching of an opponent can turn into an addictive pleasure known as the "dark side." The different ways that individuals have come to be desensitized to the harming of others and the ways it is attempted to reintegrate them into a community are in conjunction with the training of the rearranging of the neurophysiological apparatus to successfully dominate a combative encounter is what I call the warrior's habitus. Many garroteros take an immense pride in their art as a unique development of local communities to protect themselves from a history of assault upon the integrity of the people and their land. Part of a set of tactics to maintain the integrity of the pueblo, Chapter 7 looks at one way garrote has been reconfigured to meet the latest challenges of modernity where ideas of openness, fairness, and a level playing field are treated as the basis for modern society. Seeking to take advantage of the state's interest in supporting popular culture, one group of garroteros through the support of the state publicizes their art through demonstrations and public exhibitions at the same time they hide and distort how the art is really done or taught to maintain their control over the art. At the same time, they earn the grudging admiration of other garroteros who see how they are deceiving those seen to exploit the cultural resources of the pueblo for their own political projects. Overall, I seek to show how these social practices and tactics continue to play a strong role in the way that practioners, friends, neighbors, and the wider rural society imagines, re-creates, and reaffirms a complex of social identities, which are bound to a historical place and time occurring against wider political-economic processes.

The social context I describe has led me to examine what was and is still a wider set of trans-Atlantic practices used in close quarter combative situations, as currently practiced, imagined, and represented in Venezuela. I am interested in how these social practices are practiced, talked about, imagined, performed, and consumed by various individuals in different social settings, and the way they link up with notions of identity, agency, and gender on an individual, communal, and national level. With this in mind, this work provides a deep look into the diverse ways a local armed combative art targets the physiological abilities, affective structures, and ethical boundaries of an individual in an attempt reconfigure the way they interact with the world in order to allow them to face life's challenges successfully and with honor.

Acknowledgments

The late ex-labor organizer, ex-guerillero, and garrotero José Felipe Alvarado once told me that "garrote is never taught for money only friendship." Sharing this feeling, I was lucky enough to meet a number of men who thought I was worthy of their friendship and could be trusted to learn a little of their most treasured possession, garrote. With this in mind, I extend my most heartfelt thanks to my principal teachers Saúl Téran, Danys Burgos, William Liscano, José-Felipe Alvarado, and Wencio Barrios. Saúl, Danys, and William especially deserve my gratitude. They took me deep into the art of garrote. They accompanied me on search for garroteros to interview in both Lara and Falcón states. During interviews, they flagged key information that I missed and persuaded those interviewed to expand on their statements. Whatever value this work has and whatever level of skill in garrote I possess, I owe to these men. A debt of gratitude goes to those men who patiently would explain things and teach me a bit of their art whenever we met: Ismael Vásquez, Felipe Vásquez, Adrían Pérez, Ervil Franco, Umberto Burgos, Natividad Apostal, Silvio Alvarado, Juaquín and Andrés Yépez, Mario Echegerrai, and Manuel Rodríguez. There are three active schools in the area as of this writing. One is led by Manuel Rodríguez and Davíd González at the Museo de Barquisimeto. Eduardo Sanoja has been teaching garrote for decades in Cabudare. Pasqual Zanfino leads a children's class in the Plaza Bolivar in El Tocuyo. All four men are very welcoming, hospitable, and highly recommended to anyone seeking to learn the art of garrote. Many thanks goes to those researchers who continue to dig into the history of their national treasure and share their findings with me, Eduardo Sanoja, Argimiro González, Dr. Miguel-Angel Chavier, Hector Ramos, and Sorraya Rojas. I especially want to thank those families who made me feel the warmth and pleasure of Venezuela hospitality, the families Colmenares, Quintero, Pérez, and Morales. Back here in the states, I extend my gratitude to my martial art teachers and their arts they shared with me. Gil Kim and his Hwa Rang Do, John "Johnny Demon" Ball, George "Chicken George" Drake, and their prison-fighting moves. Louis "Crazy Louie" Yacco and his Okinawan Kara-te. Paulie Zink of the Tai Shing Pek Kwar system, the Capoeira of Reginaldo "Borracha" Santana, Leslie Buck of Mande Muda Silat and Pekiti Tersia Kali. Maha Guro Richard de Bordes of the Hanafi lineage of Harimau Silek, and Tamdan McCrory's MMA. In Genoa, I have been studying with Claudio Parodi of the Bastone Genovese, and I have begun what I hope is a long and re-warding apprenticeship with Gregorio Vuovolo of the Cavalieri d'Umilità system and the Thai art of Krabi Krabrong. A great deal of thanks goes to Drs. Tom Green, Wojciech Cynarski, Carlos Gutirrez, and everybody at the International Martial Arts and Combat Sports Science Scientific Society (IMACSS) conferences. I was always met with a warm reception of my presentations and was always thoroughly entertained and educated listening to the projects of others. I strongly recommend presenting at a conference they host. To my anonymous reader whose identity was latter disclosed, a great deal of thanks for putting in an inordinate amount of work to make this work stronger and hopefully more enjoyable to read. Amy King and Kasey Beduhn, my editors at Lexington Press. James Wong esq. James was the first to volunteer to read this work and did great job trying to edit and make sense of the mess I had sent him. We first met at Binghamton University, and he has been my long-time training partner. Over the years, we still push each other to broaden and deepen our knowledge. We have gone on to join up with the Dog Brothers stick fighting group, whose creativity, pragmatism, and humor continues to inform both my theoretical explorations and my per-sonal practice sessions as I seek, as Marc Denny says, "to walk as a warrior all my days." At Binghamton University, I owe a debt of grati-tude to Hilton Silva from the Federal University of Rio de Janiero (UFRJ), who arrived as a one-year visiting professor. Seeing the situation at the time, he offered to set up a biocultural dissertation among the caboclos of the Amazon with me. He agreed to serve on my committee, and with Ralph Garruto to chair my committee. Although our plans fell through, Ralph Garruto continued to champion my cause. He refused to give up on me no matter what obstacles arose and saw me through to my de-fense. As a biological anthropologist, he had little interest in cultural anthropology; nevertheless, I never would have finished without him. Funding for this research came from a Clark Fellowship for underrepre-sented minorities. I met Mr. Clark once at a luncheon and remember with pleasure our all too brief chat. Laurie Kolosky at the interlibrary loan department did a great job finding the works I needed. The geology secretary, Carol Slavetskas, is an absolutely amazing woman. If you ever meet her, take off your hat and bow your head. Over the last fourteen years, she has looked out for me in every way possible—from listening to me drone on and on about theoretical issues, to futilely trying to explain the politics of university and everyday life to me. But even more impor-tant, she created a place where I could call home, something I never wanted or appreciated before I met her. With our four Chihuahuas, Bos-ton Terrier, and three cats keeping me company, I had a place where I was able to think and write. I could go out in the backyard and swing a variety of weapons to clear my head, then return to the kitchen table or backyard patio table to think and write some more. Listening to old female singers such as Bessie Smith, Billie Holiday, and Aretha Franklin reminds me of the deep devotion, humor, endurance, and strength of character that women such as Carol possess, who made everything I have accomplished through today possible. My love is eternal.

Introduction

After months of being brushed off with a number of excuses or outright excluded from Sunday group practice sessions, José-Felipe Alvarado agreed to cross sticks with me. One late afternoon, sitting under a shade tree on José-Felipe's small plot of land, I asked him as I had done so many times in the last few months to give me a little lesson in garrote. The traditional stick fighting art once was practiced throughout Venezuela. To my surprise he said "¿Como no?" (*Why not?*) "Clementina bring Miguel and me a couple of sticks. Miguel, move these benches." At eighty-eight years old, José-Felipe moved much slower then he once did, but was he was still the master of timing and distance appreciation. With our palos in our hand, we began slowly, both of us respecting the opening fixed sequence of attack and counterattack that began the *Siete Lineas* style of stick-play. He nodded and grunted quietly in an acknowledgment of my understanding of this opening sequence. Smoothly, he transitioned to a free sparring session, or *juega por la vista*, with an attack to my elbow that I avoided and countered with a blow to his wrist, which he in turn eluded, by circling his arm leading to a counterattack at my ankle. Without any hesitation, I slid my leg away and around his palo and countered with an attack at the outside of his extended bicep, which led him to prematurely stop his attack and withdraw his arm. José-Felipe's wife began exclaiming "Look at Miguel! He moves so well now." José-Felipe ever so slightly turned up the heat, and as the attacks came faster, I easily avoided them and respectfully countered, feeling comfortable and at the same time a bit unsure of how easy this was going. "Look at Miguel!" Doña Clementina exclaimed, "he has learned so well," as I avoided and countered another attack. After about a minute of this, José-Felipe stopped and said, "Enough Miguel! Let's take a little break." I pulled the benches under the shade of the tamarind tree where we had been *jugando con los palos*, and we all sat down and discussed the heat and the prospect of rain. After a few minutes, José-Felipe rose from his chair and said, "Come on Miguel let's jugar one more time." Feeling good about my new found skills, I grabbed my stick and moved the benches out of the way. The action unfolded as before, with both of us moving at about half speed, and then the action began to speed up, with Doña Clementina exclaiming how well I moved. Then it happened. José-Felipe, evaded my attack to his right knee, took a big step forward and clipped my left earlobe. The suddenness of the strike and the slight pain froze my body for a split second. During this involuntary pause, José-Felipe then struck my right earlobe, then with a series of descending horizontal whipping blows struck my left elbow, right elbow, my right thumb, which paralyzed my hand, and then my stick, which went flying out of my hand. Overcoming the shock and regaining my composure after a moment, I looked down at my now numb and empty hand and said to myself "uh oh!" I looked up at José-Felipe who just stood there with a slight smirk on his face. I figured, well, I got to keep on going, so I rushed over to grab a big boulder half buried in the dirt. Struggling unsuccessfully to rip it out of the ground, José-Felipe pleaded "No Miguel, No." I said to myself, "It's over I'm dead." I stood up and José-Felipe extended his hand and said "Come on Miguel, let's sit down and talk a while." Doña Clementina remained very quiet after this exchange. Even José-Felipe's dogs Duque and Chente, my loyal friends until then, feeling embarrassed for me had found something better to do and disappeared. We then sat and talked about the weather, the fresh cool air in the hills here above El Tocuyo, and the nice quiet nights in the area. After a couple minutes, he excused himself to have dinner and left me there alone. Sitting there looking across the fields, I felt both humbled and extremely lucky that I was able to see and feel the skill of one of the great stick fighters of Venezuela. I could not wait for my next chance to do it all over again.

Garrote or *los juegos de palos* is a Venezuelan civilian combative tradition, revolving around the mastery and use of a hardwood walking stick. The garrote was carried by most all rural Venezuelan men until well into the twentieth century as a symbol of their manhood. The garrote also acted as a formidable weapon to protect a man's person, his public reputation, or property, as the case may be. Garrote has always been considered first and foremost a survival art although *jugando con palos*, or playing with the sticks, took place in a wide variety of circumstances. The wide array of contexts and different intentions guiding how the palos could be swung foregrounds its once intimate role in everyday male life. If for example, a neighbor tried to usurp a piece of your land or divert your water supply, the sticks came out to settle the matter. If you and your friend had some free time on your hand, the sticks would come out to "get some air." At a social gathering, if someone refused to join you in a round of drinks, laugh at your jokes, made disparaging remarks about or doubted your exploits, you would take up your garrote and *invite* the unfriendly companion outside to discuss the matter in private. Reflected in training drills and oral tales and seen in the disfiguring scars of some men, all too often the sense of excitement that came from knowing of an impending brawl would lead to mass melees. At times, relatives, friends, or spectators joined in the fray, either through their desire to see a good fight or the enjoyment of getting in a few licks of their own, or to make sure their friends or relatives did not get ganged-up on. In these types of group melees, sticks, machetes, knives, other occupational tools, and, increasingly, revolvers were brought into play to prove either who was the better man or who had the better cause, or to redress an insult to a man or his group's honor. What all these modes of combat held in common was that they were impromptu duels where the death of one's opponent was not the main purpose, but merely to beat a man down and leave him bloody and bowed, but alive. Serious assaults with the intent to rob or kill were committed with a combination of machetes, knives, and sticks, and, as time went on, by revolvers, by individuals, or groups of men, complicating any clear demarcation between fighting as a way to enhance or defend one's prestige, test one's skills, protect one's belongings, or seeking to eliminate an enemy. In the recent past, death was much more an intimate part of everyday life then it is now, and people were more accepting of the risks everyday life entailed. That being said, anytime a man could be taken unprepared, such as alone on a road at night, when drinking, taking an afternoon nap, working his plot of land, or otherwise preoccupied, was seen as a prime opportunity be taken advantage of by an assailant. This meant a man had to cultivate to some degree a "warrior's habitus," or a set of dispositions and embodied practices to fit a man to defend his property or his manhood.

Dying out in the major urban centers along the Venezuelan littoral by the end of the nineteenth century, garrote continues to be passed down from family members or close friends as a means of self-defense throughout much of the country's interior. In a development that caught the attention of laity and scholars alike, during the late nineteenth or early twentieth century in one small area of mid-western Venezuela stick fighting was integrated into a cycle of dances honoring a local Catholic saint. Now known as the *Tamunangue*, this once local religious observance has become a national icon, representing the *mestizaje* of the Venezuelan nation binding all citizens in a shared mythological history of miscegenation (Guss 2000).

In addition to its perceived status as an exceptional form of self-defense, the instilling of valued character traits was, and is still, a key underlying element of the art that contributes to the persistence of this art. The idea of garrote as a "civilizing" tool was expounded upon many times during my stay. The best explanation of this aspect of the art came from one garrotero's mother. Worried about her son hanging out in the street, showing no inclination to do much of anything, she asked a neighbor to teach her son garrote to instill some character and sense of purpose in his life.

These dual aspects of garrote reflect the two principal yet interconnecting interests in this book. First, is to examine and contribute to the body of work regarding the persistence and renewed popularity of combative disciplines. Looking at the advent of the modern, many scholars predicted the eventual triumph of a rational, peaceful, and secular world.

Underlying this idea of modernity is the presupposition of a universality of humankind, where all differing political ideologies and social conflicts are ultimately reconcilable through the judicious use of reason. In this view, acts of violence are characterized as deviant, criminal, or an atavistic regression to pre-civilized impulses. Having a more jaundiced or clear-eyed view of the world, many working-class individuals and rural laborers around the world have long understood that violence can be a valuable tool to ensure one's survival, impose ones will on another, keep another from imposing one's will on you, or just a pleasurable pastime (Conley 1999; Hurley 2007).

Following up on commonly held feelings that the practice of combative arts can fundamentally reshape how a subject feels about, moves, and interacts with the world, I explore this idea by looking at different practitioner pedagogical methods and stories of training and fighting with the garrote. Among those living in the small pueblos and working-class barrios of rural Venezuela, young men's training with the garrote was geared toward the developing of one's physiological skills, emotional structures, and cultural competencies, or what I call a "warrior's habitus." Incorporating in varying degrees a warrior's habitus prepared a man to resist the institutional oppression of elites, claims against his family's land, and the need to establish and maintain one's reputation as a man to be reckoned with. In other words, there was a need to demonstrate that you were willing and able to fight to protect your reputation, your family, or your community from any and all outside threats. Garrote, as it was often explained to me, is not a "martial art" but is a people's art *un arte civil* or *un arte del pueblo.* Assuming this vantage point situates garrote in a set of historical contingencies and processes of the emergence of rural and working-class Venezuelans. Principally of indigenous, European, and African backgrounds, these were the men and some women who contributed greatly to the making of the modern Venezuelan nation, yet whose histories still remain largely unexamined. With this understanding, I seek to examine how these local embodied knowledges—themselves the result of the trans-Atlantic migration of peoples, ideas, and technologies—were co-opted, refined, transmitted, and manifested as a tool of cultural and physical resistance. All too often, these were the people who carried the brunt of progress and change undertaken by elites while reaping little to none of the rewards promised as accompanying modernity.

MODERNITY AND VIOLENCE

What makes a study of the combative traditions of Venezuela compelling today is the fact that Venezuela has been for decades in the forefront of Latin American countries that embraced a North American modernity.

Venezuela was for many years an exception to the political norm in the region. Beginning in 1958, when the military handed over control to a democratically elected civilian government, Venezuela had appeared to prosper. Losing political parties, instead of taking to the streets or allying themselves to elements of the military to foment a revolt, took on the role of a loyal opposition. After the return to civilian rule in 1958, successive regimes instituted a series of progressive social reforms, contributing to a higher standard of living for a rapidly expanding middle class. The economic crisis of 1989 and the failed military coup of Colonel Hugo Chávez in 1992 were the first signs that Venezuela had not escaped the problems accompanying the embracing of a North-Atlantic mode of modernity that had beset other Latin American nations. The recent death of President Chávez and the current political, social, and economic upheavals that have roiled Venezuela make the persistence of local forms of armed combat a rich subject to mine in order to better understand the way people feel about, look upon, and engage with the world around them. Looking at the reasons men come to fight, how they decide to fight, how they adjudge victory and defeat, and how they deal with the consequences of these acts brings to the forefront the sometimes contradictory demands of modernity and tradition young people often face in midst of negotiating the travails of everyday life.

My primary engagement with modernity centers on the persistence of enduring dispositions many social scientists once predicted would fade away with the triumph of a modern rational secular society. At first glance, this prediction would appear especially relevant in Venezuela, where the onset of the twentieth century was accompanied by a sudden and lucrative demand for its petroleum reserves. The intersection of the increase in the spending power of a newly expanded upper and middle class, with a concomitant increase in global flows of information, technology, and peoples in what David Harvey referred to as "time-space compression" (Harvey 1990), resulted in a new set of configurations transforming the Venezuelan economy, social relations, and popular culture. The shape-shifting nature of modernity and the ways it has developed and experienced in Venezuela can be seen through a look back at key events occurring in the twentieth century. The increasing demand for Venezuela's oil by the United States and Europe resulted in the newly expanded elites turning their back on once valued European ideas of culture, instead welcoming many North American pastimes, such as baseball, boxing, and beauty pageants. For years, those of the Caracqueño middle class would regularly fly to Miami or New York on weekends to shop and pick up the latest fashions. The end of the 1980s ushered in a series of economic crises leading to a reduced standard of living for most all Venezuelans that have only worsened over time. US cultural hegemony, once paramount, has been continuously decentered over the years to where many Venezuelans embraced such trends as

Colombian Vallenato and Jamaican Raeggaeton music, Mexican soap operas, and East Asian martial art cinema, reflecting the global nature of modernity. However, these events should not occlude the fact that cultural patterns of consumption and ways of being a Venezuelan continues to be based on a system of racial hierarchies and exclusions, originating in the colonial era silencing or erasing the major demographic and cultural input of indigenous and African communities. Traveling through rural Venezuela, a visitor readily sees, hears, and feels a strong sense of integrity of the pueblo where, depending on the region, indigenous, African, and European syncretic traditions are practiced and valued (Martínez 2002). The significance placed on honoring traditional practices, imaginaries, and artifacts points to the need for a more nuanced examination into the relationship between acts of resistance and accommodation subjects engage in their everyday life (Mahmoud 2005). Within this crucible of the modern and the traditional in everyday life, the value of learning combative disciplines continues to the present day. Oral traditions claim these practices were handed down to carefully selected family members or close friends. Up through the present, it is within these semi-restricted groups that concerns about morality, gender, violence, honor, and the future of the youth are struggled over, discussed, and embodied through the practice and transmission of these body disciplines.

The idea of modernity has for a long time been linked to the entity of the homogenous nation-state and the idea of the bounded rational individual (Anderson 1991). The ascendance of a centralized authority characterizing the nation-state was due to the success of those championing a statist form of government to monopolize and legitimize the use of violence to itself. The imperialistic, domineering aspect of modernization accompanying the nation-state has long interested anthropologists (Carneiro 2003; Childe 1941; Haas 1990; Service 1975; High-Turner 1971). One aspect of this process is the expanding role of state institutions into the realm of the civil sphere, a process where the state increasingly regulates and proscribes the rights and privileges claimed by non-statist corporate groups and individuals, such as the right to resort to violence to protect one's interest or status (Emsley 2005; Ikegami 1995; Pitt-Rivers 1995). Looking at the shifting parameters of these claims and counterclaims regarding the legitimate uses of violence as they occurred in Western Europe, the historian Norbert Elias developed the idea of a "Civilizing Process" to understand how learned intergenerational ideas and practices of interpersonal violence have changed over time in relation to the state (Elias 2000). Within Latin America, the increasing criminalizing, stigmatizing, or labeling as deviant any self-help acts of violence had waxed and waned through the colonial and post independent eras. By the early twentieth century, polices aimed toward the eradication of these practices reached a nadir. For example, in the port towns of Brazil, local expressions of capoeira and other Afro-Brazilian combative traditions were driven to extinction in many areas. In Trinidad, staff-wielding Afro-Trinidadian battled both *Lathi* swinging South Asian immigrant laborers and local policemen in the streets during Carnival, until the *Boismen*, or stick men, were convinced to retire their sticks (Cowley 1996). In Argentina, Curaçao, Colombia, and Venezuela, the propensity to hold impromptu duels in the street or at social gatherings with knives, machetes, and or sticks of varying lengths was likewise repressed in the name of hegemonic discourses such "Law and Order" and the "March of Civilization," as the latest generation of Latin-American elites rushed to embrace a North-Atlantic modernity. Other defining characteristics of this striving to be modern focused on the sponsoring of wholesale European immigration and the rebuilding of the cities or the nations' infrastructure to strengthen their export market. Accompanying these developments were the gentrification of minority communities from downtown areas and the widespread repression of public religious or secular expressions of many of these local communities. Oftentimes, these were seen as blight upon the country's image and a perennial police problem. Coming across this trait throughout his career, anthropologist Michael Herzfeld saw these cultural struggles as an example of the "Global Hierarchy of Value," where certain material or cultural traits of a community seen by locals as unique to their culture are held to be signs of backwardness or primitiveness by those who seek to emulate contemporary Western ideas of culture (Herzfeld 2004; Shyrock 2004). Within this context of nation-state formation, I suggest local community practices of non-European or subaltern social and cultural embodied knowledges relating to the way men organized themselves hierarchically or resolved interpersonal problems through the use of violence were driven into extinction or into the shadows of the barrio or the pueblo. Only recently has this unbalanced history of everyday Latin American modernity begun to be corrected.

SCHOLARSHIP ON COMBATIVE TRADITIONS

Over the last few years, the reemergence of a scholarly interest into the different ways people come to physically dominate one another has resulted in a number of well-researched and well-written books rich in ethnographic detail highlighting different aspect of Chinese Kung-Fu (Boretz 2011; Farrer 2012; Judson and Nielson 2015; Sharar 2008), Indonesian and Malaysian Silat (Farrer 2009, 2012; Wilson, Ian 2009, 2015), Brazilian capoeira (Assunção 2005; Downey 2005), South Indian Keralapayitt (Zarilli 1998), North Indian wrestling (Alter 1992), and the increasing popularity of mixed martial arts (Spencer 2012; García and Spencer 2013). The publication of *Martial Arts in the Modern World* (Green and Svinth 2003) and the latter companion *Martial Arts of the World: An Encyclopedia of History and Innovation* (Green and Svinth 2010) were important in the emerging field of "Martial Studies" in that it brought attention to a number of combative systems around the world still currently practiced as practical methods of self-defense, recreational activities, traditional warrior disciplines, or as attempts to recreate systems found in old treatises and instructional manuals. Documenting these systems was a first step in acknowledging the everyday role that violence plays throughout much of the world. Within a number of communities around the world, there is the need to have at least a basic knowledge of fighting just to survive everyday life, calling attention to the pragmatic orientation of combative disciplines. Among others communities, combative disciplines are practiced as a traditional or ethnic marker of belonging to a community. Reflecting the value people still place on these practices can be seen in the financial rewards or employment opportunities that can arise from being crowned a champion.[1] Equally noteworthy is the number of combative arts that owes its development and practice to disreputable marginal or stigmatized communities co-opted by the state and crowned with the title of a "national art" or "intangible cultural heritage" communities. All too often what happens in incorporating these arts into a state's pantheon of cultural accomplishments is the art is reconfigured to make it accessible or palatable to the wider population. Accompanying this domestication is a rewriting of history, suggesting an ongoing marginalization and active forgetting of the contribution of disreputable sectors of the popular classes to their respective nations.

For example, in Latin America the interest of scholars in African–New World links first noted by the anthropologist Melville Herskovits and reflected today in the global popularity in Brazilian Capoeira has overshadowed other Latin-American combative pastimes, combative rituals, and street-oriented combative traditions. Wrestling is an almost universal among the indigenous communities in the New World, yet only the wrestling of Central Brazil (Wagley 1977), the Paraguayan Chaco (Grub 1904), or the Tarahumara of Northern Mexico (Fontana 1977) has been given brief notice. A few articles have been devoted to the Quechua and Aymara fist fighters of the Andes (Chacon et al. 2007; Wibbelsman 2009; Zorn 2002). Recently, a novel was published about Surinamese-Javanese Pentjak-Silat exponents searching for the roots of their art (Khozali 2010).[2] In the histories of Latin America, the knife, stick, and machete fighters from Argentina, Chile, Brazil, Colombia, and Venezuela, or the "stick licking" arts of the Caribbean, have only begun to undergo any serious notice by scholars (Assunção 2014; Desch-Obi 2008, 2009; Osornio 1995; Ryan 2011). Alternately, they have been dismissed as the street brawling of mean or crazy drunken old men by locals who still remember these times. For too long the dismissal or marginalization of the way people choose to fight betrays an adherence to an elite Western discourse regarding violence, privileging East Asian or similar combative traditions that claim an overarching spiritual dimension to their art that transcends the mere physical that continues to inform many sectors of a society.

One well-known case of the ongoing globalized exoticizing and domesticating of local combative traditions is seen in life trajectory of the famous Vicente Pastinha, who first learned and practiced capoeira as a form of self-defense around the beginning of the twentieth century. At first he learned the art to protect himself against bullies, but soon graduated to the position of head of security for a popular gambling house, while gaining a reputation among the police of the city of Salvador as one of the principal troublemakers in the area. Marrying and subsequently retiring from his street activity to raise a family sometime in the 1920s, he later returned to the Bahian capoeira community in the 1950s to take a leading role in its re-popularization. During this time, he became known for promoting a "traditional" capoeira, oriented toward fostering physical health, emotional maturity, and sportsman-like conduct. Pastinha's project to modernize capoeira was one of many competing views of the art at the time. Whereas Pastinha envisioned capoeira as a form of self-cultivation, others focused more on refining a street-effective fighting method or continued to practice the local variations of the art they had learned but whose names and ways of playing capoeira have faded into obscurity (Assunção 2005; Capoeira 2002; Olivera 2005).

THE PERSISTENCE OF ARMED COMBAT

The rise in popularity of unarmed forms of combat in today's West, as reflected in internet content, academic literature, and the rising popularity of MMA, ignores the fact throughout the world, including the United States, that most confrontations involve or quickly escalate into an armed conflict. Far from excessive violence, the use of weapons has the pragmatic goal of neutralizing or eliminating a threat quickly and efficiently. Long understood by those men who have fought hand to hand under battlefield conditions; the last thing you want to do in a hand-to-hand combative encounter is fight hand to hand. Once a weapon is introduced, the stakes of the outcome rise exponentially. Armed combat between two serious antagonists last mere seconds with only a few blows exchanged before someone falls to the ground dead, gravely injured, or disfigured, while the other flees the scene. Equally important in regards for this research is the way men choose to fight. Choosing a weapon, whether it be fists, knives, swords, or firearms, often possesses a symbolic aspect, such as entailing the recognition of the other man as being of similar social standing, of being coeval, and a worthy opponent. For example, out of the California prison system comes the adage "fist fights are for friends, stabbing is for enemies." Ethnographic and historical accounts abound with tales of men pitting themselves against each other in impromptu duels with similar weapons over questions of precedence or violations of parameters of respect. Looking into these events, it becomes evident how individuals sharing a sense of coevalness often chose weapons that served as an identifying marker based on ethnicity, class, occupation, or neighborhood. The way a number of these types of combative acts ideally rely on all men being similarly armed foregrounds the ritualistic aspect of male hierarchical contests or dueling. Another component that these acts share is they are between two equals who have agreed upon the best way to resolve any disagreement through recourse to arms where death is a real possibility but not the main goal. As Pindar was supposed to have said, "Prowess without danger has no honor among men." The archaic era Greek poet recognized long ago how important it is for young men put themselves in risky situations on a regular basis while showing no more concern than taking a stroll in the park. An attitude of studied indifference to danger the Italian Castiglione in another time and place called *Sprezzatura* (1967:66–68). Another common element seen in a number of dueling traditions with percussive or bladed weapons is how men choose less dangerous weapons or use them in such way as to reduce but not eliminate the risk of inflicting mortal injuries. In the choosing of a less lethal weapon to engage in a duel with one's peers in what can be seen as a "fair fight," the role of intercommunal cultural norms designed to minimize the consequences of unrestrained violence within a community becomes clear and subject to examination. (Emsley 2005; Gallant 2000; Shoemaker 2001; Spierenbeg 1998).

Growing up I heard a number of times from older teenagers and adults that if a conflict arises between two people, they should retire to a secluded area and settle their differences. In what was called a "fair fight," each could test the other's courage and abilities to see who is the best man or possessed the most just cause. Another reason for retiring to a secluded area was to avoid the real possibility of receiving a great deal of pain and possibly serious injuries from a "fair fight" with someone as strong, fast, and determined as yourself.[3] Alone, both men could bluster and posture before settling their disagreements through talking without being egged on by those wanting to see a good fight (Falk 2004). In Venezuela, the ideal scenario of how one-to one duels are supposed to take place could and did often take place with two men entering the dueling ground walking and only one leaving the same way. Altogether, the diverse ideologies and culturally accepted ways of moving the body, in conjunction with material technology governing the proper way that men should fight, suggests that aggression is not a simple biological impulse, nor it is located outside of history. More accurately, it can be said fighting is shaped, mediated, and informed through current cultural values in conjunction with a material technology and manifested in a way that would be seen as practical, efficient, and normal by one's community.

Garrote and the Body

With a tight stomach and sense of nervousness with what I was about to ask, I crossed the small bridge spanning the small stream that flows down to the Tocuyo River. Walking up a steep hill, I approached the house where I spent many wonderful hours listening to Ricardo Colmenares and his extended family tell me about stick fighting and other aspects of life in the mountains. Arriving in front of his house, I saw Maestro Ricardo sitting on a chair on the porch relaxing and enjoying the Sunday morning sun. I greeted the sixty-nine-year-old farmer who practiced a form of stick fighting passed down from his grandfather. Sitting down on his porch drinking a cup of fresh coffee brewed from the beans of his family's farm, we discussed the weather, our families, and the seasons coffee crop. Finally, I blurted the real reason I had been coming to visit him. I asked if he would consider teaching me how to swing the sticks in the way he learned from his father. His eyes widened and he leaned back as in shock, "What! You want to learn how to jugar with the palo?" he asked incredulously. "Well, yes, if you have the time," I mumbled, preparing for the impending rejection. "Well," he said, recovering his composure as he leaned forward, putting both hands on my shoulders and gazing earnestly in my eyes. "I will tell you what my father told me when I was a young man," he paused. "You better go to the store and buy some salt for your bruises because these sticks hit hard!" He then threw back his head and laughed uproariously. Maestro Ricardo was not far off the mark. By the time my fieldwork ended, I had contusions all over my ankles, shins, forearms, and head from practice sessions and demonstrations from different people showing me a few moves "done easy," as I was reassured. Maestro Ricardo's humorous advice highlights the central role that the body, in conjunction with material technology taking place within a relationship of apprenticeship, can act as a starting point for this investigation: how the poles of modernity and tradition are thought about, imagined, negotiated, and lived-out in everyday life.

For scholars in the 1980s, the seminal article by Marcel Mauss on "Body-Techniques," acted as a launching point for what has been called "the re-turn to the body." In his essay, Mauss describes how, when he was among a community with no tradition of spitting, he taught a young child with a cold to spit (Mauss 1979, 118). This simple act contributed to his realization of the pragmatically oriented embodied nature of culture. Throughout the twentieth century, a number of scholars from a wide array of the social sciences developed a number of theoretical concepts to talk about the myriad ways the body is enculturated, targeted, or comes to be socialized within a wide array of social and political regimes, often drawing on variations of the old Aristotelian idea of the "habitus." Among the profusion of studies attending to the interrelationship between local political-economic regimes and the way the body becomes

enculturated, Loïc Wacquant's stint in a predominantly low-income
African-American neighborhood boxing gym in Chicago was key in presenting Bourdieu's idea of the habitus, or the unspoken ways that people
come to know the proper way to think about, act toward, and judge a
situation or event (Wacquant 2004). Asking why many lower-class men
chose boxing as a career, Wacquant came to understand how boxing
provided a way for some men to distance themselves from street-life,
while maintaining the respect from street denizens, as they sought to
transform their bodies in order to "punch their way to success." Drawing
on the Bourdieu's idea of "Capital" as that which is valued within a
community and can be used to raise one's station in life and is exchange-
able for other forms of capital, Wacquant focused his attention on the
ways men cultivated and refined their natural physical attributes or
physical capital through a regime of extreme physical austerities in order
to maximize their chance of success in the ring and then out of the ring.
What he found was that boxers often sought to convert their finite "physical capital" or their body and any subsequent local/national fame, "symbolic capital," into a more stable financial success (i.e., economic capital)
(Bourdieu and Wacquant 1992). With increased financial success, they
could attempt to escape low-paid wage labor, the nihilistic cycle of violence and imprisonment that made up "street culture," or the monastic
discipline demanded by the ring.

In the realm of martial art studies, the concept of the habitus has been
used to examine the way Vietnamese refugee communities in Australia
promoted the relevance of Vietnamese martial arts to resist the physical
and cultural assaults of Anglo-Australians (Carruthers 1998). In Indonesia, the state has long worked on harnessing the ethnically diverse and
numerous local practitioners of local civilian combative systems known
popularly as Pencak Silat to quell any unrest by local ethnic, political, or
religious groups through the promotion of a national martial art. Traditionally, these combative arts have strong ties to specific ethnic groups,
guilds, castes, or villages. During the Second World War, under the direction of a number of ethnic Javanese, generals seeking to create a modern
nation-state have sought to secularize and sportify Silat. To this end, they
increasingly eliminated its predatory tactics and secularized its spiritual
connections to local spiritual beliefs by promoting its own sport version
of Silat with a corresponding state sponsored ideology of *Pancasila* (Wilson and Wilson 2002; Wilson and Wilson 2009, 2015). The growing popularity of mixed martial arts (MMA) has been analyzed through the lens of
a "Civilizing Process" or a type of communal habitus where the gym acts
as a social laboratory for practitioners to cultivate a physical body and a
set of gender attitudes and practices in order to produce a respected and
successful fighter (Spencer 2012). In the wrestling Ashrams of North India, anthropologist Joseph Alter does not explicitly draw on the habitus
but draws on much of the same underlying ideas to describe a totalizing

disciplinary regime. For wrestlers in the city of Varanasi, practice went beyond simple physical training to include such minor acts as brushing ones teeth or evacuating one's bowels in order to produce an ideal state of physical health and spiritual purity identifiable as a "Body of One Color." Achieving this state, the wrestlers' body is seen to reflect a morality and compassion able to counter the effeminate and debilitating practices of Western modernity (Alter 1992).

Looking deeper into the workings of the habitus, some scholars have looked how the habitus can change through time. Others have focused on the interrelationship of a subject's agency and habitus regarding an individual's dedication or competency of a body discipline. Learning how to *jogar capoeira* (play capoeira) in the city of Salvador, the anthropologist Greg Downey came to see how capoeira cultivates little known or obsolescent physiological apparatus or body movements to affect a change in the way a practitioner understands the world. Reflecting on the fact that not all those who learn capoeira advance at a steady rate, or plateau sometime during their journey or never reach a level of mastery, Downey linked recent insights in the neurological and cognitive sciences with French phenomenological philosophy and anthropological studies of apprenticeships to begin to apprehend the heterogeneous, contingent nature of the habitus. Reaching beyond strict disciplinary boundaries, Downey strengthened earlier ideas of the unstable fragmentary nature of the individual's habitus, furthering our understanding of the porousness between the physical, biological, and cultural realms (Downey 2005, 2007, 2010, 2012).

Running across a wealth of different peoples and situations during the madness of WWI trench warfare, Mauss concluded that a great deal of culture is expressed and transmitted through habitual body movements in conjunction with material technology. Being able to dig a trench fast and quickly was not just the sign of a disciplined soldier, but could mean the difference between life and death. Back then, English trench shovels were built with an enclosed handle on top, while French shovels had a horizontal cross-piece handle. In an atmosphere of flying shrapnel, machine guns spraying bullets and snipers picking off exposed targets there was a high motivation not to end up as a "daily wastage," as death ensuing outside of set battles was referred to. During adrenal-induced, stress-filled events, the issuing of French manufactured shovels to Englishmen requiring a different type of grip compromised the ability of soldiers to dig quickly and efficiently. In turn, this led to the issuing of more culturally familiar shovels to battalions of different nationalities when relieving each other in a trench sector (Mauss 1979, 99). In this mundane act, Mauss identified the key role material technology and the physical body in a relationship of apprenticeship plays in the enculturation and subject-formation of individuals. Recently working from a variety of disciplines, scholars interested in material studies have convincingly argued that both subjectivity and social networks emerge out of the primordial relationship of an individual with the environment or material technology (Ingold 2000; Miller 2005; Tilley 2006; Warnier 2007, 2011). Seeking to understand the role that material technology plays in the way bodies are enculturated and knowledge is transmitted, this work examines the manner in which Venezuelan men learn to fight with walking sticks, machetes, and knives and how this traditional practice contributed to the development of physical skills and a distinct masculine comportment still valued and practiced today.

At a time when gunfire is ubiquitous in the streets of Venezuelan cities and a murder occurs every twenty-one minutes, garrote is still seen to be a deadly art by practitioners and deeply regarded by many rural peoples (Venezuelan Violence Observatory 2014, 12). One common response among those I interviewed in regards to the value of garrote today was that they felt garrote as a discipline cultivates such attitudes as fearlessness, aggressiveness, steadfastness, and cunning, which can serve good stead throughout one's life. But even more importantly, for those who decide to pass on garrote to the younger generation there is a concerted effort to cultivate the moral and ethical dispositions of those they accept as students.

In many parts of Europe and Latin America, ideas and practices of honor are tightly bound up with ideas and practices of masculinity.[4] Throughout the world among working-class or rural peoples, one's public masculine identity is often bound up with public opinion. In the arenas where men congregate and socialize, men are evaluated through their success in balancing two contradictory approaches to life: that of a "hale fellow well met," and a cunning individual, or a dangerous man to disrespect or take advantage of. Trying to navigate and live up to these two contradictory sets of dispositions often lead to a number of extreme public acts, both to maintain one's honor and or burnish their public reputation (Campbell 1965; Herzfeld 1985; Paine 1989). Examining how people come to be socialized beings, a number of scholars in the twentieth century, working independently in their own fields, have come to similar conclusions—that it is through a subject's own agency of reflection and reflexivity that allows one's subjectivity to emerge. Through these acts, individuals are able to transcend their immanence or Cartesian solipsism and open themselves up to the representations and judgments of the "Other." Out of this this ability to incorporate the views of others, modes of self-identifications, such as, gender, class, ethnicity, and subject-hood, are lived through. Far from being fixed, unchanging identities, individuals continuously constitute and reconstitute their subjectivity in multiple sites over time as they meet with the various obligations of society (Cooley 1956; Crossley 2001; Mead 1967; Sarte 1960).

Although, up until recently, around the world there was a greater need for men to have some mastery of armed combative methods to walk the streets, there is a wealth of anecdotal evidence suggesting parents of working-class or rural children still stress the importance of young men learning to standup for themselves. The old traditional, standby, fear-inducing threat—usually uttered by a single overworked and worried mother to her son—"you better worry about the beating I'm going to give you rather than that kid outside" is always a good motivating speech to cultivate the attitude of aggressiveness, but does little in teaching someone how to fight who has never fought before. Other more pragmatic help might be passed along by older neighbor teenagers, relatives, or neighbors in quick informal training sessions in a garage or behind a building when no one is around, to a more pedagogically organized, yet vicious, informal apprenticeship.[5] After all these years, I still remember the barrage of stinging slaps to my face, the laughs and jeers of others in my high school P.E. class, and the encouraging words of my self-appointed teacher of slap-fighting telling me to keep my hands up and other bits of advice. What all these diverse modes of teaching share is the necessity of teaching an individual to cultivate and harness the various physiological structures, affectual attributes, and cultural competencies needed to negotiate successfully through the often contradictory and confusing travails of everyday life.

Methodological Considerations

Data from this study derived from two periods of fieldwork in Venezuela in 2005 and 2013, when I spent seven months and six weeks there respectively. In order to elicit information, I had originally prepared an open-ended interview schedule and continued to revise it during the first couple months of my fieldwork as I began to interview garroteros. However, this only resulted in basic demographic information and could not elicit the type of information I was searching for. Another issue was the lack of students of many garroteros I interviewed and who I had hoped to be my main source of information. Those who I could find and acknowledged training garrote were not available to be interviewed, nor were they very forthcoming at all about their training. Due to this situation I relied on a relationship of apprenticeship to learn the art of garrote, to gain the trust of garroteros, and to get them to open up about their lives, their views on the world, on teaching, fighting, and the value of garrote in a modern world. These responses would not come easily, and only after I had proved myself worthy to ask questions. These men who accepted me as a student not only took me deep into the technical aspects of their art, but sought to teach me the culture of the garrotero. To this end they followed me around when I looked for other people to interview to ascertain their reliability, to explain my presence, to them to get them to open up to me and show me moves. They flagged key statements informants made and persuaded these men to expand upon their statements. All this and more in an effort to help me truly understand this art we all cherished. I ended up interviewing forty-one people in 2005 and trained intensively with five men in four different lineages. In 2013, I interviewed a further seven people in Falcón and Guárico states, reinterviewed a number of people I interviewed earlier, and trained intensively in two different lineages. At the end, my teachers grudgingly admitted I could "play a little."

The external validity of the data is difficult to ascertain due to the level of secrecy surrounding the art. But after numerous conversations with my teachers about those we had met or heard about repeatedly, we all felt I had made contact a with a fair number of practicing garroteros in the area. Internal validity was based on the promise of confidentiality and anonymity of all those who desired it. Finally, I relied on my own background in martial arts. My experience in martial arts is difficult to talk about not only due to the desire to remain humble and avoid any discussion of my purported skills or achievements, as most all my teachers sagely advised, but because my record is far from admirable. Beginning with the time after I left high school and said good-bye to schoolyard fist fights, I have been beaten down, stomped down, knocked down, and body-slammed more times than I care to remember. While I am not proud of my uneven record, I am grateful that those who beat me left me alive and fairly intact or were slow runners. In addition, I am still amazed with the number of combative exponents who I have come into contact with whose skills left me speechless, humbled, and in awe. On occasion, these men scared the daylights out of me and caused me to look for an unobtrusive way to get away from them as quickly as possible without letting on I was terrified of them. I began to study Korean Hwa Rang Do for eight years. After a while, I began to go to punk rock shows in Los Angeles. I regularly would get high and drunk and get into a number of fights with varying levels of success. After a year of this, I reduced my consumption of drugs and alcohol and regularly invited a couple of friends from other martial art academies, where we would look for bullies or gangs harassing weaker or smaller individuals and we would jump in and fight them. Tiring of this, I left on an extended hitchhiking trip around the world, where I fought or defended myself against bullies or robbers in migrant labor camps, back alleys, and country roads. Returning to Los Angeles, for the next seven years I studied Monkey Kung-Fu and Capoeira. During this time, for a couple of years I worked as head doorman in Huntington Beach, California, where again I regularly fought every weekend with patrons, band members, and other security personnel, again with varying levels of success. Upon finishing my undergraduate work, I conducted reconnaissance ethnographic projects in the Andes, the Brazilian Amazon, and the city of Bahia, Brazil. During this period, I was involved in a machete, a stick, and a knife fight. Returning again to the United States, I moved to Austin, Texas, where for three years I studied Pekiti Tersia Kali and Mande Muda Pentjak Silat and regularly attended Harimau Silat seminars in Dallas. Here, I felt I finally learned some understanding of armed combat that aided me immeasurably during my times in Venezuela investigating and training garrote. Moving to Binghamton, New York, I studied MMA for one year with Tamdan McCroy and have recently been attending Dog Brother martial arts seminars at Ryan "Guard Dog" Gruhn's school in State College, Pennsylvania, where he has hosted Marc Denny, Eric Knaus, and Benjamin Rittner. I have made two brief trips to Italy, where I briefly trained stick and knife fighting from the Batstone Genovese and the Cavalieri d'Umilita schools. I hope to make Italy the site of my next ethnographic project.

NOTES

1. See "Wrestling Boom Sweeps Senegal," Rose Skelton. BBC Africa Business report, April 13, 2010, http://news.bbc.co.uk/2/hi/business/8617738.stm. Accessed April 20, 2016.

2. The author sees the roots of Javanese Silat in Brazilian capoeira, ignoring the numerous oral and written histories of these arts.

3. To my eternal gratitude, Johnny "Johnny Demon" Ball was the first person to back me up in a fight. Afterward, he explained to me, "When a fight is about to begin, go right up to him nose to nose and let him know you are ready to fight right here and right now! Nine times out of 10 the guy will back down." "The tenth time," he said with a wry chuckle, "be prepared for all hell to break loose."

4. It can be difficult at times to distinguish motivations of instrumental from symbolic violence due to the long and complex histories between individuals. For example, see Santos (2007).

5. See Canada (1995), Hernandez (1985), and Jingoes (1975) for examples of more informal types of training.

ONE
This Is Garrote

Not too long ago, looking for material on the existence of Venezuelan stick fighting would lead a martial arts scholar to a number of works treating garrote as a local manifestation of a number of folkloric stick-dances found throughout Latin America and Europe (see Guss 2000). It took the efforts of one local martial artist who actually listened when he was told by garroteros that garrote is a stick-fighting art that preceded its incorporation into the Tamunangue. Seeking to set the record straight and chronicle a dying art, Sanoja wrote the first book that treated garrote as combative discipline of the Venezuelan people (Sanoja 1984).[1] Since then, an increasing number of works have been published treating garrote as a distinctly Venezuelan combative discipline (Assunção 1999; Canelon 1994; Chavier 2009, 2015; González 2003 a, b, 2004; Ryan 2011, a, b, c, 2015; Sanoja 1984, 1996). Far from being a commemorative practice of a long ago past with little practical relevance in the modern world, these works all treat garrote as those men who have practiced the art for decades have seen their art, as a means par excellence of self-defense. Treating garrote as a combative art with roots in a number of local traditions of combat in the military and civilian spheres can help shed light on possible avenues of transmission contributing to the development and refinement of garrote as we have come to know it today. As it took shape in the Segovia Highlands, the emergence and development of garrote appears to be tied in with the changing attitudes toward violence in the late seventeenth-century Europe and brought to Venezuela by governing elites, merchants, and settlers substituting the open-carry policy of rapiers with hardwood walking sticks and sword canes as a means of self-defense. Co-opting this foreign prestige item, a number of local communities of indigenous, African, and mixed-blood communities treated the carrying and use of the garrote as one tactic of many to resist and renegotiate the racially based caste-like social hierarchy and state policies that continually sought to reduce them into landless proletarianized and hispanicized laborers. Supporting this view is the existence of garrote in other areas of Venezuela where the persistence of stick and machete fighting among African and African-indigenous communities persisted for many of the same reasons, to protect their property and to be seen and treated as men equal to all others. Lest one reduce the complexity of the development of Venezuela and the art of garrote to a uniform set of conditions, the different histories of migration, colonization, resistance accommodation, and coexistence that make up the history of Venezuela call for sensitivity to the historical forces that shaped the local communities and unique developments of garrote.

GARROTE IN THE SEGOVIA HIGHLANDS

Built in the 1950s, the Trans-Andean Highway, in addition to allowing the quick deployment of armed forces to quell any civil unrest, also improved the connection of Andean coffee farmers with Caribbean port towns and expanding global markets. Bypassing the small town of El Tocuyo, El Ciudad Madre, the mother city of Venezuela suffered a further blow to its illustrious history in its slide down to its current status as a Podunk town in a backwater region of Venezuela. Yet for three days each year, El Tocuyo regains its former glory as it has increasingly become well known for their local religious ritual dedicated to the thirteenth-century Franciscan monk Saint Anthony of Padua, venerated for attempting to convert the Moors of North Africa from Islam to Christianity, or from one religion of Abraham to another.

Beginning every June 13 around the towns and hamlets in the southern half of Lara state, the faithful turn out to ask for favors or repay favors bestowed by Saint Anthony. These *promessas* or *velorios* are also held throughout the year when an individual or group of individuals will pool their resources, hire a group of musicians, and prepare food and drinks for the neighborhood. Instead of an elaborate dais, a small simple alter is constructed to house a statue of the patron saint where he is surrounded by flowers, candles, and incense. Lying at the foot of the altar are garrotes, machetes, knives, or lances. Depending on where it takes place, the ritual consists of an introductory instrumental song, a duel, and a number of paired dances. Depending on the village or town where it is performed, the Tamunangue will have five to eight *sones* or dances. For each sponsor who contributed to the ritual, a complete cycle of sones are repeated. After a few cycles, everybody takes a break to eat tripe stew or other prepared foods and take shots of the locally made alcoholic drink *Cocuy*, which means the ritual can continue for hours.

The opening of the promessa begins with an instrumental piece known as *La Salve*, calling attention to all concerned that the ritual is beginning. After a few minutes, the musicians switch to *la batalla*. At the direction of the *Capitan-Mayor*, who along with the *Capitan-Mayora* guides the event, two individuals approach the altar and, after taking a weapon from its base, engage in a mock duel. During this time the Capitan-Mayor acts as traffic cop, permitting people to duel and controlling the duel and then leading the couple out so a new couple can duel. Keeping the rhythm of the ritual going, the Capitan-Mayor finally brings this section of the promessa to a close and indicates when the other sones should begin and end, repeating this cycle over and over again until all promessas have been made (Guss 2000; Linnarez 2003; Liscano 1951).

The annual public velorio is slightly different as a float of Saint Anthony is carried by an ever-revolving group of men around the main church in the small villages or around the local churches in bigger towns. Preceding the float are two men engaging in what is usually a mock stick duel. Finally, setting the float down in front of the main church, the promessas are performed and repeated long into early evening. After the close of the ritual, in El Tocuyo at least, portable stages are set up downtown around the Plaza Bolívar. There a number of traditional and modern bands will play, and revelers will alternately dance, drink, vomit, fight, make up, and pass out on the sidewalks and gutters into the early hours. Committed party-goers will get a few hours' sleep in order to gain the energy to do the whole thing again the following afternoon.

The Tamunangue has long been regarded by scholars, both academic and laity, as one of the most beautiful folkloric dances in all Latin America (Liscano 1951). Recognizing the increasing interest in the local ritual, government officials in the early 1990s commissioned a sculpture of a man and a woman each holding a garrote, as if dancing the Tamunangue.

Placed in the traffic circle at the entrance of El Tocuyo, I often gazed upon the piece as, over time, I learned more about garrote. Over a period of months, I began to see how the final appearance of the sculpture resulted from the juxtaposition of many overlapping, contradictory histories, desires, and representations; revealing the complex fragmentary, largely unknown history of the popular classes of Venezuela.

The struggles of the modern nation-state to impose a centralized power has left its mark on the Tocuyo Valley. There is the now abandoned military base built above the town to ensure its loyalty during the guerrilla uprising in the 1960s. During this same period, a dam was built above the Tocuyo River, submerging many radical workers' homes while aiding the large agro-industrial plantations in the valley below. As another piece of architectural display, the commemorative monument acts as another highly visible symbol designed to enforce a state sponsored disciplinary regime through enshrining and privileging a government-approved representation of a local religious ritual. Yet this had not silenced

Figure 1.1.   Statue of Tamunangeros outside El Tocuyo

the multiple voices that continue to surround and shape each velorio and the development of garrote. With the rise of practice theory in the 1980s, scholars began to realize that rituals are not unchanging acts with fixed meaning, but undergo changes in the performance and meaning through time With this insight, local scholars have speculated that the first accounts of the Tamunangue written about in the 1940s was not a fixed ritual but rather a synthesis of prior ways of paying homage to the saint.[2] For those interested in this festival what they see is more of an open-ended process that continues up through the present, where devotees and more secularized individuals continuously rearrange and change the way the ritual is performed in order to actualize their needs, desires, and meanings (Guss 2000).

Learning of the Tamunangue and its relation to garrote, led me back to El Tocuyo over the next few years with the intent of finding someone who would teach me stick fighting. I would see a lot of stick fighting during the festival. All too often to my disappointment, I would see two men using their wrists to twirl thin sticks with braided cotton yarn handles at each other from a safe distance in prearranged patterns, or a couple of drunken fools who had no idea how to swing a garrote. In their enthusiastic bumbling way, they would jump or lurch out of range of one person's wild swings and then take a big step forward and respond with some wild flailing of their own, while the defender stumbled back out of reach. On occasion, I would see older, smaller men who looked like they worked outdoors in the nearby sugar cane plantations their whole lives, and sometimes a few younger men who would swing their sticks with a purpose and meaningfulness. To me it was more than an exciting display, but hinted at a still extant sophisticated practice of armed combat in El Tocuyo. Seeing these men, I was determined to meet and learn from them after the festival concluded.[3]

Let's return to the sculpture and focus on what, to me, is the obvious mismatching of the intentions of the two figures. Looking at the statues individually, the man takes an aggressive forward leaning pose, as if inviting a strike to the head, preparing to block the incoming attack and counter with his own strike. On the other hand, the woman looks as if she were holding her palo like it was a bouquet of flowers as she dances to an imaginary rhythm. At other times, the sculpture presents the more disturbing appearance of a drunk and angry husband about to give his wife a beating for fooling around dancing when she should have had his dinner on the table when he got home. The role of gender relations in the Fiesta de San Antonio, however, takes us off track. More relevant to this subject is the incongruous disparity of intentions foregrounding the conviction among garroteros today that la batalla is not considered a *son* but a duel. The Tocuyano garroteros I spoke to took pains to stress a *son* is "danced" between a man and a woman, but a duel is a *juego* or antagonistic struggle between two men. Expressed in this work of art promoting the cultural heritage of El Tocuyo is a set of power relations occurring on multiple levels, subsuming and marginalizing the a priori and independent existence of local civilian combative methods, reducing them to a category of innocuous folkloric stick, and sword dances reinforcing the hegemonic attempt to delegitimize all acts of violence emanating from outside state approved channels (Martínez 2002).

The slippage between the sacred and profane, blending secular combative practices with religious acts, that we see here in southern Lara that may seem jarring to Westerners today was once common in medieval and early modern Europe. All too often religious festivals and secular acts of recreational violence coexisted alongside each other with little concern evinced by local elites about what is now seen as the incongruence of these blurred genres. Englishmen celebrated Shrove Tuesday in part by meeting in teams of up to a thousand people each to participate in ball games. Some men would go so far as to show up armored or on horseback to play (Dunning and Elias 1987).[4] Up to the nineteenth century, Irish stick and ball games such as Hurling and Scobeen, the forerunners of hockey and golf, served as a backdrop for mass brawls acting as a training ground for faction fights and later careers as professional soldiers (Hurley 2007). Inter-village brawls were common in rural France until the seventeenth century. In Ivrea, Italy, today, rival groups participate in orange throwing battles during a festival reliving in a toned-down way the once common rock-throwing, stick fighting, and fist fighting matches once held throughout Italian city-states, both on religious holidays and sometimes when things got a little too quiet (Davis 2009). The most well-documented case of these recreational modes of combat comes from Venice, where hundreds of men from opposing factions would meet on bridges to belabor each other, at first with fire-hardened, sharpened stakes and later their fists, in grand melees, finally being repressed in the seventeenth century (Davis 1994). Serious injuries and death could and did occur during these events but were an accepted consequence of participation and were used as fuel for renewed mass brawls to extract revenge while losing oneself in the joys of a good intense brawl.

"Without San Antonio, there is no garrote." Encapsulating the raison d'être of garrote, the garrotero Ricardo Colmenares indexes the close and intimate relationship existing between the juego de garrote and popular Catholicism in this region of Lara. In fact, the Fiesta de San Antonio is often claimed to be the main reason that garrote still exists here, while erroneously believed to have disappeared everywhere else in Venezuela. Local historians speculate that the spectacle of dueling was added to the beginning of the Fiesta de San Antonio sometime in the early twentieth century. It seems possible, though, that the introduction of a formal dueling element to the honoring of Saint Anthony under the supervision of a skilled stick fighter acting as a mediator could be the end result of a prior "civilizing process." In this scenario, there was an attempt by community leaders to limit the widespread anarchy of drinking, wild brawls, and other forms of rustic jollities felt to be antithetical to the subdued decorum and gravity local elites felt Western Europeans conducted their celebrations. At the same time, there was a concern to indulge the desires of young, risk-seeking men, seeking to display their skills, avenge a grudge, or lose themselves in the excitement of a good brawl that was a traditional part of rural masculine everyday life.

The popularity of honoring the saint through dueling with sticks, machetes, knives, and lances in the southern region of Lara state should not occlude the existence of garrote in many parts of Venezuela—notwithstanding the comments of garroteros from Lara claiming all garrote originated from the Tocuyo Valley or garrote has only survived in one area. I have met and interviewed such men from such diverse areas as in the mountains of Falcón and Miranda states and the foothills of Guárico state who disparage what they see as the performance-oriented garrote of Lara; so different from what they feel is an authentic or traditional combat-oriented garrote they still practiced and cherish. Nevertheless, the way garrote in southern Lara has become associated with the cult of Saint Anthony of Padua highlights the ambiguous status of such issues as secular/profane, fighting/playing, and the problems inherent in using analytical terms such as "martial arts" to understand the wide array and at times overlapping or contradictory goals, intents, and values that shape the way combat could be manifested in everyday life.

One recent example of the transcendental nature of combat that makes strict classificatory systems unwieldy and unusable are the serious outbreaks of violence that still break out during these celebrations. One of these acts was witnessed by one of my teachers in the small village of La Piedad just a few years ago. During a local celebration of the Tamunangue where individuals now engage in a performance-oriented display of garrote, two middle-aged laborers honored the saint by having a good amount to drink, then asking the Capitan-Mayor to "cross sticks" in honor of Saint Anthony. The prior imbibing of alcohol distorted both men's distance appreciation and power generation to the point where they were increasingly struck by the other palos harder and harder as they tried to get the other person to ease up on their strikes. Finally, losing his patience with the other man's lack of control, one man exclaimed "*Carajo*! I am through putting up with all this bullshit." Throwing down his stick, he pulled up his shirt tails with one hand, withdrew a machete from a sheath he had hid down the front of his pants, and began to stalk the other man. In response to this latest affront to his good nature, the other man responded. "To hell with you, I will teach you some manners, asshole." Likewise, he, too, threw down his palo in return, and pulling up his pant leg took out a large pocketknife from his sock, opened it up with both hands, and began to hunt down his opponent. Now properly armed, both men began to engage in an old fashioned duel until the Capitan-Mayor, relatives of both men, and other bystanders were able to separate the men and convince them to put their weapons down and walk away to get their wounds tended. Here the ambiguity and transcendental nature inherent in all social encounters is visible where the boundaries between what was considered an innocuous folkloric celebration, a *juego duro* or hard game, and an outright brawl or *la riña* could quickly shift, depending on one's intentions and the perceived intentions of the other subject. In any encounter with garrote, there is a real chance that one might lead to another and back again in a heartbeat. A man claiming to be a garrotero had to know how to respond quickly to this reframing of the modality of a combative encounter and respond accordingly as a man who is not to be trifled with or have his good nature abused, but at the same time respecting the community values and ideas at large.

With the publication of Eduardo Sanoja's seminal book on garrote, we first find the practice of Garrote Larense laid out in a triparties division of la batalla, el juego, and la riña (Sanoja 1984). A few of my teachers used this distinction in teaching me, for example the late José-Felipe Alvarado of the Siete Lineas style. On occasions, José-Felipe explained to me that a strike to the shoulder was the target for a juego or agonistic match, but a strike to the back of the neck was reserved for la *riña* or an antagonistic fight. To counter a strike to the chest with a blow to the bicep was a juego, but to thrust the tip of you palo to the throat of the person you are facing was a riña move. There is an inherent ambiguity in these distinctions though, as seen in a common strike to the chest or *pechero*. This is considered an acceptable strike for a performance-oriented la batalla, or agonistic juego modes of combat. However, this strike whose target is the side of the heart was continually stressed to me to be a dangerous move that should be done with care.

On the other hand, other garroteros from the same generation as José-Felipe felt there was only one mode of garrote, as the late Natividad Apostal of Barquisimeto explained one afternoon in his bodega:

> La batalla is the same as la riña, what happens is that in la batalla one strikes a blow to the head and the other avoids it. But in the riña one attacks with a blow to really strike and one avoids it. This is called "floreo," for example, one strikes a blow to the head and the other avoids it, and moves his leg out of the way. One must move the body so the strike hits the ground. It is done in an exchange. We make a juego, but the strikes are hard. The strikes in the juego are the same as the riña. (Natividad Apostal, interview by author, Barquisimeto, April 24, 2005)

Through my introduction to the practice of practice of Brazilian capoeira back in the late 1980s, I began to realize the difficulty in devising suitable analytical frames to discuss the practice of not only capoeira, but many other early modern popular practices that have resisted attempts at institutionalization or sportification. Analytical frames such as "martial art," "sport," "game," or play often fail to fully to describe how a system of combat was set up to deal with specific types of combative encounters such as the battlefield, civilian self-defense scenarios, or recreational contests. Neither are they able to contain the way these practices are embodied by local subjects. Ultimately, any classificatory scheme is unable to capture the transcendental nature of the lived experiences of individuals who may use combative moves learned in a number of different combative encounters with varying results. Within the sphere of combative practices, this can be seen in the unspoken, often ambiguous informal agreements that regulate who participates and under what conditions, what kind of attacks or defensive actions are acceptable, and how a situation is judged and talked about later by participants and spectators. Local practices that are continually negotiated and reconfigured within broader contextual frames of "tradition," or "ways that our fathers did it," all too often shift through time and space as some aspects are forgotten or deemed unsuitable, or new aspects are introduced as a return to the "traditional." Looking at how people actually construct, negotiate, and participate in events calls for a phenomenological approach that asks what types of power relations or types of capital are cultivated and to what end? How have specific aspects of the powers or capital evinced in combative practices been employed at different times and places? How have the powers or capital cultivated by practitioners changed in importance, and how do these changes effect the practitioners in how they move their bodies in what are considered meaningful ways in different social contexts? Finally, how do these changes affect the way they experience the world? These questions will be addressed in forthcoming chapters.

THE ORIGINS OF GARROTE IN VENEZUELA

Gazing upon the physical characteristics of the statues that welcome visitors to El Tocuyo to see how the sculptor portrayed the national ideology of miscegenation that forms the background of so many Latin American countries, I would think back to comments by local Venezuelans asking about news reports of racism in the United States. Telling the unpleasant truth often resulted in a disapproving pursing of the lips and the smug response, "Here we have no racism, everybody is equal." Among Venezuelans, it is common to assert they live in a racial democracy where all forms in inequality are class based. In conjunction with Venezuela, a number of other Latin American countries celebrate the idea of *mestisaje* as key to their unique historical development and concomitant lack of racism (Wright 1990). In the case of Venezuela, the manifestation of Tamunangue is treated as an iconic example of this process. What gets left out in these grand narratives of inclusiveness are the ongoing racial hierarchies and exclusions on which the nations of South America were built and still wrestle with today (Naím 2001; Ruette 2011; Salas 2005). At stake in the embracing of these national origin myths is in the act of raising a local practice to the level of a national treasure often occurs through the covering up or marginalization of alternative subaltern or popular histories that do not fit the needs of the political elite.

North Atlantic Military and Civil Combative Traditions in Venezuela: Iberian Influences

Available data suggest the stick, machete, and knife fighting practices found in the Segovia Highlands today are best treated as part of a larger constellation of civilian combative traditions found throughout Latin America and the Caribbean, whose roots lie in the military and civilian combative traditions once current throughout Europe and Africa.[5] As garrote in the Segovia Highlands is practiced today by those who began to learn in the 1930s and 1940s, the art evinces strong European influences seen in the way these men hold and move their bodies and weapons in comparison to other African and Afro-Caribbean stick-fighting styles that I have been exposed to.[6] These impressions are supported by archival research that shows the majority of immigrants into Venezuela before World War II originated from Spain (Lopez 1999). Investigating the existence of armed combative traditions of Western Europe suggests that sword-, knife-, and stick-fighting traditions were once common among the popular classes until the beginning of the twentieth century. In addition to the well-known martial abilities of the Spanish soldiers in the early modern era, there are a number of fragmentary sources that suggest a wealth of civilian combative arts revolving around the use of agricultural, herding, and craftsmen tools (once widespread in Western Europe) could have contributed to the development of garrote (Bishko 1953; Perry 1980). Nevertheless, it was the knife, the machete, and the stick that became the principal weapons associated with much of Latin American combative traditions (Assunção 1999; Foote 2010; Markoff 2005; Osornio 1995; Ryan 2011).

What makes Venezuela unique in the Luso-Hispanic valorization of the blade is the preference for the walking-stick length both as a symbol of being a gentleman as well as serving as a fearsome weapon. One likely source for the popularity of stick fighting in Venezuela dates back to the late-eighteenth century when the carrying of a walking stick was a part of the everyday dress among European males. As modern forms of state governments were beginning to exert their legitimacy to monopolize the use of violence, there was an increasing intolerance for dueling, brawling, and vendettas that characterized masculine social life. In response to these changing attitudes toward violence, elite and middle-class urban dwellers had begun to replace the carrying of rapiers and other thrusting types of swords developed for urban combat with walking sticks, sword canes, and weighted sticks (Amberger 1999; Wolf 2002). The unique trajectory of combat among the elite and the expanding merchant class should not exclude the continued practice of armed and unarmed combative arts continued among the popular classes in Europe that equally might have had an influence on the development of garrote.

For example, in many parts of Venezuela where garrote persists, instead of carrying a palo of walking-stick length, some men prefer carrying a shorter and thicker two-foot-long braided handle stick that served both as a riding crop for mules and for self-defense. From this use, it follows that another possible root of garrote lies in the practices of livestock raising and herding cultures of southern Spain. The uncertainty of definitively pinning down the origins of stick fighting in Venezuela notwithstanding, the variety of combative traditions practiced as methods of self-defense, as a recreational pastime, or as religious celebration points to the diversity, sophistication, and ubiquity of combative traditions through the region and a number of possible avenues of transmission into Latin America.

On a technical level, there are a number of similarities that point to major influences from Europe. One is the way that if the fighter is right handed, he will stand with his left foot forward and hold the stick in his right or rear hand. This is contrary to many Afro-Colombian stick and machete styles where the weapon is held in the front hand, where a man who is right handed will stand with his right foot forward and hold the weapon in his right or lead hand. To muddy the waters even more, there are a number of Caribbean stick-fighting styles where walking sticks are held at both ends and alternately swung at the opponent. Further parallels to Europe are seen in the beginning of a juego de garrote. Here two men will often circle each other while whirling their palos similar to what Irish Shillelagh fighters call "wheeling," an act which recalls how European saber fighters would make wide circular blows before closing with the opponent (Hurley 2007). Of course, there may be equally persuasive alternative explanations for these similarities; however, taken as a whole, the evidence does point to roots in Iberian combative practices.

GARROTE AND THE AFRICAN DIASPORA

Leaving aside the influence of possible Berber or Tuareg combative traditions and their influence on Iberian combative traditions for another study; *Isleños* or immigrants and their descendants from the Canary Islands have contributed to almost every major event in Venezuela history. In the oral histories of garrote collected around the Tocuyo Valley, the role of immigrants from Canary Islands have influenced at least two contemporary stick-fighting styles that developed during the late nineteenth and early twentieth centuries. A major difficulty with trying to understand the demographic impact of Canary Islanders in the development of garrote in Venezuela is that after lodging passenger manifests with the authorities at their port of departure in Spain, many ships then stopped at the Canary Islands, picking up additional passengers destined for Venezuela, leaving no paper trail (Parsons 1983; Rasmussen 1947). Over the last twenty years, researchers from the Canary Islands have explored and documented the wealth of stick-fighting and wrestling styles on the island chain. Many times only a few families on each island continued to practice these traditions. Investigators from the Canary Islands have also gone to Cuba, Venezuela, and Louisiana searching for the existence of a Canarian form of stick fighting, known as *El palo chico*, done with a walking-size stick or a small stick (Rodríguez 1987).

At present, there are two schools of garrote that claim a strong Canarian influence in the Tocuyo Valley. Moving to a little house near the banks of the Tocuyo River near the barrio of Los Hornos in the early twentieth century, a Canarian immigrant, Temeré Pacheco, is remembered for being the teacher of one of the most renowned garroteros in the city of El Tocuyo; Juan "Cartorce" Yépez. Maestro Temeré was known for his *juego pachuquero*, where an operator holds a walking stick by one hand in the middle and thrusts either end at an opponent in rising and descending "figure 8" motions; a unique method it was said he used to defeat all the local competition (González 2003).

A few miles away up in the foothills above the Tocuyo Valley, the *Siete Lineas* style of El Molino owes its development to the son of a Canarian immigrant. From 1884–1891, León Valera was taught a version of Canary Island stick fighting, as well as Spanish saber techniques, while accompanying his father as a traveling merchant on his trips to the town of Puerto la Ceiba on Lake Maracaibo. One day on the beach, León Valera claimed to have saved the life of a drowning Englishman. As a way of thanking the young man, the Englishman taught him a thrusting type of stick fighting.[7] In conjunction with techniques of Tocuyano stick fighting that he had been exposed to, Léon Valera developed a style of garrote he called the *Siete Lineas* or the "seven ways of attack" style, which he demonstrated to the public during a promessa to San Antonio in the village of La Guarajita outside of El Tocuyo in 1925 (González 2004).

Although I find the existence of these oral histories fascinating, I find problems in the available evidence that make the claims of Canarian stick fighting difficult to accept wholeheartedly. Beginning with the premise that garrote was developed for antagonistic combative modalities, any changes that reduce its efficacy in ending an encounter must be seen as increasing the danger to the operator and therefore unlikely to be a long-standing tactic. As noted by many stick fighters around the world, most fights last only a few seconds with a few blows exchanged before someone drops and another hurries away before the police or friends of the vanquished appear on the scene. The manner in which those who train in el palo canario today stands in stark relief to the needs of a man facing a determined enemy. For example, holding the stick in the middle as is done at present when garroteros demonstrate the *juego pachuquero*, as it is called, means the operator is giving up the advantage of distance in an encounter where supposedly the opponent is gripping the butt end of a regular length stick. Now this by itself is not bad, as I have met Italian, Filipino, and Venezuelan stick fighters who prefer wielding a shorter stick to get inside the range of the longer-stick fighter and wreak havoc on the opponent. However, when performed today both men grasp the stick in the middle so the whole idea of demonstrating one's superior skill in closing the gap against an individual with a longer range weapon is negated. I have yet to see any garrotero who knows the juego pachuquero use their palo in this way with another person using their palo by grasping it near the butt end. Finally, the stick is used to thrust up and down in forehand and backhand moves and cannot generate sufficient power to inflict any stopping power on an individual determined to do someone lasting harm. In the final analysis, instead of being used in antagonistic modes of combat it could be the juego pachuquero is the embodied memory of a style of fighting with the stick that has devolved into a performance type of combative display where two men could entertain a crowd without unduly risking their bodies.[8]

A number of scholars claim that garrote Tocuyano is related to the numerous West and Central African stick-fighting styles around the Caribbean. This blanket statement is difficult to uphold and distorts the diverse historical patterns of local immigration patterns and interactions with local indigenous populations as they took place in different areas of Venezuela over the centuries. In addition to the presence of Afro-Iberian conquistadores in the area during the conquest, approximately 121,000 African slaves were imported in to Venezuela up until 1797, although slavery was not abolished outright until 1854 (Curtin 1969; Salas 2005). Of these people, the majority of them were brought in from other Caribbean countries, making their point of origin difficult to discern. The majority of Africans were settled along the Northern coast where a plantation economy developed. Here in the mountains of Falcón, Guárico, and Miranda states, many of the descendants of these people live and possess their own traditions of stick fighting that has yet to be fully explored. Both written and oral evidence suggests that urban afrodescendente or Afro-Caribbean stick-fighting styles did exist in the port towns of Maracaibo, Puerto Cabello, Tucare, and nearby islands of Curaçao, Trinidad, and Tobago. The only evidence of links between Tocuyano styles of garrote and these coastal styles come from the life experiences of the garrotero Baudillio Ortiz. Working as a laborer in the port towns of Puerto Cabello and Tucare in the 1930s, he claimed to have learned a few stick- and machete-fighting techniques from afrodescendente dockworkers that he then incorporated into his personal style of garrote, which in turn he taught to only six people in his lifetime (Sanoja 1984).

In an attempt to prove the African origins of garrote, some scholars have grasped at the fact that a confradia of freed blacks in the eighteenth century was given permission to hold a festival commemorating Saint Anthony in El Tocuyo. Supporting this view is the fact that in the late nineteenth century, the commemoration dedicated to Saint Anthony was known as *Los Sones de Negros,* or "the Dances of the Blacks." All in all, the evidence is fairly tenuous and unconvincing. More robust evidence of Afro-Venezuelan combative traditions with links to indigenous and European relationships in complex ways and yet to be fully understood are found in other regions of Venezuela. North of the Segovia Highlands in the neighboring state of Falcón, I met a ninety-seven-year-old afrodescendente garrotero who as a young man both himself and his friends style of stick fighting preferred a smaller heavier palo of Vera wood than used in midwestern stick styles.

Continuing, in the same vein, to the east toward the coastal mountain ranges of Miranda and Guárico states in central Venezuela, there is another style of stick fighting practiced by the predominantly rural afrodes-cendentes. Also different from practitioners in Lara, the sticks here are often a thicker and heavier and cut from a Vera tree. To further compli-cate any easy generalizations linking ethnicity to fighting arts, in the foothills of Guárico, local indigenous and afrodescendentes have a long history of the exchange of goods, ideas, and cultures to suit their needs. One local scholar recognizing the key role that this area has played in the meeting of African and indigenous traditions calls this area "the Sierras de Bandola," using the eight-string turtle backed guitar known as the bandola that is played through the region to stand for the continued exchange between peoples (T. Rojas 2010).

In addition to traditions of stick fighting in Venezuela, there are nu-merous fragments of evidence that point to a wealth of armed and un-armed combative traditions being introduced, practiced, and refined throughout the area at different times throughout history. Robert Farris Thompson claims to have interviewed practitioners of foot fighting or *Broma* in the afrodescendente region of the Barlavento (Thompson 1992, xiii–xiv). Head-butting tactics were observed in a number of recreational games or civilian self-defense encounters that seem to have disappeared. According to the historian Desch Obi, "knocking" is a Central-African tradition of head butting where two men bend at the waists and rush at each other, clashing heads or butting an adversary in the torso, which was found at one time throughout the Americas. Head butting by contrast, according to Desch Obi, relies more on using other parts of the head to attack an opponent when in grappling range (Desch Obi 2008, 84–86). One difficulty with marking the practice of head butting and knocking as an exclusive ethnic marker of African combative traditions is that it ignores the ubiquity of head butting and knocking in other parts of the world. In early modern England, for example, both types of head tactics were once seen as widespread and popular (Shoemaker 2001, 196).

From a scholarly point of view, any claim of a combative movement acting as an ethnic marker needs to be treated with care and placed within a historical context of their use, the way they were used, and the meanings, if any, behind these acts before any broad claims are present-ed. An example from Venezuela supports the validity of the claim of head-knocking as an ethnic marker of West-Central African commu-nities. Also implied in following anecdote, however, is that other non-African individuals were familiar with these tactics or were able to quick-ly discern the weakness of these types of movements demonstrating the Hobbesian or evolutionary struggle of combative movements, which means only the most effective tactics persist. During the time when Simón Bolívar began recruiting and landing veterans of Wellington's pe-ninsular campaign, a banker witnessed a set-to between an African and Irishman. Taking place at the port of Angostura on the Orinoco River, a number of African slaves were unloading the trunks of soldiers from a ship to the wharves by walking along a series of planks connecting the two. At one point during this time, one particularly strong and resentful African dockworker would casually mishandle the soldier's gear, even letting it fall off his back into the mud of the shore. Aggrieved at how his property was treated, one soldier called the dockworker to task for his mishandling of his trunk in a very insulting fashion. Adding injury to the insult, so to speak, as the dockworker was bending over to pick up some more boxes, the aggrieved soldier struck the dockworker in his head with a well-intentioned punch. In turn, the soldier was promptly head butted in the stomach for his pains, knocking the wind out of him as he went reeling across the deck. Seeking to teach the insolent man a lesson, a number of other European soldiers each rushed the dockworker, only to be butted and sent flying in turn. Finally, an Irish soldier asked the commanding officer if he could have a try at the man. Given the go-ahead, he hailed the fellow who in response lowered his head and charged at the soldier who merely stood there. At the last moment, the soldier twisted out of the way, driving a knee to the face then landing a hard right behind the ear that knocked the dockworker down and stunned him but failed to dampen his ardor. Lowering his head and charging again with a renewed will, the soldier side-stepped the attempted head butt once more and gave him a knee to the face that flipped him right onto his back where he lay knocked out cold. With such a conclusive ending, the other dockworkers showed more concern to handle all the remaining soldiers gear with more care (Eastwick 2013, 83–85). Minor scuffles such as this one must have been a common occurrence throughout Venezuelan history. In the innumerable oft-forgettable events of everyday life in the frontier regions and the rear of battle zones, men would be thrown together and end up fighting for a number of reasons. The consequences could range from a couple bruises to life crippling injuries or all the way to death. Never making their way into the history books, nevertheless, out of mundane acts of violence such as these is where garrote developed was refined and persists in Venezuela today.

GARROTE AND INDIGENOUS PEOPLES

From the beginning of the conquest when the self-appointed governor Carvajal and his men drove the Tocuyo Indians from the river valley up into the mountains, the spurs of the Andean mountains have long served as places of refuge, resistance, and the setting up of semi-autonomous communities (Arvelo 2000; Querlaes 1997; Yarrington 1997). Here, out of the reach of colonizers, groups of corporate indigenous and detribalized communities, African maroon, and mixed blood farmers had for centuries settled these lands to avoid the harsh demands of hacenderos and recruiting officers. Being out of easy reach of hacenderos and agents of the state also allowed them to control and manage to some extent their contact with local landowners and merchants. Throughout Venezuelan history, indigenous peoples have taken part in every major event in the area.

During the wars of liberation, the Cacique Reyes-Vargas from the area around Baragua in Lara state led a number of Ayaman indigenous warriors alongside Capitan Domingo Monteverde and a few dozen men of his men to overthrow the first Venezuelan Republic. At the time of the Federal Wars in the mid-nineteenth century, a number of Ayamaran Indians served under General Falcón. During the same time, roving Indian bands armed with bows, arrows, and lances sacked the hill town of Sanare in Lara state (Silva 1993). One of the great caudillo leaders was the Camacho Indian Raphael Montilla of Guaitó. From the late nineteenth to early twentieth century, Montilla would rally a number of detribalized Indians and mixed-blood laborers and farmers under his banner, leading his men down from the Andes in to the Segovia Highlands to fight the corrupt and exploitative polices of hacenderos and local caudillos loyal to the *Godos* cause.

What makes the contribution of indigenous peoples difficult in Venezuela is the edict proclaimed by President Gúzman-Blanco in 1881 decreeing that the only indigenous groups to be formally recognized are in the far northwest of Venezuela around Lake Maracaibo and the extreme south in Bolivar State (Ruette 2011). Among other old garroteros, after we had come to know each other, we would often discuss our shared indigenous heritage, leading me to understand that many peoples here still claim indigenous roots in spite of government and ethnological expert's views to the contrary. Strands of evidence such as these lead me to suggest over the last couple of centuries an increasing number of detribalized indigenous men continuously co-opted and refined elements of European cultural technology and values such as garrote to proclaim and defend their sense of coevalness with those claiming a Spanish heritage and were prepared to defend these claims in a very intimate and immediate physical manner. As opposed to a bow, arbequeses, or musket, fighting with a stick or machete one can look into another man's eyes and see hatred, fear, or pain. One can hear the crack of a stick against bone and hear the labored breathing of exhaustion or grunts and moans of pain. Many times the sweat, saliva, blood, and vomit of an opponent would cover one's weapon or body, making the act of engaging in combat with a palo, machete, or knife with an opponent a very intimate process, as combatants battled to affirm their humanity with others who would seek to deny them this status.

CONCLUSION

There is an old boxing adage that goes along the lines "styles make fights but rules make styles." However, as this case study suggests, ultimately, it is the man who fights. It is a living subject whose determination, skill, and luck or random chance must be included in any account of how a combat or any social interaction takes shape and the meaning that emerges from these encounters. Attempting to trace the genealogies of the number of combative traditions that came to Venezuela as a result of the incorporation of Venezuela into the North Atlantic political-economy, it is clear that men continued to bring with them sets of values, norms, and practical understandings regarding the proper use of combat. Throughout history, men understood that combative encounters could occur in a wide array of modalities, ranging from recreational sparring between friends to civil-based contests over questions of honor or property disputes, to all-out battlefield combat. Men also realized how different combative modalities could call upon different weapons or different usages of the same weapon to shape the end result of the encounter. Furthermore, these embodied knowledges, values, and moralities were often transmitted, co-opted, refined, and changed continuously, incorporated in varying degrees into existing systems of armed combat through the many local regions of northern South America that became known as Venezuela.

NOTES

1. This should serve as a warning for all aspiring anthropologists to distrust all previous scholarly claims regarding the status of an aspect of a community's culture.

2. For example, see Castillo (1908).

3. I first learned about garrote wandering through the library at the University of California Los Angeles in 1992, when I found a book by Eduardo Sanoja. I made one-week trips to Venezuela in 1998 and 2004. I spent seven months in the Segovia Highlands and Andes in 2005 and made a six-week trip to the Segovia Highlands, Coro, and Guárico in 2013.

4. For an example of these old ball games, see the early modern expression of Florentine football or Calcio Fiorentino on YouTube, where twenty-six men compete on each side with little rules or regulations. Looking at the video and the brawling you will even see the men fighting over the ball at times. http://www.youtube.com/watch?v=WsRqSNSjy3E. Video: Calico Storico Fiorentino.

5. In Europe, see Amberger (1999); Caçador (1963); Conley (1999); Huggins (2000); Hurley 2007; Wolf (2002); Spierenberg (1998); Yilkangas (2001).

6. My exposure to Caribbean combative practices is limited to looking at videos on YouTube and Vimeo.

7. I saw Pasqual and José-Felipe Alvarado engage in this style of stick fencing once. Facing to the side with their weapon hands forward and in a right-legged forward stance, they used their palos to thrust at the head and upper body of each other while using their left hands that they kept high near their right shoulder to parry attacks.

8. During my last trip to Barquisimeto, I saw a photograph of an old palo used in the juego pachuquero style. There was a braided handle one-third of the way up the palo. This supports my idea of an imperfect transmission of the art and its corresponding loss of any combative potential as it becomes a purely spectator driven act.

TWO

The Civilizing of a Nation

Here I will mark out the general historical development of Venezuela as it relates to the locating the practice of the garrote and machete within a larger North Atlantic political-economic sphere. Within this frame of reference, I claim the transmission of garrote until the present is a result of a "civilizing process," whereby elite political factions engaged in a century's long struggle amongst themselves to impose their vision of at first a well-governed profitable colony and then as independent nation-state. Not only fighting amongst themselves, elite factions waged an equally long and ferocious campaign against the non-elite indigenous, afrodescendentes, and small-hold farmers, who have up until the present continued to resist attempts to dispossess them of their land, strip them of their history, and reduce them to hispanicized landless laborers. Shaping and being shaped within these political and economic struggles was an equally intense ideological struggle regarding the rights and the limits of both the state and individuals to engage in acts of instrumental, symbolic, and recreational violence. Limiting myself to a few key developments, this chapter aims to foreground some of the economic and social structures that shaped the unique development and contributed to the persistence of combative arts in Venezuela. In addition, the groundwork is laid suggesting garrote is best conceptualized as a set of heterogeneous civilian combative practices that took shape and continue to develop based on the needs of each generation, as well as their exposure to other communities, goods, and ideas. To this end, the role of the immigration of different ethnic communities whose natal communities themselves have long-held traditions of armed combat is highlighted. Within this matrix of different peoples, I claim a civilizing process took shape within Venezuela, resulting in the unique manifestation, development, and persistence of Venezuelan civilian combative traditions.

37

CONQUEST AND THE COLONIAL ERA

Sitting on the northern coast of South America, the Bolivarian Republic of Venezuela has one of the most diverse ecosystems in South America. It is also one of the most urbanized countries in Latin America. A recent census counted over 31,000,000 people, with approximately 73 percent of the total population of the country living within a fifty-mile belt of the northern coast (http.//earthtrends.wri.org. 2000:1). The story of Venezuela began on August, 24, 1499, just a few years after Columbus made his final voyage, when Alonso de Ojeda sailed into Lake Maracaibo. Accompanying him was the Italian cartographer Amerigo Vespucci. Looking upon the wood stilts houses over the surface of the water reminded him of the canals of Venice and so named the region *Veneziola*. Alternately, it could be the indigenous inhabitants of the area called themselves "Veneciuela" (Thomas 2005, 189). Nevertheless, from this point the conquest of Venezuela began in two separate locations: the northeastern coast where a pearl extraction industry was set up on Islas Cubagua and Margarita (Baños 1987). Here at great cost to Indian lives, pearling proved to be the first profitable industries for the conquistadores until the end of the sixteenth century when the pearl beds became exhausted. (Baños 1987). The reliance on export–oriented natural resources, with its cyclic boom and busts, continues to characterize the Venezuelan economy, shaping its political and social realms up through the present.

More relevant for the conquest to the settlement of Venezuela was the expedition of Capitan Juan de Ampués, tasked by the Audencia Real in Santo Domingo to reassert control over the rampant and unregulated slave raiding, providing labor to the plantations on Santo Domingo and other Caribbean islands. To facilitate this project, the town of Santa Ana de Coro was established in 1527 in northwestern Venezuela. Shortly after the founding of Coro, the Spanish Emperor Charles V sought a loan from the house of Welsers to shore up and defend his European holdings. As collateral for the loan, Charles granted the house of Welsers the privilege to settle and exploit Venezuela. After twenty years of ruthless plundering, slave raids on Indian communities, and many failed attempts to find the golden cities of El Dorado or El Gran Patite, the emperor terminated their lease. Newly appointed as governor, Juan Pérez de Tolosa was sent to Coro to administer the province. Preparing conditions for his upcoming duties was his chief officer Juan de Carvajal. On his way to Coro, Carvajal forged a set of papers to pass himself off as the new governor. Received suspiciously by local officials, Carvajal's men confiscated all the weapons and horses they could collect. Carvajal then bullied and threatened 200 men into following him into the interior of the country. Setting up camp in the Tocuyo Valley, Carvajal and his group met up with the German former governor of the province returning from an expedition. Sharing dinner that night, an argument ensued between both men over whose authority took precedence, leading to Carvajal attempting to arrest the German leaders and being arrested in return, although he was soon released the next morning. Both parties agreed to set off to Coro separately to settle their dispute. Leaving for the coast, the German party was ambushed by Carvajal's men, who then proceeded to hack off the heads of the leaders with a dull machete. Afterward, after driving the indigenous Tocuyanos up into the surrounding hills, and on his own authority, Carvajal set up the town of Nuestra Señora de la Pura y Limpia Concepción del Tocuyo in 1545. Shortly after, the actual governor arrived in El Tocuyo and, according to differing sources, had Carvajal hung from a Ceiba tree in either the center or outside of town. Due to the valleys fertility and healthier climate, El Tocuyo soon became the seat for the Captaincy-General of Venezuela from 1545–1569, from whence it was soon transferred to Caracas. Out of these struggles, El Tocuyo became known as *El Ciudade Madre*, the mother-city of all Venezuela. For decades, the majority of exploration, conquest, and settlements were led by contingents of Tocuyanos or worked their way down the coast to set off from El Tocuyo (Baños 1987). As it relates to this book, many Tocuyano garroteros and foreign scholars have long asserted the Tocuyo Valley is the birthplace of garrote.

Historically, Venezuela has lacked the large mineral deposits and highly centralized indigenous political systems, found by conquistadores in Mexico and Peru, with large bodies of readily available cheap labor. Lacking in obvious advantages, Venezuela quickly slipped into the margins of the Spanish empire. Compensating for its obvious deficiencies, Venezuela developed a strong trade with both its colonial neighbors and trans-Atlantic markets, with at first Andean wheat and then cacao being sold to Mexico and the Spanish fleet. In addition to this trade, conquistadores took advantage of the lands fertility to set up *encomiendas* (Ewell 1984; Hellinger 1991). Encomiendas were grants by the crown of a certain number of indigenous workers from nearby indigenous villages or a resettlement camp of indigenous peoples known as a *Doctrina de Pueblo*. Indigenous males were coerced into providing a fixed amount of produce or corvée labor to the encomendero. In exchange for this labor, encomenderos were enjoined to protect and care for their charges, as they were incorporated into the emerging colonial system. All too often, these series of obligations and duties were observed more in the breech than the observance, leading to attempts to reduce communities to outright slaves. In turn, this led indigenous communities to draw on a wide range of tactics of resistance and accommodation, such as relocating to nearby hills or migrating to different regions where they could seek to establish more advantageous trading circuits. The propensity of indigenous and other non-elite communities to draw on strategies of spatial relocation in response to oppressive conditions led to a never-ending stream of complaints from local hacenderos and politicians about their inabilities to maintain an adequate labor force, until the mid-twentieth century when a shift to state subsidized agro-industrial practices did away with the need for a large labor pool in favor of seasonally employed wage-laborers.

The role of Africans in Venezuela begins with a small number of Afro-Iberian conquistadores accompanying Iberian adventurers. Africans were first imported as slave labor by the German banking house of Welsers in 1528, followed by the Basque cacao cartel. After their lease was revoked, many of the great European powers supplied slaves to Venezuela, not only from Africa but from other Caribbean countries. Altogether a total of 121,000 individuals found themselves laboring in Venezuela as a result of the Atlantic slave trade (Curtin 1969). Scholars have begun to uncover the history of these peoples and their tendency to set up semi-autonomous communities just outside the de facto control of landowners and local militias, actively developing their own relationships of trading with or raiding local communities (Herrera 2003; Ruette 2011; Tardieu 2013). Bolivar proposed the abolition of slavery at the Congress of Angostura in 1819, but slavery was not constitutionally outlawed until 1854. From this time onward, afrodescendentes have continually struggled to have their corporate identity recognized, as well as land claims (Perozo 2001; Ruette 2011). During my last trip to Venezuela in 2013, I encountered a strong afrodescendente presence in the mountains of Coro and the coastal mountain ranges of central Venezuela, where I learned stick fighting still remains an important yet hidden part of everyday life.

Political and socially, Venezuela is still organized by a strict racial hierarchy whose workings are still occluded through a national discourse of criollo-ness. The ideology of criollo-ness that emerged out of the apocalyptic destruction of civil society of the Federal Wars of the mid-nineteenth century claimed that all ethnic communities had become so mixed as to make any racial distinctions utterly untenable. Consequently, while Venezuelan has struggled in the past and continues to struggle with problems of inequality, these struggles are claimed to be based on class alone and not race (Salas 2005; Perozo et al. 2001; Wright 1990). The official ideological myth of racial miscegenation has been embraced by people from all walks of life throughout Venezuela; nevertheless, looking at the historical record presents a different story supporting an alternative narrative told by indigenous and afrodescendente groups. Indigenous communities who never suffered a major population decline were deprived of their land and legislated out of existence with a number of decrees throughout the nineteenth century.

Archival records of ship registers show that prior to the 1940s, the majority of the European population that came to Venezuela originated out of the Iberian Peninsula. The demographic impact of Canarian immigrants is difficult to determine. Many times after lodging passenger manifests with authorities, ships often stopped and picked up a number of Canarian immigrants who left no paper trail (Parsons 1983). The first attempt to create reliable census of the Venezuelan population in 1873 revealed a population of 1,743,411 people (XIV Censo Nacional 2014, 12). These numbers changed little over the years, and immigration never proved to be a major source of demographic growth until the end of the WWII. During this time, politicians and other elites influenced by a "Positivist" philosophy that was popular among European elites at the time sought once again to encourage European immigration in order to "whiten" and bring progress to the nation (Kritz 1975, 518). From 1948 until 1955 when immigration was sharply curtailed, about one million people flooded into the country, primarily from Italy, Spain, and Portugal, accounting for 7 percent of the total population (Kritz 1975, 520–521).[1] At the same time, the rural areas had begun to emerge from their feudalistic past while undergoing a rural to urban pattern of migration that had begun in the mid-nineteenth century and continues through today, resulting in the majority of the population residing in urban areas along the coast.

INDEPENDENCE, POST-LIBERATION, AND CAUDILLISMO

Venezuelan independence arose out of the Napoleonic take-over of Spain, when in 1810 Napoleon gave the throne of Spain to his brother. Believing any allegiance to the crown had come to an end, the Cabildo of Caracas constituted itself as a representative body, called itself into a special meeting, and declared its independence from Spain. Over the next ten years, armies made up of civilian levies, ex-slaves, outlaws, a great number of independent indigenous communities, and those under the administration of religious orders were impressed or joined a revolving number of royalist and national leaders who took turns taking and losing Caracas. Finally, after ten years of battles Simón Bolívar, fresh from liberating Colombia, drove in from the west and defeated the royalist troops at the Battle of Carabobo in 1821. With this victory came an end to major fighting in the area and guaranteed Venezuela its independence at a cost of one-third of its population. (Hellinger 1991, 23). At first part of a grand union of Colombia, Venezuela, and Ecuador, Venezuela soon broke away from this Bolivarian state and set up an independent government under the presidency of the great caudillo leader from the Llanos, José Antonio Paéz.

During the nineteenth and the first half the twentieth century, caudillismo was the dominant form of government throughout much of Latin America. Referencing the historian Gilmore's definition of caudillismo, Gilmore writes of it as "the union of personalism and violence for the conquest of power. It is a means for the selection and establishment of political leadership in the absence of socials structure and political groupings adequate to the functioning of the representative government" (Gilmore 1964, 47). Caudillismo arose out of the destructiveness of the wars of liberation that wiped out almost all civil institutions and left a political vacuum in the area. The ensuing lack of social and political stability was filled at first by charismatic or powerful local men who could gather and hold together veterans, ex-slaves, bandits, ruined farmers, or detribalized Indians. Caudillismo soon became institutionalized and legitimized over the next 100 years, with these men fighting over who would gain the right to exploit the workers and the revenues of the custom houses of the Venezuelan ports. With the democratic election of a civilian government in 1958 can one say that the institution of caudillismo finally came to an end. Characterizing these men, Gilmore shows they:

> were chiefs, heads of clans, great landowners, like Diego Colina who at a word could call out the cane-cutters of the southern sierras of Coro. Or like General Ramón Castillo who could draft a thousand men from his family properties or like the Tellerias who through family connections occupied most of the higher and many of the middle and lower posts of state government could use the resources of the state of Falcón. (Gilmore, 52–53)

Acknowledging the propensity of caudillos to institute a regime change through violent means a newspaper once wrote:

> Venezuelans are accustomed to the "revolutionary" uprisings called in creole slang a "leap from the woods" or assaúlt in which an inquiet señor, a rancher, or owner of an coffee, cacao or other agricultural hacienda "gave the cry" on his property and took to the bush accompanied by 400 peons armed with chopping machetes or even ancient blunderbusses. (Gilmore, 78–79)

During this time the increasing dissatisfaction with the distribution of political patronage from Caracas led a number of local caudillos leaders from the west to mobilize their workers to affect a regime change. Events soon got out of hand, and what began as an elite coup exploded into a full-blown jacquirie, or class war, with strong racial overtones and all the concomitant scorched-earth tactics accompanying this type of violence. From 1858 until 1863, the Federal Wars, as this time became known, led to the deaths of approximately 40,000–100,000 people or 5 percent of the overall population, the destruction of all organized economic activity, and the end of all functioning government (Hellinger 1991, 25).

Toward the end, the governor of the state of Coro, General Falcón, drove in from the west, took Caracas, and assumed the presidency. Falcón tried to secure the peace by dividing Venezuela up into twenty states, each ruled by a caudillo who was accorded regular subsidies, allowed to distribute local political offices, and attack other regional caudillos (Marsland et al. 1954). Finally the caudillo leader Gúzman-Blanco took Caracas in a bloodless coup in 1871. President Gúzman-Blanco is remembered for trying to turn Venezuela into a modern nation along the lines of France. Railroads and telegraphs were built to ease the exporting of raw material to shipping ports and the number of competing warlords was reduced from twenty to nine with the consolidation and reorganizing of internal boundaries.

As part of a project of modernizing Venezuela, Gúzman-Blanco strengthened ties to a North Atlantic political-economic sphere, forging a dependent relationship with foreign businesses to maintain the newly built infrastructure. The historian John Lombardy points out, for example, how the importation of Winchester repeating rifles into Venezuela and the conscription and arming of regularly paid soldiers had profound political consequences as "no longer could a provincial caudillo collect his peons, armed with lances and knives and march toward Caracas with any chance of success" (Lombardy 1982, 196).

The advent of the twentieth century for Venezuela was preceded by the last of the successful regime changes for almost half a century. In 1891, exiled attorney Cipriano Castro and Juan V. Gómez, along with sixty of his relatives and dependents, invaded Venezuela from their place of exile in Colombia. Avoiding major contact with opposing forces until reaching the city of Valencia, the armed levies of Castro entered Caracas peacefully and took up the reins of power. During his reign where he dedicated himself to hedonistic excess, two events occurred that bear upon this study. The first was a naval blockade in 1902–1903, imposed by the United Kingdom, Germany, and Italy in retaliation for the reneging on the repayment of debts incurred by previous administrations. During this time, oral histories tell of local Venezuelans being upset at the cavalier and arrogant attitudes and behaviors of foreign sailors and marines occupying the ports of La Guairá and Puerto Cabello. The late garrotero from El Tocuyo Baudillio Ortiz recounted to investigator Eduardo Sanoja how, as a construction worker in Puerto Cabello and Tucare, he used to listen to stories from fellow construction workers about how their fathers and grandfathers would often end up fighting against these soldiers with sticks and machetes (Sanoja 1984).[2]

The next was the "Liberation Revolution" of 1902–1903, which proved to be the death knell of the once independent provincial caudillos. Facing their first trial by fire under the leadership of Juan V. Gómez, the newly armed and trained Venezuelan army pitted itself against a coalition of provincial caudillo militias in a three-day inconclusive battle that proved to be the tipping point in favor of President Castro. After hostilities had ceased, the caudillo coalition broke up and went their own ways to make terms with the government or fight it out on their own. Following this battle, a further 210 smaller battles were fought at the cost of 12,000 lives in order to secure Castro's rule (Ewell 1984, 45).

For the next ten years, Gómez acted as Castro's loyal and obsequious second in command. Gómez then led a coup in 1908 when Castro was in Europe seeking medical care. Taking advantage of a renewed global demand for Venezuelan coffee, Gómez used this economic bounty to crush or co-opt all opponents or potential opponents. Among his major actions was the abolishment of the federal council in 1914 ending the caudillo system, even though revolts occurred in 1918, 1921, and 1929. In 1919, Gómez instituted another ban on the carrying of weapons and set up collection points where all arms must be surrendered. This effectively reversed the course of events that began in 1830, when President Paéz distributed arms to all militia members, who were to store their weapons at home. Further consolidating his power, Gómez added an amendment to the constitution outlawing all militias in 1925. According to local narratives, during the downtime between training and campaigns was a prime time to learn and or practice one's skill with the garrote.

The death of Gómez in 1935 unleashed a three-month period of revenge against his ruthless followers and policies. Suggesting once again the ubiquity of machetes among rural Venezuelans and their willingness to use them to resolve personal disputes, a Caraqueño newspaper reported that on Christmas Eve, a group of rural laborers went up to their boss's house:

> Senora Muñoz asked them what they wanted and [the leader] responded that they had come by the order of the government to kill, burn, and exact justice for seven years of tyranny. The senora demanded that they show the papers authorizing such horrors and he responded that he did not have to show her any papers, shouting "long live the liberty of the Poor, down with the Rich!" . . . they hurled themselves through the portico that separated the house from the crowd, destroying it, and they began to spread kerosene . . . smashing the furniture and other belongings to pieces with their machetes. (Hellinger 1991, 52)

After the death of Gómez, Venezuela was ruled by a series of officers from the Andean provinces. Up until the 1950s, rural Venezuela still possessed a semi-feudal structure with patrons having a free hand to exploit and mistreat their laborers. In the urban areas at this time, officers, civil servants, and businessmen took advantage of the restricted electoral requirements to maintain control over the government and the distribution of offices and public work contracts. The rising power and increasing demands of a newly expanding urban middle class strongly influenced by various socialist ideologies coming out of the oil fields around Maracaibo were balanced against the old oligarchy of businessmen and landowners. Another military coup in 1945, and the subsequent handover of the government to civilian rule in turn was overturned by one final military coup in 1948. After ten years of military dictatorships, the banding together of disgruntled officers in conjunction with a general strike ended the military dictatorship and ushered in a series of civilian governments that have lasted until the present.

CONFLICT IN LARA

Looking at the political history in Lara state, a geopolitical divide appears during the nineteenth-century wars of liberation and continuing up through the early twentieth century. Acting as the dividing line, the city of Barquisimeto and the surrounding area at first separated royalist forces and then centralizing forces in the north and east from the liberationist and then Federalist loyalists to the south and west. Serving as prime battleground to settle their differences, the southern regions of Lara state has been the site for over sixty-four battles and years of low-level endemic guerilla warfare until the 1960s. Over the years, competing caudillos regularly mobilized, unpaid relatives and laborers who would march back and forth across the area, wantonly destroying any remaining infrastructure remaining from earlier conflicts and trying their best to strip clean the farms and towns they came across of livestock and crops to feed and transport themselves.

One of the last major revolts occurring in Lara took shape as part of the attempted coup by former Gómez loyal officer General José Raphael Galbadón. Responding to the ruthless repression of a student riot in Ca-

Figure 2.1.   An old hacienda in the Tocuyo valley

racas that included his son, General Galbadón wrote a public letter to President Gómez asking that the oppressive polices governing Venezuela be lifted and there be a return to constitutional law. Interpreting this request as a threat to his rule, Gómez ordered the arrest of Galbadón, forcing him to take up arms. Launching a coup from his hacienda in the countryside of Guanare state in the Andes, men loyal to his cause moved down into the Tocuyo Valley where the local elites threw in their lot with the general (Heredia 1974; Rojas 2009).[3] Among the men who made up his army was a local contingent led by Sandalio Linnares of the hamlet of Guarajita just outside of El Tocuyo.[4] Under his command were the well-known garroteros Frolian Torrealba, Martín Fernandez, Gregorio Agüere and his sons Goyon and Lino Agüere, Augustín Linnares, Luís Felipe García, Rito Aguilar, León Valera, and Antonio Linnares. In addition to training other volunteers in machete tactics, they acted as a shock force preceding the main body of men or engaged in covert operations. One night, under the leadership of Linnares they took off all their clothes and with their machetes in their hands snuck into El Tocuyo and captured the *Jefe Civil* of El Tocuyo (González 2003, 40–41). Taking advantage of his newly built rail system, Gómez dispatched five armies from different direction to surround General Galbadón and his men and drove them back up in to the mountains and to his hacienda, where he was surrounded, captured, and imprisoned. As a result of this uprising, Gómez installed his sadistic brother Eustacio as governor of Lara to terrorize and cow the local population. Following the death of President Gómez in 1935, and as reported by the *Chicago Tribune* in its Christmas edition of 1935, Eustacio himself was shot down in the presidential palace at point-blank range by the brother of one of his victims when Caraqueños stormed the palace. Then, in a strange turn of events, the ex-general Raphael Galbadón was made the new governor of Lara.

Not surprisingly this time was characterized as a time of economic stagnation for the area, reflecting the feudal nature of rural Venezuela exacerbated with warring caudillos and guerrilla bands roaming back and forth across the country. Up until the 1940s, Lara was ruled by oligarchy of absentee landlords and merchants. In the early twentieth century, another surge in the global demand for coffee led to the extension of the Bolivariano railroad from Barquisimeto to the port of Tucare and contributed to the development of Barquisimeto as a gateway center for midwestern Venezuela, until it was replaced by Valencia in the late twentieth century (Rojas 1996, 2002). Accompanying this period of economic prosperity was a major earthquake in 1950, destroying 80 percent of the local infrastructure and causing a large loss of life, which contributed to a pattern of rural to urban migration that continues up to through the present. Also accompanying these times were an ongoing series of organized strikes and labor unrest throughout the country, which were brutally put down until the return to civilian rule in 1958.

A Cuban-inspired uprising in Venezuela held a strong place in the memory among a number of rural people in the country when I wandered around the area looking for those who would speak to me about garrote. The Simón Bolívar Front in Lara was headed up by the grandson of the revolutionary leader José Raphael Galbadón, Argimiro Galbadón, up until his death in a car accident in 1964. The villages south of El Tocuyo are still remembered as a *zona roja*, a liberated zone where the Venezuelan military would not enter unless accompanied by heavily armored trucks. Although eventually suppressed, the uprising is largely remembered as part of a series of struggles for freedom by the local inhabitants of the area from unjust rule. The garrotero José-Felipe Alvarado often made this connection explicit through linking stories of his times with the guerrillas with his grandfathers and his garrote teacher León Valera who fought as a colonel in the guerilla army of General Montilla. Raphael Montilla Petaquero (1859–1907) is still remembered today among many older local Venezuelans as swooping down from the hills with his army of volunteers to fight against the centralizing and oppressive polices of conservative Venezuelan presidents and their caudillo allies who tried to expropriate the land and water rights and oppress local Indian communities and small farmers (Tapia 2010).

CONCLUSION

Shifts in the political-economic modes of production and distribution had profound consequences for the practice and transmission of garrote in the Segovia Highlands. Foremost was the emergence of a strong centralized state able to monopolize the legitimate use of violence, leading to the military taking the lead in controlling regime changes. Transformations in the relations of production, the increase in the distribution of government funds, as well as changing social relations, acted as a "civilizing process" resulting in a growing intolerance or embarrassment toward wild expressive public behavior. In this new type of environment, the hard-drinking, hell-raising, mule-riding, stick-fighting type of individual had little place in the new order of things. However, these men who were seen as an embarrassment to those embracing the increasing wealth the new order had brought were also seen as guardians of traditional local ways of dealing with the world that could serve as a good stead for those facing the vagaries of an often ruthless and pitiless world.

NOTES

1. Approximately one-half of these peoples had returned to their countries of origin by 1961.

2. Even now there is supposed to be a two-handed method of stick fighting still practiced in Puerto Cabello in the state of Falcón. I planned on visiting the area in 2013 but was dissuaded by some people who told me it was only a children's dance. I now have reason to believe there is a combative element to the art as taught by some teachers.

3. Drawing on laborers from his hacienda, relatives, and a few supporters, his army numbered 400 men and began their revolt with 25 Mauser rifles, 30 other rifles, 40 revolvers, and 100 machetes.

4. A bust of Linnares was erected in 1987 to commemorate his dedication to the freedom of the pueblos. Linnares died of malaria in 1931 in the nearby state of Yaratigua, where he was buried.

THREE

Sites and Pedagogies of Garrote

Now we move to an examination of the sites where garrote was taught and the diverse pedagogical methods that were used and are still used to today to transmit the art. One element I want to point out is the wide variety of settings and diverse teaching methods that militates against the idea of garrote diffusing from a core location at one point in time. The admittedly incomplete record of teaching sites that have come down to us of what was once much more widespread phenomena suggests the importance that garrote held among men not only as an icon of one's manhood, but also as a practical tool of self-defense. In turn, this leads to a consideration of the palo and auxiliary weapons a man might draw upon when needed. To this end, I provide a brief description how a tree branch is chosen and modified in order to transform it into a weapon able to withstand the blows of other palos or machetes, while at the same time possessing an aesthetic beauty that can reflect the character of the man who has made and carries it. I then provide a brief overview of a number of other weapons that are taught under the rubric of garrote at present.

I once asked one of my teachers if there were any other styles or schools of garrote in his village? He replied that he knew of two different styles or schools of garrote. In addition to his own style that was brought to the area and taught to his grandfather back in the 1930s, there was another one that no one really knew anything about. My teacher did however know a couple of men by sight who was purported practitioners of this local style of garrote. One of the men, an older man, lived deep in the country far away from everybody and would never admit he knew anything; "what the hell are you talking about, I don't know anything about garrote, get the hell away from me," he would respond when asked. In regards to his own style, his knowledge of his art stretched as far back as his grandfather picking it up from a Clarencio Flores, who

49

came to the area to work the sugarcane fields around 1930. In keeping with this lack of historical concern was a similar nondescript name of the stick fighting style la *riña con palos* or fighting with sticks. The casual disinterest in the history of the art or the matter-of-fact name of the art betrays the mundane existence of the art as just another aspect of everyday village life. Just as a cooking pot was called a cooking pot and was used to cook with, a palo was called a palo and was used to fight with. Be that as it may, accounts have come down from the mid-twentieth century that suggest among some there was a concern to organize and hierarchize a body of knowledge in order to present it in a gradual and comprehensive manner to students. What is noticeable in the act of setting up a school is a concern to properly equip the younger generation with a set of skills that a young man needed to possess.

FORMAL TRAINING SITES

In Barquisimeto, there were at least three schools of garrote in the early to mid-twentieth century that we know about. One was led by Asunción Alvarez. The policeman Ishmael Colmenares ran a school of garrote on the outskirts of Barquisimeto in the mid-twentieth century.[1] Not far from the local university, Félix García ran a garrote school out of his shoe shop from the early 1950s to 2002. One of the fullest descriptions of training comes out of early twentieth-century El Tocuyo. In a history of the town, a local chronicler described how a group of young elite men would meet in the courtyard of a family known for cultivating and supporting the arts and other intellectual pursuits to learn garrote from ethnically or otherwise marked members of the popular classes:

> In the house of La Nigua, so-called because in the center of the large courtyard there was a beautiful Nigua tree whose dense and green foliage was twenty meters in circumference. It was famous as the Nigua tree of the unforgettable Valentin Pérez.[2] For quite some time, in this house the first tocuyano press was housed, where the illustrious priest Leonardo Antonio Colmenares taught typesetting, where the inspiring musical composer Don Hildebrsand Rodreiguez began his divine art and where in the courtyard, the juego de garrote was taught by the watchman of Lara Plaza, Juan "El Morocco." On occasion the class was led by Juan "Cartorce," so-named due to the 14 stab wounds he received thanks to an enemy who attacked him when he was sleeping in his hammock. (Bujanda-Yépez 1969, 164)

Much as Capoeira in the city of Salvador evolved around the same time where lower class, ethnically marked males who gained reputations in the streets as good fighters were hired to teach their art, garrote as it took shape in the Tocuyo Valley underwent similar processes. Holding classes at enclosed sites such as gymnasiums, military bases, or private residences, young upwardly mobile elite males could safely practice a street art felt to be a valued local cultural tradition and a healthy and somewhat risky pastime.[3] Reading on, the author continues:

> One afternoon one of the onlookers that was older than the usual crowd asked Juan "Cartorce" why he had let himself be stabbed without defending himself, as he is supposed to be a master. He answered him with open contempt, that if he were not sleeping, not one hair on his head would have been touched by the villain. To demonstrate this and to preserve his honor, he lay on his back on the floor of the courtyard and ordered one of his most advanced students to hit him with a palo; a request that was immediately complied with and at great force. However, Juan Cartorce escaped unharmed in a spectacular proof of his abilities. With amazing rapidity, he sat up, disarmed his attacker, and threw him to the ground in such a way that drew roars of laughter from the onlookers. (164–65)

What stands out in this passage is the way training with the palo is conducted in a semi-private space, limiting the gaze of the curious and comments of onlookers. The unusual commentary from the sidelines foregrounds the public sphere where men built and maintained their reputation against all those seeking to burnish their reputation at the expense of others. In this vein, touched to the quick by this questioning of his skills in an upper-class courtyard where he would not have been able to confront the man head-on at the cost of offending his elite sponsors and spending time in jail or at least the possibility of losing his job as a teacher, Juan Yépez chooses to show his mastery of garrote from disadvantaged positions with one of his students, demonstrating that garroteros regularly trained to meet and deal with assaults in all types of situations.

From this point the author shifts to how a typical class was led through its paces:

> With the fighter Juan Cartorce leading them, he soon had them gasping for breath then led them to a large earthen jug of water. . . . Next, he began what he called the theoretical part of the course . . . because you have to know how to defend yourself from wild animals. With his Vera wood palo in his hand, he then ordered one of his students to stand in front of him, stick in his hand and positioning himself in an appropriate ready stance quickly shifted his body from one posture to another as Juan attacked him with different blows of the palo. He quickly learned, that if he were too slow he would get a Vera wood stick across the head "so that you don't fall asleep" as the Master used to say. This warning as Roberto Montesinos used to say with his fine irony qualified as the highest teaching method. (164–65)[4]

In what he called a "theoretical part of the class" designed to deal with what he called "wild animals," the idea of garrote is reinforced as an important factor in the education of young men. The training instilled in the student a set of physiological skills and character traits esteemed by those in power. Men who could defend themselves from those "uncivilized" enough to have recourse to violence whether they are four-legged or two-legged beasts. The theoretical aspect of the class appears to consist of restricted sparring. Students were trained to recognize and respond to unrehearsed attacks or the cultivation of *vista,* the ability to see and respond in a way that was seen as efficient, practical, and culturally normal. The striking of the students in order to keep them from "falling asleep," and characterized ironically by one of the students as an example of a highly refined teaching method, is a way to bypass conscious reflective thought, which is too slow to follow the motions of the stick. Instead, the body must learn how to avoid pain and injury by learning how to see and respond appropriately to an incoming blow without recourse to conscious thought. The sense of ease that Juan Yépez felt about striking his social betters on the head and the willingness of these young men to accept these blows in an extremely conservative, racially marked hierarchical society suggests a bond of trust between the master, the students, and the parents of the students as a necessary part of a toughening up process that the juego de garrote is supposed to cultivate. *Palo por Palo* or blow for blow is often the rejoinder when somebody suffers a slight, insult, or attack and the recipients are dealt one in kind right back. The resilience to take a blow and deal one right back at someone is still a valued attitude among rural Venezuelans and admired in garrote encounters.

Reading over the description of training an underlying concern becomes apparent among the Tocuyano elite in what the anthropologist Carruthers called a "pedagogical anxiety," or a concern on the part of the older generation to inculcate an appropriate physical development and traditional moral practices among their sons (Carruthers 1998). A pedagogic anxiety is apparent in the willingness to permit a marked lower-class type of activity to be held in a courtyard of an illustrious local family. Additionally, the hiring of an unskilled laborer to teach their sons a form of dueling that could be seen every weekend at parties and nearby drinking establishments by drunk, jealous, or hell-raising lower-class, ethnically marked men suggests that some valued masculine attributes were seen as best found among the popular classes. Altogether, this regular class session in stick fighting suggest a resistance on the part of some elite Tocuyanos regarding the debilitating effects of European modernity as manifested in the education and physical pastimes gaining popularity in Venezuela at the time such as baseball, boxing, and bike riding. The idea of garrote as a traditional character building discipline was brought home to me when speaking to the mother of one of my garrotero teachers who told me that she asked a neighbor to teach her son garrote back in the early 1990s to toughen him up and give him some character because she worried about his teenaged dissolute ways after school.

INFORMAL TRAINING SITES

A common meeting site for Venezuelan men was the *pulpería*. Pulperías are still commonly located in front of people's houses or independent stands where general merchandise and alcohol is sold. The locally made alcoholic beverage Cocuy, tobacco paste or Chimú, and garrote are often linked in Venezuelan practices of leisure time among rural men. Of all the fights that made it into the criminal court system of Barquisimeto from 1830 to 1930, fully a third of them began at or around a pulpería (Assunção 1999, 75). One local historian from the hill town of Sanare remembered these times where: "The excessive drinking of Cocuy created a belligerent atmosphere to where they wanted to bring out their braided sticks and knives. Where they once had grand fights, where Félix Mendoza, Goyo Mendoza, Vicente Colmenarez and Chilao Fernandez were always in the thick of things" (Silva 1993, 45).

Pulperías acted as the principal social site where men could gather, buy supplies, drink, trade news, and gossip. For at least one garrotero, the pulpería doubled as an informal training hall. During the mid-twentieth century, the garrotero Raphael Peraza once ran a pulpería out of the front of his house. During the late afternoon when business was slow, he often would order any students around at the time to review the basic moves of his art. However, after warming up with some basic drills and beginning in earnest, he would order them into the interior courtyard where the public could not be able to "observe their agility, their knowledge and the quality of their juego" (González 2003, 44–45).

Embedded in this memory surrounding the Casa de la Nigua and seen in other accounts is the distinction made by garroteros between public and private realms of practice, an aspect I will explore in more depth later. At this point I want to draw attention to the way these diverse remembrances and anecdotes reinforce the access to a restricted type of practical knowledge that can increase one's public reputation and safeguard one's economic standing. The way knowledge was held and disseminated is noted in the spatial distinction between the *casa* and house and the *rua* or street as explained by the Brazilian anthropologist Roberto de Matta (1991). Treated as archetypal types, the *casa* or house is where one is safe and treats others with dignity, respect, and trust. The *rua* or street is by contrast a Hobbesian war of all-against-all, or a barrel of crabs where everybody is struggling to crawl over each other in an attempt to escape. Even today, due to the inherent danger of "garrote conferences" or training with different groups, a few garroteros I talked to or trained with would avoid meeting garroteros from other groups to avoid potential trouble. If they can be convinced to attend, they will complain to any who will listen that they are too ill or injured to engage in any exchange of friendly stick-play. Illustrating the problems that can easily arise during these meeting of different groups, one garrotero from another group tried to take advantage of the safe training version of garrote Danys Burgos uses to reduce the number of potential injuries with training partners or those seeking a friendly exchange of skills. Mistaking this more recreational modality of a *juego* as a structural weakness of his art, one man from another school took advantage of the way Danys would deflect a forehand horizontal blow to the heart by striking and deflecting the opponents palo from underneath, instead of striking his elbow where it could cause a good deal of pain.[5] Choosing to dismiss the safer alternative targeting as a form of concern for the other, the man blithely lifted his palo up and over Danys palo to hit him square in the face. "Flipping the switch" so to speak, Danys immediately stepped out to his left with his left leg and attacked the man with a downward diagonal strike to the left side of the man's neck. This was just a trick to get the man to commit to a solid block. Taking advantage of his opponents committed block, Danys then stepped again to the outside and slightly behind the man with his right leg and let loose a full power downward backhanded strike to the back of the man's right calf dropping him to the ground. While members of the man's school looked on with concern, Danys assuaged everybody with the feigned comment "Oops sorry about that, my palo must have slipped." Rising again to try conclusions with Danys again, Danys again baited him to block an attack that ended up striking him in the right kidney dropping him to his knees. "Ooops! My mistake, sorry my friend, are you all right?" By this time, this man's teacher and his friends were remonstrating quite loudly in chorus with Danys telling him to "take it easy." "Sure," he said, "No problem," and proceeded to drop him yet again with another blow at which point the man withdrew from the *juego*. Responding to the storms of protest from members of the opposing group, Danys quietly and in a dignified manner let it be known that if one wants to jugar easy with him, he will respond in an easy fashion. However, if somebody wants a hard game or *juego duro*, that's how the sticks will be played.

Accounts of informal apprenticeships are even more difficult to uncover as one goes back a couple generations due to the contingent, haphazard nature of training. In spite of the lack of documentation, the role of informal teaching seems to be in the past and up until today a common mode of transmission for passing on the skills of a garrotero. One shortcoming of informal modes of transmissions is that it can often be short on pedagogical niceties and quite brutal times. Often this meant an ability to pick things up quick or to weather a storm of abuse was a key trait needed to advance in these settings.[6] Late one night sitting with my garrotero friends, I was complaining how difficult it was to learn from José-Felipe Alvarado due to a lack of an organized progression of moves. In turn, they confessed to me how surprised they were that José-Felipe as an avowed die-hard communist would let a North American stay on his farm with him and teach him garrote in such a gentle fashion. Gunter went on to tell a story how much he had changed over the years. Seeking to pass down the art he loved so much to his teenage son, one day with great anticipation he took him out back of his little plot of land. Here among the avocado trees he handed him a garrote and told him to defend himself. As befitting the old style of training, he hit his son full force with the garrote to teach him to move or block without relying on conscious or reflective thought. Angered at what he saw as deliberate abuse of his body and good nature, his son responded by angrily throwing down his palo and saying, "to hell with you. I am out of here; I am not putting up with this crazy old bullshit." Deeply disappointed by his failure to impress upon his son the value of the gift he was trying to pass on to him, José-Felipe waited patiently for the next generation to come of age. Years later, his son having children of his own, the day he had been waiting for so long had finally arrived. His teenage grandson he believed was ready to accept and appreciate the value of the gift he was about to bestow on him. As he had done years before, José-Felipe struck his grandson with a series of full-force blows. Instead of wincing with pain and trying to block or deflect the oncoming blows like a warrior, the young man just stood there without moving and cried, much to the disgust and sorrow of the old man. Then, in what may seem as if the gods may have a sense of humor and to José-Felipe's eternal mortification, his grandniece took to his teaching and reached a high level of skill. To be fair, José-Felipe had greatly toned down his rough way of teaching by this time. He was also very proud of his niece and would continue to teach the female relatives of his students, a few who have reached a high level of skill. The whole while keeping his feelings about what he felt was an inappropriate gender activity to himself.[7]

Reflecting a more gradual type of learning progression that also indexes the diversity of pedagogical approaches extant at the time, Saúl Téran told me stories he heard from his father and uncles about how they learned garrote from their elder relatives on the tocuyano sugar cane plantations where they labored. During the afternoon siesta, taking the young man off to the side an older relative would cut the top stalks off of a sugar cane plant and use these tops as *varas* to practice the basic footwork and strikes of their art. Aspiring garroteros would also learn how during harvesting as men would bend over and step and cut as if they were fighting an opponent in a way to continue their training while working. Continuing this informal nature of training little has changed in the transmission of garrote from when these stories were first told. From what I have been told, among those who train garrote today but keep their knowledge secret, the majority of training occurs on an ad hoc basis with such things as work, inclement weather, and the caprice of the teacher limiting instruction.

CONTEMPORARY TRAINING SITES

Among many of the older generation of Venezuelans I used to talk to, many of them remarked on the decline of garrote over the years. Often they would tell stories of a time not too long ago when men would always carry a garrote with them when appearing in public. A time it was said when it was necessary to have some knowledge how to fight with a garrote just to be able to walk the streets. Only in the last sixty years were the aggressive and transgressive masculine pastimes of rural Venezuela domesticated to such an extent that the public display of weapons has been decentered, where now men often keep their weapons in their cars or otherwise hidden nearby. At one time in Lara as late as the 1960s, men regularly drank Cocuy, raced horses, gambled, and fought in the streets with sticks, machetes, and knives or went off alone to settle things "like a man" where nobody could interfere. At present, many young men today lean toward drinking beer, playing baseball or basketball, racing mopeds, or learning East Asian martial arts or mixed martial arts (MMA) in formal academies. The slow disappearing of the social conditions that supported a certain aggressive and expressive type of masculine behavior may have shifted. Nevertheless, the cultural values or long-held dispositions that supported the practice of garrote still resonates among rural Venezuelans, leading a small but committed number of young men and some women to continue the practice and transmission of these embodied knowledges.[8]

In what has now become a bedroom community of Barquisimeto, Eduardo Sanoja has tirelessly promoted the teaching of garrote since 1983. Originally teaching East Asian martial arts from his backyard, one his students, Umberto Burgos, told him about a neighbor of his who taught him the old Venezuelan stick fighting arts.[9] Maestro Umberto introduced Eduardo Sanoja to Mercedes Pérez, who persuaded him with the inducement of hefty training fees to come out of retirement.[10] Taking to the art, Maestro Sanoja searched out other old local stick fighters, such as Baudillio Ortiz, Félix García, Juan Barreto, and Napolean Zapata, and introduced them to a younger generation of martial art enthusiasts that had gathered around him.[11]

Another school of garrote was until recently located in the hills north of El Tocuyo in the hamlet of El Molino. Here on his little plot of land, the former labor organizer, ex-guerillero, and renowned garrotero José-Felipe Alvarado held a school on his farm for a number of years from the late 1990s to shortly before his death in 2009. After the failed Marxist-uprising of the 1960s, José-Felipe at first fled to Cuba, where he had a long meeting with Fidel Castro (which he remembered with pride), and then back to the Venezuelan countryside in the mountains of Barinas state to avoid any possible government retaliation. After an amnesty was granted to guerilleros, José-Felipe came back to the Tocuyo Valley where he laid low and grew enough food to feed himself and his family, still fearful of government reprisals. Around 1995, a group of young men interested in garrote persuaded José-Felipe to teach the art he had learned from León Valera. Every Sunday around 10:00 a.m., students, friends, and visitors would make their way to his little farm where they would all sit under the shade of a couple of Mamón and Tamarind trees to talk, socialize, and learn garrote while kicking up a cloud of dust that would slowly cover everybody. Opening up the gate that led to his farm and greeting or shooing away his two dogs Duque and Chente, the visitor would greet José-Felipe and all others. Everybody would then catch up on the latest news for a while and then someone would ask José-Felipe if he would care to "jugar a poco." "Como no," he would reply, and jugar garrote with a succession of students and visitors. After tiring, he sat down while a revolving number of people took turns to jugar garrote while getting pointers or some hands-on tips from the maestro. This would go on and on until lunch, when we would disperse to eat and seek relief from the afternoon heat.

Living on José-Felipe's farm with the intent of learning an art still held to be a gift between close friends or relations, I was able to see the networks of power that infused this site, subjectivizing and differentiating people both vertically and horizontally in the way they were able to learn and competently engage in the juego de garrote. These networks of power that control one's access to the cultural capital of garrote and shape one's subjectivity are best seen in the way individuals were treated when they came to José-Felipe's farm to jugar. As I had written earlier, José-Felipe taught in an old fashioned way where he would strike at the student in front of him. Thankfully, he had mellowed in his old age and would not strike hard. The student would then try to block or avoid the blow and counter. José-Felipe would easily riposte and lay his palo against a student's vital area again and wait for the student to move again, sometimes with advice from the maestro. This went on for a few minutes until the student became confused and frustrated or José-Felipe tired. In this way, a flow of give and take would ideally develop, allowing the student's body to recognize the trajectory of incoming blows and be able to move and counter in a type of flow without recourse to conscious thought, in other words to develop his own style of play.[12]

The top echelon of garroteros were those who had learned the Siete Lineas style from their fathers or uncles, or in Pasqual's case, a fellow student of José-Felipe Alvarado. Except for Pasqual, who would come regularly to check up on the old man, hone his skills, and help with the training of students, most visitors would come to spend some time with José-Felipe and jugar garrote with him as a way to visit a relative or connect with a traditional form of masculine sociability, as well as to keep their skills sharp. In these instances, the flow between the two men was an amazingly fast give and take, where the sticks would fly faster than the eyes could see. Strikes just grazed over the other's body as they were barely avoided, until José-Felipe struck one or more light blows and disarmed the other, sending his palo flying through the air. Other times, José-Felipe would move in and catch the other man with a trip or a leg-lift, unbalancing the other man and causing the student and teacher to laugh at the skill and cunning of the old man. Both men would then stop, hug, and sit down.

Many times they would discuss what had just happened, with José-Felipe giving some bits of advice about the match. After the top echelon of garroteros had their turn, the second tier of garroteros would take up the palos and begin to jugar with each other and sometimes with the upper echelon of garroteros. The second tier was composed of a few young men in their twenties and thirties from El Tocuyo who initially befriended Pasqual, who had previously learned the Siete Lineas from Juan Yépez, another earlier student of León Valera.[13]

To be invited to José-Felipe's farm, it was necessary to receive an invitation from Pasqual. In order to judge the worthiness of potential students, Pasqual would advise them to train at a friend's wushu academy where he was a high ranking teacher and helped out on many occasions. Both the principal teacher, Pasqual, and the investigator, Argimiro González, were high ranked practitioners of this modern gymnastic folkdance (wushu). I believe they primarily learned their art from a number of instructional books.[14] After being vetted for a few years, Pasqual would invite those he approved of to join him at José-Felipe farm to learn garrote.

The third and last tier were the curious and investigators who with the company of Argimiro or Pasqual would come for an afternoon or a few days to see the art, drive around the area meet a few of the old garroteros, and maybe learn a few moves.[15] This is the category where I fell in. I was different in that I was the first to ask to stay for an extended time. I first met Argimiro and Pasqual during previous one-week visits to El Tocuyo in 1998 and 2004, when I was taught a couple of moves. In 2005, Argimiro, Pasqual, and José-Felipe agreed that I could stay on his farm and learn garrote. After moving in, on my first Sunday morning, I saw José-Felipe sweeping up thick layers of leaves that covered the practice area in front of the wattle and daub shacks he and his wife called home. For about an hour, we swept up leaves into a burlap sack and then walked to the gardens in back of his house to dump the bags of leaves on his garden to "feed the plants," as he would say. All too often as we were finishing up, a gust of wind would blow and shake the trees, causing another great defoliation where it seemed like we were in a snowstorm of leaves. "It's like a carnival!" Jose-Felipe would say, grinning as we redoubled our task to clear the ground before the class began. People began arriving about 10:00 a.m. Usually about four to six people would show up, and after everybody had caught up with each other, begin to jugar garrote. My first Sunday, Pasqual invited José-Felipe to jugar garrote with me. I already had a couple lessons with Pasqual earlier that week at the wushu school and had a basic idea about what to do. But after two minutes I was totally confused and unable to move without José-Felipe's palo barring me every way I turned. I sat down and observed for a while, got up, and tried again with José-Felipe and Pasqual a couple times before we all broke for lunch.

After class, it was arranged that I would continue to meet with Pasqual and another student, Julio, at the wushu school for further instruction to help make sense of José-Felipe's teachings. Arriving at the school on a Tuesday night, Pasqual showed up and told me he was going to teach me the *la batalla* or the folkloric, performance-oriented mode of garrote, as this was composed of the basic moves of the Siete Lineas style. "This is a good place to start," I thought to myself, as we began. The first two weeks went by quickly with actual class time with the palo lasting about five minutes, and then listening to Pasqual talk about a number of subjects about ninety minutes. For a while, I thought it was the Venezuelan way never to work up a sweat. During the week, I would ask José-Felipe to teach me, and we would go out back to his garden, and using a palo to clear a spot free of leaves and move any snakes out the way, he would teach me finishing moves or la riña. This meant we would go back and forth for 20–40 seconds with a set of five to six traditional opening moves to develop a flow, and then he would end the flow with a variety of finishing blows to vital areas or trips or throws that would have knocked me down on the ground if he had exerted any force. Through this varied training, I was confused how I could make these moves work in an unrehearsed flow, as my previous training with Filipino Kali and a couple of street encounters had given me an idea how a stick fight unfolds.[16] I was happy to be collecting information though and figured it would eventually come together. After a couple weeks, I had picked up the six attacks that make up la batalla. Pasqual then began to show up increasingly late at the wushu school. During this time, one night he showed up and pointed out two wushu students whose relatives taught them garrote and asked them for a little demonstration. They tried to beg off, but finally agreed. Doing the most basic attack and defense two-man routine of la batalla, they continually complained their arms hurt, they were tired, or late arriving at home where their parents would be waiting worried. Pasqual then asked one of them to jugar garrote with me and then said "he only knows la batalla, only do la batalla with him." We did these basic moves for a few minutes before he begged off and everybody left. As we were leaving the school, Pasqual asked me what the old maestro was teaching me. After I told him, he responded vehemently "No! No! I am going to tell him to only teach you la Batalla." "Ok," I thought, "he wants to keep me on a narrow pedagogical ladder." By then another student asked me to work out with him during the week. The following

Sunday, Pasqual had heard about this extracurricular training and questioned me about it. I told him we were working on the moves you showed us. "No! No!" he said, "a student should have only one teacher." He just grunted when I tried to explain we're just going over the moves he, himself, had showed us. By then, Pasqual had quit showing up during the week to teach me. Also by this time, José-Felipe and the others would not invite me to jugar garrote with them, only my new training partner Gunter would jugar garrote with me for a few minutes and without any commentary from José-Felipe or Pasqual. During the next few weeks, I would ask José-Felipe for a lesson, who would regularly respond with such comments as "maybe tomorrow," "it's too hot now," or "I'm hungry, it's time to eat." My training had effectively come to an end. Confused but continuing to talk to the people in the groups such as the two regularly appearing students Julio and Gunter, I was told that José-Felipe and Pasqual had both told them they had reached a level where they should quit learning from them and begin to develop their own style without any further input from them.

Soon after this, I hired a car and driver and organized a trip with Argimiro to visit a number of garroteros. In typical Venezuelan fashion, Pasqual, Julio, and José-Felipe invited themselves for the trip. Along with some informative interviews, I witnessed some great demonstrations and kept on thinking to myself that I could not use anything I had learned against the moves I was seeing. As we continued to drive around the area, Argimiro would ask me "Hey Michael, are you thirsty or hungry? There is a stand here that sells drinks and lunch." "Sure," I replied. "Hey, everybody," cried Argimiro, "Michael is buying us all lunch." Or later that evening, "Hey Michael, ever hear of Padilla's, there is a stand over there, you want to try one." "Sure," I said. "Hey, everybody, Michael is buying us all Padilla's." This openhanded hospitality at my expense, combined with what I had been experiencing, gave me a lot to ponder on how this investigation was progressing.

Soon after the trip, I was laid out with dengue fever, which gave me even more time to figure out what was going on and what I was going to do next. After recovering, I decided to find myself one or more garrote teachers. I began to take advantage of Sunday, a traditional visiting day, to search out the garroteros I had been impressed with and ask them to teach me. I soon had three teachers who I would visit between one and five times a week. In every case, I was their only student they had in years. I learned eagerly and recorded all our sessions and then every night went back to Gunter's house to review with him what I had learned and test it against him. Finally, after about a month I was able to hit Gunter at will and easily block or avoid all his attacks. At times, he would get so frustrated he would throw down his palo and yell "That's it." We finally figured out how we were being taught a watered-down version of the Siete Lineas system that would not work against a non-cooperative opponent. While Gunter continued to attend the Sunday classes out of a mixed sense of friendship and obligation, I continued to visit my other teachers, and occasionally during the week asking the old maestro for a small juego every once in a while, where he would dismantle me. By this time, I understood enough to have an idea what he was doing and was able to begin to steal his knowledge and practice it on my own. After I left the area, the school continued on as before until José-Felipe died in 2009. As of the spring of 2013, Pasqual had begun a children's class at the Casa de la Cultura in downtown El Tocuyo.

By 2012, a few students of Félix García, under the direction of Manuel Rodríguez and Davíd González, began to teach their art openly in the courtyard of the Barquisimeto museum. Afraid that the traditional environment of secrecy, violence, and extreme machismo was killing the art, Manuel and Davíd, with the help of others, began to take part in demonstrations and posting video clips of these events on YouTube in order to attract students. For the first six months, they waited in vain for someone to show up. Finally, after about a year there was a core of eight students who show up twice a week. Teaching in the painfully slow method they learned, where a move must be perfected before moving on to the next one, attendance flagged, until Manuel and Davíd began to offer a controlled, free-sparring session during one night as a way to retain students. As of 2013, the class is going strong.

EL PALO

Among the many different styles of garrote I was privileged to see, each had their own preference in regards for the choice of wood and the preparation of the stick. Among the types of wood chosen to make a garrote were a variety of hardwoods, whose choice was mainly dictated by one's ecological niche. In contrast to other stick fighting systems I am aware of around the world, in Venezuela garrotes are chosen from the secondary branches of the main horizontal branches of a tree. This means that a garrote tends to taper, with one end being slightly thicker and heavier than the other. The garrotero will grip the thinner end and, in this way, use the heavier thicker end to make contact in either whipping or snapping blows, where the velocity and impact are increased by the uneven weight distribution of the garrote.[17]

There are a number of types of wood used to make a garrote, some are more prized than others for aesthetic reasons. But as it was stressed to me by a number of garroteros when talking to them about acquiring a palo, it was enough to go out in the woods where one lived and find a suitable hardwood tree and cut your garrote from that tree.[18] Generally, it takes about two to three weeks to prepare a garrote from going out into the woods and cutting a branch to the curing and tempering of the garrote.

Usually a garrote is cut around midnight when the moon is waning right before a full moon. The stick is left to dry a few days to concentrate the sap; the stick is fired to remove the bark and then soaked with sheep or goat fat, soap, or motor oil until it cannot soak up any more and then left in the sun to dry. Recounting his first experiences with fabricating garrotes, Félix García remembered:

> I learned from my mama, because since I was a child, I liked the sticks back from the time I saw men jugando garrote there on the corner. I was like eight years old. Then my mama used to see me over there out back of the house where it was all full of Armargosa trees, you know the Armargosa's that grow straight, then I used to cut some sticks and jugar garrote by myself. The she told me "look, the sticks have to be fired," so she fired them and after she fired them she put them in a corner until they were good. I learned from her and then made the sticks and fired them and put them away for 15–20 days so the sticks dry and don't bend. One stands them straight up in a corner so they don't bend. (Félix García, interview with author, Barquisimeto, April 23, 2005)

There is also a tradition of braiding handles and adding decorative frills for a garrote that appears related to the use of a garrote as a riding crop, pointing to possible influences of Mediterranean herding cultures. Along these lines, some garrotes drilled a hole through the butt end, threading a leather thong to be slung around the wrist of the holder. Reflecting the highly personal nature of these fighting weapons, many garroteros disdained the use of any handles, as it interfered with the striking ability of the garrote. For garroteros who would alternate using the left and right hand in using their garrote, they felt the use of a wrist thong left a man vulnerable to wrist or elbow wrenches by an opponent who could catch the palo and twist the man's arm. The garrotero Santos Pérez was known for hiding a small steel spike on the end of his garrote that he covered with a small metal cap. During an encounter, Santos would remove the metal cap and swing or thrust the spiked end to wound or disconcert the opponent. From what I understood, the spike was too small to actually kill anybody, it was just for harassment and disfiguring an opponent.

Knives, Machetes, and Lances

The knife and the machete, or its relatives, are tools used in rural areas throughout the world on an everyday basis. The present day disinclination of urban professional people to carry a knife in public, as many of these people carry a cell phone, should not occlude the fact that knife fighting has been raised to a high degree of refinement throughout many parts of the world and is used in encounters every weekend. I am familiar with two types of knives commonly used by peoples in rural Venezuela. One is called a *Pico e' Loro*, or Parrots Beak—a folding type of pocketknife with a 4 1/2 inches long blade set in a wooden handle. The blade has a wide curving end, much like a carpet cutter, and is perfect for the agricultural worker who needs to trim, slice, or cut things open. The other type of knife is a fixed-handled knife with a blade of about 10 inches. The handle was made out of bone and covered in goat skin. This knife I saw used among garroteros fighting in knife against knifeand espada y daga drills. The knife was used both in a traditional saber grip and a hammer grip, allowing both slashes and thrusts to be used although with different trajectories.

I saw two types of machetes used among garroteros in Lara. One was a short 18 inches long blade with a squared off top used to cut sugar cane. The other was a curved pointed blade of approximately 28–32 inches long. Although I was told that many styles of stick fighting could be easily transposed to the machete, some of the older garroteros told me this is wrong and, through a number of drills, showed me that the machete demands to be used in slightly different ways to take advantage of its unique properties. From the recently deceased garrotero Natividad Apostal, I heard of the late Diman Gutiérrez from the hill town of Bobare who used to perform in velorios to Saint Anthony with a 6-foot lance held with both hands in an overhand grip and would jugar against men armed with machetes and walking sticks. What is interesting about this is that the use of a lance is its link to agricultural cattle prods such as the Spanish garrochas, or *dejarretadera*, and its use in the numerous nineteenth-century civil conflicts. Its shorter length than traditional garrocha or *dejarretaderas* leads to more questions about its origins in herding animals and any possible influences on the art of garrote.

The mandador is a type of whip once used by muleteers, who provided the main form of transporting produce and goods until the mid-twentieth century. The garrotero Adrían Pérez of El Tocuyo, drawing on his memories as a youth, practices garrote with a mandador made out of an untreated piece of Jebe wood approximately 28 inches long with a rawhide thing approximately 36 inches long tied on one end. At times he will use a mandador in his right hand and a knife in his left hand. The mandador is still used in other areas of Venezuela as a herding tool. Because I had not been introduced to them at the time and at the risk of hoping to make contact with them later, I did not ask if they have any knowledge of using the mandador in combat. Danys Burgos once showed me a rawhide blackjack or *Cachachappa* that Maestro Ramón Aguilar gave to him. This is a very brutal and effective weapon for use in close quarters, handily bringing any type of rowdy behavior to a quick close.

CONCLUSION

From the accounts that have come down to us, the wide array of teaching sites and styles that characterized the teaching of garrote in the past continues through today. Despite the renewed sense of openness found among some garroteros, the restrictive semi-secretive nature of these combat practices continues to shape the art. Strategies such as self-teaching, picking up of moves from different people, and practicing with friends or trying out ones moves in various contexts of agonistic and agonistic contests occur regularly. Describing the days before he was accepted as the last student of León Valéra, José-Felipe told us how young boys would try to learn garrote:

> Yes, when I was a boy, I was 13 or 14 years old and we used to crack each other's heads. This is what we use to do, we would meet up at the bottom of a dried-up streambed. We would take a rubber ball and we would put it here (pointing to the top of his head) and put out our hat over it. Latter we would go back to the house. What happened to you? Well, I fought with so-and-so and he cracked my head. And you, what did you do? Well, I gave him a strike but did not crack his head. Well then tomorrow you have to go back and fight him again because if you do not fight him I am going to give you a beating. It was like that they would tell me. Well, and this was certain, I went there the next morning and fought three times, three times. Finally, they (their parents) went to my parents and in a respectful manner, one father to another their father said, they would not stand for this learning how to fight. Then the parents brought together all the boys and gave all of us blows with the palos. Then we became friends; this was nothing, boys to the end. Well, I have told you something there, I had a liking for it, I used like it. (José-Felipe Alvarado, interview by author, El Molino May 29, 2005)

For generations, the knowledge surrounding the way a tree branch is converted into a weapon was not just that of fashioning a utilitarian object, but creating a socialized, fetishized tool. Many rural Venezuelan men worked with agricultural tools on an everyday basis to butcher livestock, harvest crops, and build and repair buildings or tools. Men understood all too well how an understanding of the basic principles of standing and moving with a garrote could be transposed to a number of other implements when faced with a potentially dangerous situation, from a loose aggressive dog to someone diverting one's water supply, or an envious neighbor casting aspersions upon one's family. Responding to these challenges by grabbing a handy agricultural tool when one's garrote was not readily available suggests the way that material technology influences the way the body can be moved and points to the fundamental relationship between the body and technology. Among other combative systems, the material technology associated with a practice is recognized as being a key element in the dialectical coproduction of material and subjectivity. Bringing attention toward the relationship between subjectivity and material technology also has the effect of decentering the boundaries between subject and object, highlighting the little understood way subjectivity is often fashioned through the use of material technology in an environment of apprenticeship.

NOTES

1. Both maestro Natividad Apostal and his cousin Silvio Alvarado tell how Ishmael Colmenares would only teach at night on the side of a stable with only one lantern for light to discourage anybody trying to see what he was doing. Personal interview with Natividad Apostal, interview by author, Barquisimeto, April 24, 2005.

2. A famous garrotero and one of the few students of Baudillio Ortiz.

3. This seems to be a common domestication trajectory of combative arts. For example, in Los Angeles in the late 1990s the Israeli army combat system Krav Maga and the Brazilian art of capoeira, once the purview of rough and hard men, were now taught as aerobic classes. While the domestication of these modes of combative practices is amusing, on the flip side of the coin the writer Doug Century wrote an account of an aspiring rapper who was trying to break away from his drug dealing past. This man was a practitioner of the African American hand-to-hand fighting prison refined art of "52 blocks" among other names. Internet chatrooms buzzed with middle-class men and women seeking to find teachers of this art. Doug Century explained that these men were hard core criminals who had lifted weights rigorously and been engaged in violence for years and trained by going "all out." These men, he reminded those seekers, did not have the mentality to deal with the safety concerns of young good-looking girls looking for self-defense lessons, or competitive middle-class young males eager to learn the latest ghetto art or test their own skills against these types of men. See Doug Century's *Street Kingdom: Five Years Inside the Franklin Avenue Posse* (2000) and the seminal article by Tom Green (2012).

4. Roberto Montesinos, the son of a famous Tocuyano doctor, Don Roberto, was a poet, journalist, teacher, and political dissident against the dictatorial regime of Juan V. Gómez.

5. One school of garrote calls this strike a "palo electrico" as the effects of hitting what is popularly known as the "funny bone" can feel as if the one hit had a jolt of electricity shooting through his arm.

6. Other times it was the one most scared to quit as he feared the wrath of the teacher when he would fail to show up for class more than he did the usual beating he would receive as part of training.

7. In my time in Venezuela, I was aware of two older women in the Segovia Highlands whose skill with the garrote was acknowledged by male garroteros. One had died a few years before I arrived. The other would greet me but never allow me to interview her. Of the female students of José-Felipe who were in their thirties, none would make themselves available to be interviewed. Other highly skilled female garroteros I had heard of was the granddaughter of Domingo Escalona, the first student of León Valera, the granddaughter of Félix García, and the teenage daughter of Olegario Pérez, another Tocuyano garrotero who I saw play garrote with José-Felipe a few times. I interviewed one female who studied with Los Hermanos Yépez. Soraya Rojas, a cultural historian and chronicler from Guárico state, learned garrote from the Natividad Rom, who at one time had a school of garrote in the area until shortly before his death in 2002.

8. For Southeast Asia, see Farrer and Whalen-Bridge 2011.

9. Recently Dr. Miguel-Angel Chavier, seeking to uncover the roots of the style of garrote taught by Mercedes Pérez Ramon Aguilar, Danys Burgos, and William Liscano, followed a number of leads back to the little hamlet of La Riconanda where a man now 101 years of age related how his father had taught garrote for years underneath a Cotoperi tree in the village square (e-mail to the author 08/05/2013).

10. William, a friend of my teacher Danys, lived about a half-mile from Mercedes Perez's house. Confessing that back in the 1980s when they were just young boys, they were too intimidated by his skill and reputation as a skilled garrotero to ask to learn anything. Instead they settled for peeking through the gate and over the wall of his house to watch people train.

11. To place this in proper context, in Barquisimeto, Félix García, with help from Eugenio Leal, Napolean Zapata, and others, was still actively teaching in his shoe shop from the early 1950s to the early 2000s. So it is more accurate to say that Sanoja brought some of these older men out of retirement and introduced them to a wider circle of young men interested in the art who have continued to spread the art.

12. The late highly esteemed Filipino Kali maestro Sonny Umpad felt the ability to develop one's flow was one of the most useful skills a Kali student could develop.

13. This was another Juan Yépez, whose two younger brothers Andrés and Joaquín Yépez still live and teach in El Papelón.

14. Devoid of all combative moves wushu was developed by the Chinese communist state during the 1950s to develop a new citizen who, while treasuring old traditions, refused the secrecy, superstition, and hell-raising anti-social aspects of martial art gangsters, secret societies, and other marginal peoples. Later, the government reversed its strict nonviolent policies, developing and promoting *San Da* or a form of kickboxing. All the routines they taught were in books they had and would refer to when teaching.

15. Many of these investigators were professors or graduate students from Venezuelan universities driving around taking a casual interest in the cultural heritage of their country. In 2004, a couple of professors from the University of Las Canarias in Tenerife came to the area as part of a larger project to look for evidence of Canarian stick fighting in Venezuela, Cuba, and Louisiana. They spent a week around El Tocuyo, driving around meeting and interviewing and engaging in friendly bouts of stick-play with the garroteros they met.

16. In other words, the knowledge of how to set up the delivery of the final or finishing blow was being omitted and had to be "stolen" if one sought to master the art. See Herzfeld 2004 on the role of "stealing knowledge" among traditional Cretan artisans and their apprentices.

17. In an interesting example of how the same type of stick can used in different ways for the same purpose among the stick fighters of Apulia, here a 4-foot-long shepherd staff that is cut from the limb of a tree and therefore is tapered much like the garrote. They prefer to hold the stick by one hand on the thicker end and use the thinner end for the point of contact.

18. Over the years, there has been a number of prized woods. But due to the severe deforestation of the Segovia Highlands, I refrain from providing a list of woods used.

FOUR

Secrecy and Deception in Garrote

From here, I move to an examination of the social and cultural structures of everyday life among garroteros. In this section, I explore some of the attitudes, affects, and dispositions common to Venezuelan sociality, but honed to a high degree among those who sought to master the garrote. Among those who depend on their fighting skills for survival, the importance placed on managing the flow of information can mean the difference between life and death. As many fighters have come to know, the element of surprise and getting in the first strike is the most common and most successful form of attack. This hold true from a neighborhood bar brawl to one nation attacking another. The advantage of surprise is of such a great value that a veil of secrecy is often a key to one's survival in many parts of the world where one's fighting skills are part of everyday life. Walking through life with one's sensitivity heightened to any possible attack is not a form of deviancy or paranoia. All too often it is a common intersubjective stance toward the world where awareness of one's surroundings acts as a mode of survival. Especially in areas where low-scale violence is endemic, state control or police presence is weak, and there is a tradition of self-help and a concern with one's public reputation.

Speaking of the way that garrote is still cherished and guarded, a friend from the Andean hill town of Sanare recounted one afternoon that "among the old garroteros if you told them you were hungry, they would say, 'come in my friend, pull up a chair and share my food.' If you had no place to sleep they would say, 'please come over my friend and share my roof.' If you were lonely, they would say, 'Please come over and meet my sister, she is very pretty' but, if you want to learn garrote, they would say, 'Ahhhhhhh! That's different, that I keep close to my heart.'" The hard-won wisdom of not willingly baring one's throat to a wolf is also reflected in an old Persian tale of a wrestling teacher who taught his best student 359 throws. Later the student comes back to challenge the teacher and is thrown by a 360th throw he has never seen before. "Master," he was supposed to have said, "why did you never teach me, your best student, that throw?" The master was supposed to have replied, "The dog that you feed from a puppy will always bite the owner one day" (Gilbey 1992, 25). This, and countless other stories about garrote like these, exemplifies Simmel's claim that every relationship between two individuals will be characterized by the ratio of secrecy involved in it (Simmel 1906). The practice of garrote has been and remains for the most part unknown, ignored, hidden, dismissed as old fashioned drunken street brawling, or increasingly seen as a harmless folkloric dance. For this reason, I look at the general role that secrecy, competitiveness, and the asymmetrical distribution of knowledge plays among practitioners of garrote. In the anthropological literature, the role and function of secrecy have been investigated through many different approaches and in many different places (Bourdieu 1962, 1965; Goffman 1956; Johnson 2002; Herzfeld 2004; Piot 1993; Urban 1997). What these works all share though is the claim that there is a basic agonistic aspect in all societies manifested in acts of hierarchy, competitiveness, and deception. The attitude or stance toward the world is referred to here as a form of "strategic secrecy" or the general view of society as an inherently unfair or morally neutral place.

STRATEGIC SECRECY

There is a wall of secrecy, dissembling, and distrust that is an integral part of everyday life in rural Venezuela that goes beyond any facile historical explanations and is found throughout a number of communities recorded in the ethnographic literature. As regards to Venezuela, in a recent work dealing with the changing fabric of Venezuela folklore as it was created and subsidized by at first the state and now transnational corporations, the anthropologist David Guss captured one artisan's feelings about the propriety of setting down in writing his teaching methods and skills as akin to a form of treason:

> I don't have any written method my methods are not written down! Anyway I'm very jealous with that. When I die no one will know shit about how I gave classes, or what I based my classes on. Method? Are you crazy? Ask the people at NASA to give it to you. That's the way they do things. It's like asking for formulas. It's the same thing . . . besides; people have been learning music without writing it down for ten thousand years, so why do I have it now. (Guss 2000, 113–114)

The role of secrecy as it relates to the art of garrote can be seen throughout the available sources we have about garrote in El Tocuyo. A generation later and a few miles down the road from where a group of young elite Tocuyanos once learned garrote from Juan "Cartorce" at the Casa de Nigua, a young José-Felipe Alvarado recalled how he would surreptitiously watch older men practicing garrote. Struck with a burning desire to learn to fight with the sticks, he got up enough nerve one day to ask some of the men to teach him a few moves who answered, "sure, OK, why not," and then preceded to ignore him when he returned later in anticipation of learning (José-Felipe Alvarado, interview with author, El Molino, March 03, 2005). A generation later, continuing further up the road into the foothills above El Tocuyo, Joaquín and Andrés Yépez were faced with a similar situation when training with Domingo Escalona, one of the first students of the garrotero León Valera.[1] In this case, Maestro Domingo consented to teach them, but after a while they both figured out they were learning nothing of real value and they gave up. After the catastrophic earthquake of 1950 that struck the Segovia Highlands, alongside with many others the Yépez brothers packed their bags and moved out of the area, in this case ending up at a *caserio* or hamlet outside of a sugar cane plantation outside of Cabudare. There, they met José Sequera, a son of León Valera, and were finally able to learn a number of Tocuyano styles he had previously picked up, such as the Siete Lineas and the Juego de Lamadero.[2] Even almost fifty years later when the value of stick and knife fighting has declined with the increasing easy access to firearms, the transmission of this knowledge is often tightly guarded. I had written earlier of the unwillingness of members of the Siete Lineas group in El Tocuyo to teach anyone anything of value. Seeking to find other, more open teachers of garrote, I met with a less restrictive attitude toward their art by many men, although they did test my desire to learn.

Exasperated with the stonewalling I received in El Tocuyo, I went in search of those garroteros I had previously met and whose art had impressed me. One Sunday, when Venezuelans spend the day paying social calls, I put on my best clothes and went in search of Maestro Ramón Aguilar of La Riña con Palos lineage. Remembering only how the area looked like from a quick visit a month earlier, I took a variety of busses in the general direction of where the maestro lived and wandered around for four hours looking for familiar sites until I met a couple of neighbors who pointed out his house to me. Calling out his name, I was invited up on the porch where I was given a chair and hot cup of coffee. After a few minutes of small talk and pleasantries, Maestro Ramón asked me outright why I had come to his house. Being completely forthright, I told him that when I saw his garrote, I thought it some of the greatest stick fighting I had ever seen and had developed a burning desire to learn his art. He leaned back and smiled and said, "thanks," but he worked nights as a security guard and had no time to teach anybody. I was deeply disappointed at this news but smiled and said, "that's all right," and silently tried to figure out what was going to be my next move. We continued talk about the weather and my views of Venezuelan food, when out of nowhere he asked me "So if you could train, when could you come over?" I looked him straight in the eyes and responded, "I will come over anytime and anywhere." "All right, let's train right now. Paula, go get me a couple of sticks, Daniel, put these chairs away, we're going to do a little training." Happy beyond belief at my luck and a little confused, I followed Maestro Ramón downhill and across the street to a trash littered empty lot with a set of broken cement stairs and landing shaded by mango and palm trees. Standing in front of this broken landing was a couple of shirtless men drinking beer passing the time and watching us curiously. Unnoticed at the time were a group of teenagers further off. Grabbing a handful of mango leaves hanging above the landing Maestro Ramón balled them up and drew a three-foot-long X on the concrete and then with a few more handfuls of leaves drew a circle around the X. Finally, at each point where one of the arms or legs of the X touched the circle he made a small half-circle inside the larger circle (see table 5.1: I).

Standing up and handing me a stick, he told me, "you stand here on this line," pointing at the 2 legs of the X. He then stood both of his feet on both arms of the X, so we were facing each other. From this point, he had us walk clockwise around the X while swinging forehand and backhand blows at each other's knees that were blocked by the other man's strike at his partner's knees. Then he called for one of the teenagers, who he introduced as his nephew, and repeated the sequence with him while telling me this is the basic footwork that acts as the foundation for the entire art. "Look," he said, "I never even practiced with this kid before but look how well we move together—this is because we have good footwork." After about thirty minutes of teaching me a couple of two person drills, he called an end to the session, "that's enough—did you like it?" "It was fantastic," I responded. "Good, when can you come back?" he asked. We made plans for next week; he told me how to get back to El Tocuyo, and I left well pleased at my luck.

Early Tuesday morning, I got up early and left for Maestro Ramón's. This time I arrived in only three hours. In order to keep up a good impression, I disappeared into a vacant field of high weeds and changed my shorts, tank top, and sandals for a pair of Levi's, a long-sleeve shirt, and a pair of boots. Walking up to his front gate, I yelled out "Buenas dias, Maestro Ramón!" Then a minute later, "Hello Maestro Ramón!" Meeting a wall of silence, I again yelled out "Buenas Dias Maestro Ramón!" until finally his daughter came running out of the house and said, "I am sorry, but my dad is not here, he is working, can you come back tomorrow?" "Sure," I said as I left and headed back to Barquisimeto to do some archival research. The next day, I got up early and took off, arriving this time in two hours. I waited an hour near the truck stop near the entrance to the road to his house, changed my clothes, walked to his house, and called out his name. His daughter came running out of their house again and said, "My dad says he is sorry, but he had to work all night, can you come back tomorrow?" "Sure," I replied and turned around back to Barquisimeto and the archives. The next day, I got up early, got off the bus at the truck stop, changed my clothes in an empty field, came up to Maestro Ramón's fence, and called his name. His daughter came running out one more time, and this time she said, "My dad is too busy working and helping his son clear a plot in a nearby squatter settlement—its best you go back to El Tocuyo, and he will call Argimiro González to notify you when he is available to teach." Seeing how Argimiro and I were no longer on speaking terms, this left me nonplussed. Not knowing what to do, I said thanks and began to walk away when I remembered that teenager Maestro Ramón had used as a partner to show me how to move. I returned and asked the daughter where the young man lived. I was told to keep on walking until the road ends then take a few more turns on a dirt path. After about thirty minutes of walking, I came to a lone house blasting Beatles music. "Hello!" I yelled out over and over. Eventually, a woman stuck her head out the window. "I am looking for your son; I want to ask him some questions about garrote." "He is out on the farm, come back tomorrow." After thanking her, I turned back around headed toward the archives. The next day, I made my way back to his house and saw him there helping his dad fix his car. I asked to interview him, and then after the interview, I asked him if he would teach me garrote. "Sure," he responded, "come back tomorrow." I came back tomorrow, and he was there waiting for me. He began to teach me some moves, but he kept on being interrupted by his father, who stuck his head out from underneath the car at regular intervals, yelling out remarks like, "why are you teaching him to move like that?" "What's the matter with you! You know better than to do that," "No! No! No! You are doing it all wrong!" "Look at him he is stepping all wrong!" Finally, after the class ended, his father wiped the grease off his hand and introduced himself as Snyder. He told me his son didn't know anything and that I should come over tomorrow afternoon and he will take me to meet his teacher Danys Burgos, who lives nearby.

The following day, I showed up; he put me in his jeep, and we took a short drive and met Danys. A neighbor showed up and offered me a beer, but before I could respond, Danys invited me to his backyard. We ducked under some clothes hanging on the clothesline, shooed some chickens and a flop-eared rabbit out of the way, cleared a space of the leaves and branches with a few kicks, and then we began. Danys handed me a palo. With the other palo, he drew an X in the dirt and enclosed it with a circle and then drew little half–circles around the arms and legs of the X. After class, he asked me how I liked it and invited me back to train every day after he got off work. After the first few weeks, Danys' friend William, who offered me the beer, myself, and Snyder were the only people training regularly. Finally, it was just Danys, William, and I. Danys said I was his first student in over five years. A few months later, Snyder came by to say hello and confided to me that he had first asked Maestro Ramón about me and asked if he should introduce me to Danys. After a couple months of training, Maestro Ramón himself rode his bicycle to Danys house to check on my progress and loan me a videotape Argimiro González had shot of him. So after testing my determination, resourcefulness, and character, Maestro Ramón gave his approval, and I began an extremely rewarding apprenticeship and friendship with this group of people.

I often used to relate my experiences trying to learn garrote in my interviews with people to explore in greater depth the enduring power of secrecy and dissembly that surrounds garrote. The most common response I received from urban middle-class people is that it was a symptom of the low mentality of the rural laborers. Among local practitioners of garrote, it was suggested that the locals saw us as government agents, tax collectors, or somebody with ulterior motives. Among the elder generation of garroteros, the common response was that it was an example of pure selfishness, or *egosimo,* or the need to keep a tactical edge in combat. One interesting explanation came from a man who related to me how the older generation of Venezuelans loves to keep secrets. They take pride in knowing a secret and knowing how to keep a secret. In addition, they take pride in knowing that other people know they have a secret. In other words, there is the attitude of "we are all equal here, but I am just a little bit better then you."

As seen in other craft activities around the world, possessing the determination or the wiliness to steal garrote was often seen as a first step to determine the aptitude of a young man seeking to learn the art as seen in the following story. Speaking of his experiences learning garrote, José-Felipe related how he used to see Maestro León Valera at local parties or social gatherings, where he would be continually rebuffed by the old man in his attempts to learn garrote due to his reputation as a troublemaker:

Miguel: Why did you like to jugar so much?

José-Felipe: Ah, well I used to like to jugar, because precisely I did not want to swing a stick like a jackass. Then later when I would see the men jugar, I would go up there and look, and there was another opportunity and I took the chance to ask them if they would teach me to jugar, but they would not teach me.

Miguel: Nothing?

José-Felipe: No, no they did not teach me anything, they told me, "Sure, OK why not," and then they would teach me nothing.

Miguel: Did you watch?

José-Felipe: Ah yes now—this is what then happened, I had a great opportunity, a great opportunity that Maestro León Valera had Santos Pérez teach me—Santos Pérez was a good jugador and he told me that he would show me some moves—he would take the earth beneath his feet, well, well, well, and we stayed good friends until his death, so that between us if he ever needed a Bolivar, I would bring it to him.

Miguel: There were a lot of good feeling between you and him.

José-Felipe: And it was the same with him; if things were bad with me he would ask me how is your wallet?—it's bad—well then take this without interest and neither he nor I would pay each other back—none of us told Maestro Léon Valera that he was teaching me; we were living in the same taupora and then Maestro Léon Valera used to tell us, "No, I will not teach him," he knew.

Miguel: He knew you were a bully?

José-Felipe: Yes, it would be—I will not teach him, he is a bad man—but the badness I had was pure youthful foolishness. (José-Felipe Alvarado, interview with author, El Molino, February 27, 2005)

In a world where face-to-face interactions, patron-client relations, a tradition of self-help, and a highly sensitive preoccupation with one's public reputation was the norm, an attitude toward the world that valued the role of dissembly and the ability to discern attempts by others to conceal information in others was a key trait to resist oppression and aid in one's survival. At the same time that people seek to maintain a distance from each other, there is an equally powerful drive to create bonds of friendship and trust with others. For example, until the 1970s, when government halted the "disappearing" of ex-guerrillas from a recently concluded communist revolt, the choosing of a good friend could mean the difference between life and death.[3] The act of teaching another person the means by which they could be undone was a great act of trust that was recognized by both parties and created strong bonds between men. The depth of these links is reflected in the death of one garrotero. After a long life swinging a garrote, Santos Pérez died in 1999. His family, as devout evangelicals, was determined to give him a proper Christian burial with none of the "paganisms" associated with the popular Catholicism of the area. Even though he was specifically not invited, José-Felipe was determined to see his friend of over fifty years off right. Waking up early the morning of the funeral, he put on his best clothes, put his sombrero on his head, tucked two palos under his arm, and walked to the church where the funeral service for Maestro Santos was being held. Swinging the doors wide open, José-Felipe walked right in. Looking neither right nor left, nor speaking a word to anybody, he strode right up to the coffin. Ignoring the objections of the pastor and some members of the deceased's family, he opened the lid of the coffin of his friend and laid his favorite palo with the cap concealing a steel spike across his chest to take with him in his journey through eternity. Closing the lid, he turned around and walked out the church and back home without saying a word to anybody. Such was the reputation both men had made through their life that no one dared remove the palo from the coffin and it was buried with him.

TACTICAL SECRECY

There is often an agonistic environment and inherent ambiguousness in all social situations. In the case of early modern Venezuela, everyday ways of being a man or a garrotero meant that one's garrote was always present but partially absent to others view. While in the past most men had to have some knowledge of garrote, not all men's knowledge or skill were equal. One consequence of this was that men would often try to keep others misinformed regarding their competence with the garrote or, in the case of an actual fight, which way the stick would attack them. In the number of proscriptions, adages, street smarts, or acts of politeness where a great deal of this type of knowledge is transmitted in garrote, I group these forms of social knowledge under the heading of "tactical secrecy." In much the same way as speaking of keeping one's opponent guessing in a fight, Saúl Téran explained to me one day.

> The stick must always remain hidden, so that it is not seen, low or high, you always have to change things up with stomach, chest, and head strikes, always moving, changing hands from right to left, and after that, you attack on the high line with the punyon, that is with the thrust at the navel, the hand is always protected. After one strikes like this, low and high, then attack the stomach, chest, and head and the thrust, then use all of them together. (Saúl Téran, interview with author, Barquisimeto, April 18, 2005)

What really brought home to me the deviousness and potential danger that men had to be aware of during social occasions came from the impromptu lessons I would receive from the garrotero Ismael Vásquez. One day while visiting him at his house, he showed me some of the old tactics used to defend oneself from those people who would insist they were your friends. For example, when arriving at a party and a "friend" tries to give you a welcoming embrace, Maestro Ismael showed how he would wrap one arm around the man's shoulder then spin around 180 degrees to make sure nobody was coming up on him from behind. A simple welcoming handshake could lead to a man with evil intent to grab your fingers and bend them back, attempting to break one or more of them so you could not grasp a weapon. Alternately, he could attempt some kind of wrist lock to wrench or dislocate the joint. Only in North America is a strong firm handshake considered a form of "manliness" and not the gesture of a naïve fool. Among those individuals I have met who were raised in a warrior culture or have long-practiced combative arts and have trained to incorporate to some degree a warrior's habitus, a man would give me a slight weak "feminine" handshake, lest he leaves himself vulnerable to an attack. Maestro Ismael also showed me a drill on how to meet an ambush by multiple opponents along the road. Moving all the time forward, Maestro Ismael showed how to block and deflect a number of attacks to his legs until he could break free of the group of attackers. Along similar lines, José-Felipe showed me how to sit in a chair with my palo across the arms of the chair or across my lap where I could easily grasp it by both ends and repel an attack. In turn, Danys Burgos taught me how to walk through a doorway with my palo held in both hands, so if attacked, I could push the palo against the weapon, arm, or chest of the attacker and propel myself back out of the door and safety. With the number of fragmented and seemingly casual pieces of practical advice and body-techniques I was exposed to by a number of teachers, I learned to discern what Goffman called "lurk lines" or those environmental sites or circumstances where danger can wait to take advantage of those naïve enough to take the apparent as the real (Goffman 1971, 296). In what the Brazilian capoeirist Daniel Noronha saw as "Walking in evil" (Downey 2005, 153), in addition to learning how to perceive possible dangers, a student also learns how to competently and with aplomb deal any sudden dangerous situations that can arise out of everyday life—a social world where, as the Venezuelan fable warns, "good is always repaid by evil."

SORCERY

It has been said that Venezuela is Latin America's least Catholic country. Nevertheless, in one recent poll almost 96 percent of people claimed to be Catholic (Dineen 2001, 23). A popular type of Catholicism throughout Venezuela revolves around the veneration of local saints who act as accessible mediators between the mundane world and heaven. For example, in Barquisimeto, there is a whole neighborhood of shops devoted to folk remedies, spiritual charms, amulets, and spells. In a little understood aspect of garrote, I only met three garroteros who would acknowledge any connection with this popular aspect of Catholicism. The late garrotero Natividad Apostal was a practicing herbalist and bone setter, and Felipe Vásquez claimed to be an *espitualista*. Toward the end of my stay, the garrotero Felipe Pérez, originally from Boro Santa Teresa in the Tocuyo Valley, mentioned how in the past some garroteros would carry a *Tuura* with them to ensure victory. A Tuura was a pouch that contained special or blessed objects to obtain supernatural protection. Drawing on this form of protection connects with other more mundane concerns to maintain the body "closed" or invulnerable to harm. In his study of ca-poeira, the anthropologist Greg Downey saw the protective amulet, or *Patua,* as an expression of an experiential logic where danger is encoun-tered both on the physical and spiritual planes of existence (Downey 2005, 147). In other words, among many combative exponents I have come across in the Philippines, South Africa, Brazil, and Venezuela, fight-ers were interested in cultivating new habitual dispositions in terms of moving and carrying the body, judging and reflecting upon events, and a concern to protecting one's open portals.

Examining the macrostructural contexts where garrote was shaped and honed into a distinct combative practice of the Venezuelan pueblos, this section explored how information is managed to protect one's life and public reputation. Secrecy and deception are not mere tactics to con-trol the flow of information but are sets of affective embodied knowl-edges that are part of a repertoire of communally acceptable practices of managing acts of sociality which are reworked and deployed to fit an individual's life's projects. In a number of works, the sociologist Goffman explored how we sometimes consciously, and sometimes not, project cer-tain roles, actions, and perspectives through everyday actions, dress, and language to persuade others toward a certain point of view of ourselves (Goffman 1956, 1963, 1971). Carrying a palo in public was once a public sign of manhood and presumed a certain level of skill. Carrying a garrote lent one a measure of symbolic capital as an honorable man able to sur-vive the agonistic environment of an honor culture. At the same time though, there was an ideology of hiding one's knowledge and ability of garrote as to avoid the jealousy and challenges of neighbors, as well as to take advantage of an opponent's ignorance of one's skills to surprise him or them, giving oneself an edge. But as Simmel presciently observed, a secret is only valuable if someone knows you have a secret (Simmel 1906). Today, when men no longer carry weapons as part of their every-day dress, one young garrotero has come up with a novel way to display his prowess. Instead of carrying a palo, he wears a different shirt every day, displaying the logos of a Canary Island stick-fighting group that befriended him. In this way, he is able to maintain a pretense of keeping his knowledge of garrote a secret while announcing his connection with a foreign stick-fighting group. In addition to his dress, he regularly shows off his skills at international and locally sponsored folkloric festivals, and he teaches a couple of students basic moves. In such a manner, he main-tains an appearance of hiding his skills and he protects his restricted status, all the while displaying his knowledge and skills in the art through his participation in local festivals and his everyday dress. Men once carried a palo advertising one's secret and claiming a social capital that can only be increased at the expense of another's defeat, or the putting up of a good fight before going down to defeat. This accompanied a certain type of manhood where honor was tightly linked to one's public reputation in a small, closed environment where face-to-face interaction and ascribed achievement based on family and aggressiveness were dominant. At present, revolvers and knives are more common instruments of popular violence in accordance with acceptable everyday dress of men today and the accessibility of weapons. At the same time, ideas of honor as a publicly bestowed status have been internalized as dignity, a feeling of worthiness that all humans possess equally. Accompanying these shifts has been a declining public acceptance of rustic violent recreations or the settling of vendettas by violence. Within these broader contexts, the art of garrote has been recast and continued by contemporary practitioners.

NOTES

1. José-Felipe Alvarado was the last student León Valera accepted as a student.

2. Also known as the Juego de Oscuridad, or the game of darkness, due to the predilection of Raphael Peraza to practice only by the illumination of one or two lanterns in order to hone the students' perceptual apparatus under less then optimal conditions, in this way, providing a means for the student to protect himself and an advantage when pressing an attack under the cover of darkness.

3. Here I am referring to the Marxist guerilla uprising that occurred throughout Venezuela until the late 1960s. Eventually, they were ruthlessly repressed by the government with military and financial aid from United States.

FIVE

Belonging and the Role of Honor

Fighting and being part of a social group might appear to have little to do with each other but fighting is an extremely social act. Not only does one need another person to strike back at him to transform a beating into a fight, but one needs to be taught how to fight. One of the goals of this work has been to show how with any combative act the result is a previously tested and culturally meaningful way of moving the body in conjunction with material objects. Moreover, it is learned in a process of apprenticeship, mooring a student to a place, a lineage, or community. More than a weapon of self-defense, the garrote served as a symbol of the ability and willingness of a man to gain and maintain the respect of his community—to be seen and treated as a man of honor.

FIGHTING AND BELONGING

The link between ways of fighting and belonging was particularly made clear to one officer during the trench warfare characterizing World War I. During a trench-scrum when enemy soldiers were face-to-face in restricted spaces and unable to use grenades or rifles easily, the author found to his surprise that Englishmen preferred to use clubs, blackjacks, and their fists to dominate the enemy, feeling blades were somehow anti-ethical to being an Englishman. Moreover, elite Italian *Arditi* shock troops favored narrow-bladed daggers they could drive behind the collarbone of an enemy, penetrating the lungs and heart. West African colonial troops felt more comfortable with wide-bladed knives that they used in low slashing blows seeking to disembowel their opponents (Todd 1938).[1] What both the officer and the sociologist Mauss discerned during this time was how a number of alternative body-techniques in conjunction with material technology emerged to affect efficacious responses to simi-

79

lar challenges. As already socialized individuals finding themselves in extremely stressful situations, soldiers relied upon the use and coordination of specific muscle groups with specific types of weapons in a manner that would be seen as ethically right, efficacious, and reflecting an individual's origin or lineage.

As it relates to Venezuela, although many garroteros had differing opinions about almost every aspect of the art, one thing they all held in common as what was the most important attribute needed to master garrote was an understanding of footwork, or *pisada*, and awareness, or *vista*. Upon meeting a man who would agree to teach me garrote, my first lesson would begin the same way as it did for those countless others before me. In the countryside, I would follow my teacher out into a field and he would begin class by using his garrote to clear a space of leaves and snakes. Then with one end of the palo, the teacher would draw a geometric figure in the ground: "This is the *cuadra*; this is how you learn garrote."

Cuadras, or squares, came in many shapes and sizes; some were rectangular, others circular or triangular, some were large and others small. Some cuadras guided the way you would move your body to attack and defend yourself. Other cuadras laid out the proximal relationship that opponents would maintain in relation to each other. Underscoring the wide variety of teaching methods and the difficulty of making definite statements regarding the art, the garrotero Napolean Zapata, who hailed

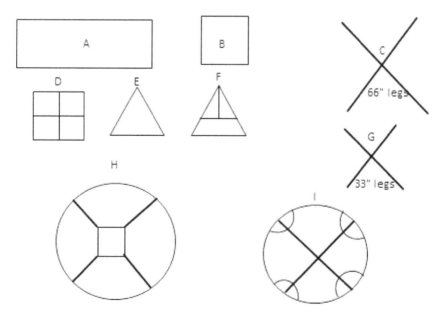

Table 5.1. A few of the cuadras used in the Segovia highlands

from across the river from El Tocuyo in La Otra Banda, did not use a cuadra at all, but taught his *Doble y Cruzado* style through the use of *Llamadas* or static challenge postures that deliberately opened areas of the body as to invite an attack to an apparent weakness or opening. To muddy the waters even further, los hermanos, Yépez of El Papelón do not focus on footwork at all and believe their students will pick it up intuitively over time, in a type of mimicry.

The apprenticeship process that opened the doors for me to seek to think, feel, and move my body in conjunction with a weapon as a garrotero began one morning when I met Saúl Téran in front of his place of business. I came in response to his invitation to show me a style of garrote with different roots than the one in El Tocuyo that I was studying and having myriad difficulties learning. Accompanying Saúl to the back of his Chinese medical clinic/martial arts school, I was hoping to see some students swinging garrotes, but we were alone. Guessing my confusion and disappointment in not finding anybody else there training, he explained that none of his Kung-Fu students were interested in learning the art. Drawing on a pedagogical progression of scaffolding, Saúl walked over to one side of the courtyard, grabbed a handful of Mamón leaves that were hanging overhead, and began my apprenticeship (Downey 2008). Using a palo he grabbed from the storeroom on the way to the courtyard, he laid out a cuadra. Gripping the garrote as if he were going to swing it, he laid it on the ground, his hand still wrapped around the garrote. With his other hand full of leaves, he made a mark where the top of his hand met the garrote and another at the striking end of the garrote. He then drew a straight line connecting these two marks. Doing this three more times he made a square. He then grabbed a couple of handfuls of additional leaves in to draw a diagonal line on each corner of the cuadra with each line the length of the garrote this time (table 5.1, H). Looking up, he said,

> You see the cuadra teaches you all you need to know. You should be able to lay the palo up against your armpit and just be able to cup your fingers around the end; that is how you know the right length of the stick. Each side of the cuadra is the same length as the palo (minus the handle) and gives you the proper distance you should maintain from your opponent, while the diagonal line, again as long as the palo, shows how the length of your stance.

After finishing the cuadra, Saúl picked up his palo and stood on the southeast diagonal line, saying "stand like me." Standing on the northeast line, I began a long process of trying to mimic his posture, the angle at which the body leans, the placement of the arms and the garrote. Throughout the next few weeks, Saúl continually reprimanded me about an errant limb, unbalanced posture, or awry stick and, as time went on, more often coming over to me to strike or move my limbs and garrote into place. Through the act of striking me, Saúl showed how this posture minimized the vulnerability of my vital areas. My front foot was slightly turned inward to protect the groin. My trunk leaned forward slightly and my shoulders turned so as to line up with my hip to protect my internal organs. My left arm was held across my trunk with the palm cupping my right front shoulder to protect my chest and to keep the left elbow from protruding beyond my trunk. My right arm, holding the stick, was laid along the back of my rear leg to prevent the opponent from guessing from which angle my attack would come. That first day after a long process of grabbing, pushing, and pulling my body and my garrote into a proper standing position, Saúl was finally partially satisfied and a little exasperated and went back to the northeast line and took up a ready posture. Both of us were standing at a 45-degree angle, or *en perfil*, to each other, further minimizing our vital areas exposure to an attack while encouraging the use of our peripheral vision.[2]

After learning how to stand in relation to an opponent, Saúl began to teach me how to move through a series of *lineas* or basic prearranged two man sequences of attack and defense, that range from one to five exchanges of attack, defense, and counter. Saúl began with a one palo linea. "Me falta un palo arriba," he said, as I aimed a rising underhand strike to his groin with the tip of my garrote. To do this, I stepped with the rear foot from the northeast line to the northwest line and, with a snap of the hips, dragged my lead foot behind me to where I was now standing on the diagonal of the northwest line. Finishing in this manner, my lead foot was twisted inward and uncomfortable: Now give an *afinca*, or stomp. In other words, I had to pick up my lead foot and move it inward a couple of inches as if scooping some leaves or pebbles out of the way and then lightly come back down. This is the basic step from which all other moves arise and return. At the same time, I was trying to strike and to monitor the movements of my body and the garrote, Saúl defended the blow to his groin, using the same stepping pattern moving from the southeast line to the southwest line while knocking my stick away from his body with a counterclockwise twirl of his own stick toward the east. After a couple weeks of teaching, when I finally began to understand how to move, instead of parrying my stick Saúl began to direct his parry at the outside of my bicep, in effect launching a counterattack, forcing me to halt my attack and evade his counter by moving, screwing my elbow back into my stomach and withdrawing my hand gripping the stick up nearby left shoulder, while leaving the tip pointed at him, thereby evading his counter. Rather than blocking or meeting force with force the use of *negavas*, or avoidances, by the arm or by the judicious use of body movements also known as a *cuerpo limpio*, or avoiding a strike without blocking, is seen as the highest proof of one's ability by many lineages of garrote.

For the first few weeks, upon first stepping on the line of the cuadra, and after completing any attack or defense, I had to constantly monitor myself, rearranging my feet, legs, body, arms, and garrote, and then my distance from Saúl. Continually and patiently, Saúl helped with this process by poking and prodding, striking, pulling, and pushing my limbs and stick into their proper position. Alternately, yelling out commands to "watch your hands, your feet, your head," as he launched blows at offending body parts, in case I misinterpreted his instructions. In this process, learning to maintain the proper distance or "use space" (Goffman 1971, 295) with one's opponents through the judicious use of footwork was key to maintaining the proper upper body mechanics to initiate and counter attacks. For this reason, Maestro Félix García would say to a student of his when he was being struck too much during training, "go back to the cuadra," meaning go off to the side and work on the basic footwork. Hearing this command always brought a titter of laughs from the other students who understood that the miscreant had failed to main-

Figure 5.2. Saúl evades Andrés attack with a cuerpo limpio

tain a basic competence of the fundamentals of the Palo Sangriento. The
need to master the basics of the movement and placement of the body
stressed by Saúl and Maestro Félix during training calls attention to the
key role social networks play both in the reshaping of a student's physiological attribute and, as important, in the reconfiguring of a student's
subjectivity.

One time after a hard workout, Saúl explained to me that while garroteros all share common repertoire of attacks, what sets a lineage of garrote apart from others is the way they defend these strikes. Knowing I
trained with a number of different teachers Saúl advised me to train only
one lineage a day as not to be confused how to move. Depending on the
garrote of lineage I was training at the time, I would seek to step off at a
45-, 90-, or a 135-degree angle. Either I sought to take a large step to outflank the opponent or take a small step and move to the outside of the
opponent's strike. Removing my body from the trajectory of the strike, I
could respond with a twirl of the wrist, directing my palo to hit the tip of
my opponent's palo to redirect its trajectory away from me and then
counter with my own attack. I could aim instead at my opponent's bicep
or tricep to force him to abort his attack. Or moving completely off-line of
the attacks where me and my opponent would be *ombro a ombro*, or shoulder to shoulder, I could safely launch a counterattack. Making these "signature moves" done at the right time in response to an attack during a
training session showed to my teacher and his friends that I had done my
homework and was beginning to understand how to swing a palo in a
way deemed to be effective, efficient, and group-specific. In other words,
I demonstrated a level of respect and trust in my teacher and that his
trust in me had not been misplaced.

Regularly, I would come to train with Danys Burgos after he was done
with work at a nearby small furniture manufacturing shop. Arriving in
front of his parent's house I would yell out "hello" until he would appear. Danys would then open the gate to his home, invite me in, call his
friend William on his cell phone to join us, and grab a pair of palos.
Waiting out back until William showed up, we would talk for a few
minutes and then begin a prearranged sparring sequence that, as time
went on and I became more comfortable with the sequence, would become increasingly a free flow match. Usually the action would start off at
a medium pace and then slowly increase. As the tempo increased and the
sticks came faster, my footwork would begin to suffer as I would fail to
step out fully to avoid the trajectory of an attack. Increasingly, I would
awkwardly twist my body out of the way and rely on blocking incoming
attacks with my palo to compensate for my lack of proper balanced body
displacement. Attempting to correct my stumbling and increasing awk-
wardness, I would begin to look at my feet to ensure I was stepping
correctly. In response to these increasingly longer looks at my feet, the
sticks from Danys or William would come even faster, compounding my

errors until I finally felt a blinding surge of pain as a garrote hit home against bone. Then William or Danys would stop, put one finger to the bottom of their eyelid, and giving it a tug say in a disapproving tone "vista," "let's do it again, this time watch out." Remembering my luck to have such a great pair of teachers, I would swallow my frustration and prepare myself for another round of "juegando los palos."

Alongside with one's footwork, one visual awareness or "vista" was considered the other key attribute in learning garrote. Earlier I discussed that vista can refer to the cultivation of a wary attitude toward everyday social situations. In a more subtle sense, vista can also refer to evaluating the emotional attitude of one's opponents: are they timid, fearless, or detached. At its most basic sense though and the definition I am referring to here, vista refers to learning to recognize the trajectory of an attack and decide if it is a fake or committed attack and respond accordingly. Among the garroteros I trained with, they all recommended I look at an opponent right in the eye, using my peripheral vision to attend to the opponent's limbs. Unpacking the ideas and practices surrounding ways of looking at an opponent reveals how combative exponents around the world and through history often call upon little used perceptual attributes mediated through material technology to dominate a combative encounter. Taking the analysis a step further, a solid understanding of pisada and vista, emphasized so much during training, can be seen as a local manifestation of the warrior's habitus. Both stepping and seeing are treated as key physiological responses that have been successfully employed in the past to allow an individual to dominate a combative encounter. Varying across the area due to historical contingencies, individualistic preference, or some combination of the two, the proper exhibition of these fundamental concepts are seen and treated as group markers of belonging to a region, a family, or a lineage. In a process Wacquant identified as "Body-Work" (1995, 73), Foucault as "technologies of the self" (1988, 18), or what Merleau-Ponty saw as a "Landscape of Praxis"(Merleau-Ponty 1971, 199), moving the body in specific ways to a challenge, acquiring the ability to discern to the trajectory of attacks to recognize intentions and respond accordingly, is not merely the learning of a new skill but a total transformative process of learning to use the body in new ways in response to any ominous encounter (Downey 2007, 215; Merleau-Ponty 1962, 173; Wacquant 2004, 117). In the case of martial arts and other craft activities, this transformation usually emerges within a relationship of apprenticeship. Taking on the responsibility to train a man in ways that can be turned against the teacher or their community resulting in physical injuries and loss of respect in the community is a heavy burden fraught with peril for a garrotero who has to decide whether to accept someone as a student. In the long and intimate disciplined training, the teacher/student relationship often transforms into a deep and lasting friendship as, along with technical skills, social knowledges, world views, and moral principles held by the teacher and his group are incorporated and manifested during training and post-training social activities.

HONOR VIOLENCE AND THE PALO

Many times talking to garroteros in El Tocuyo, I was told how among those of the previous generation when two men came to have a disagreement, they both retired to the banks of the Tocuyo River where alone they could settle their differences with garrotes, like men of honor. The idea of honor and "cultures of honor" as types of meaningful realms of study was once the focus of intense debate among anthropologists. As a result of this, scholars have done much in furthering our understanding of the role of honor and shame, its counterpart, as it has been thought and used in different time periods throughout the Mediterranean and Latin America. Out of this debate the general agreement has emerged that honor and shame are indicative of the ways that collective groups see themselves and are used as a practically oriented set of attitudes to engage in and evaluate all social interactions. In other words, "Honor and Shame are reciprocal moral values representing the primordial integration of individual to group. They reflect, "respectively the conferral of public esteem upon the person and the sensitivity to public opinion upon which their former depends" (Pitt-Rivers 1965, 42). The role of group recognition in assessing one's place in society arises from the idea that one's moral worth is visible to one's peers, and as such can be measured through one's comportment, dress, or patterns of socialization. Alternately, honor can be located in a lineage, a group, a pueblo, or an individual. Honor can also be based on the sexual continence of its members, and even based on the recognition of mutual obligations of trust and honesty amongst one's peers. Honor can even accrue to those who cheat, lie, and steal, thereby devaluing the honor of others to one's own benefit (Herzfeld 1985; Paine 1989; Pitt-Rivers 1965, 1977; Wolf et al. 1967). Enumerating the great number of ways a man accrues honor reveals the oftentimes sets of mutually contradictory rules and norms that a man must negotiate successfully on an everyday basis to sustain or increase his public reputation. One element held in common in all honor cultures is that male honor often depended on possessing a reputation for bravery and an acceptance of violence (Davies 1988; Gallant 2000; Gilmore 1987; Spierenberg 1998). As it was said among the popular classes of early twentieth-century Mexico City: "Honor in Mexico City was a right that had to be defended daily against many threats and at a high cost" (Piccato 2001, 81).

As an honor culture took shape in Venezuela, it came about that many men carried hardwood, braided-handled walking sticks not only as iconic symbols denoting their manhood but as tools to manage their public reputation through the measured use of violence. One night sitting out on some chairs in the front of his farm José-Felipe explained to me the responsibility and obligations one assumes upon picking up a palo:

> In Venezuela it was that men carried about their palos in an honorable manner. Others did so less honorably, others even in a less honorable fashion, and if as a result one decides to aggressively strike someone with a blow from his stick, people said he was a jugador, but no Señor he is not, it is a sign of disrespect. The stick is very sacred and shows that a man has been taught right from wrong. He comes from a good family; he has good friends and is a good worker and shows respect to all. There comes a time when two people are going to engage in a juego, and they have something very much on their minds; respect for their reputation, respect for the public and their friends, as well as that man that he is to cross sticks with. Because imagine that you don't respect an attack that this man launches at you, is it still a juego? It degenerates into foolishness, because all of us men that possess this art that we hold dear, (Aside) we don't know that . . . I don't know anything, but I understand very well one thing—although I know absolutely nothing . . . but the first thing one has to do is acquire the discipline, the friendship, the understanding until one is able to survive in the juego. (José-Felipe Alvarado, interview with author, El Molino, May 29, 2005)

In this passage José-Felipe speaks of the palo as metonymically standing for a man's public self, as well as being a tool to maintain his public reputation as an honorable man. Up until the 1950s in Lara and the early 1970s in the more remote areas of the country, when men went outside their home to visit neighbors, have a drink at a pulpería, or attend a party, they went with a girl in one hand and a palo in the other. Many times knowing the trouble that would inevitably break out, many times the owner of a house would collect the palos of all men attending a house party, or they would hire a policeman to collect all palos at the door, to be returned upon leaving. This could be a delicate situation as trying to take away a man's palo could led to a fight or worse as occurred one night in El Tocuyo back in 1911. Court documents attest that:

> José Márquez saw Juan Domingo Colmenarez with the aforementioned stick in his hand leaving said establishment, José Marquez approached Juan Domingo Colmenarez and grabbed said garrote and pulled but did not take it. And at this Juan Domingo said to Márquez, don't take away my garrote, and taking a knife from a sheath in his belt stuck it in the hollita of José Márquez. (Assunção 1999, 84).

Here again the publicly embodied nature of man and his reputation is felt to reside not only in his body but his palo, so that any attempt to take away a man's palo was akin to symbolically castrating or publicly humiliating him in a way that could provoke a violent response. At present, men under the age of seventy do not carry garrotes in public, while only very few rural men over seventy publicly display theirs. A number of men I talked to do, however, carry their palos in their trunks or on the dashboards of their cars or strapped underneath their mopeds as befitting changing notions of an appropriate public comportment.

Coming of age in a highly unstable environment where violence was seen and treated as a legitimate tool to attain ones means, the escalation of stick fights to include the use of bladed weapons or firearms through a desire not to lose, or the premeditated ambushing of enemies with multiple armed men lying in wait to eliminate the individual, was not too long ago a common occurrence in rural Venezuela. At the same time, there was an equally strong concern to mediate the potential devastating effects of unrestrained violence unleashed on a community. I once asked José-Felipe what was his favorite weapon during his time in the guerilla. He responded an "AK-47, it was brought over from Cuba." "Not a palo?" I asked. "No, No, No, the palo was never used to kill anybody, only to gain respect." In this exchange and others that were to follow with other older garroteros, I began to understand the palo, or garrote, is seen as a culturally shaped piece of material technology meant to act as a cultural brake on unrestrained intracommunal violence.[3] The intent of an assailant to minimize the bodily harm inflicted on another with a palo was recognized as far back when assaults with a garrote began entering the criminal court system in the early nineteenth century. The penal code of Barquisimeto of 1832 stated those found guilty of fighting with bladed weapons or firearms were to pay a fine of four pesos or spend three days in jail. In contrast, the use of a stick would result in a jail term of no longer than 24 hours (Cañizales-Verde 1992). Further supporting the idea of the garrote as culturally significant piece of material technology to reduce the consequences of intracommunal violence is borne out in homicide statistics, where in the province of Barquisimeto during a one-hundred-year period beginning in 1830 until 1930 when the number of complaints drops sharply, the stick was involved in only 7.4 percent of homicide cases and 24.5 percent of injuries (Assunção 1999, 75).[4]

One result of the establishment of a modern state in Venezuela was an increasing acceptance of laws governing the carrying of weapons in public and other forms of extreme behavior. The once common site of seeing a man carrying a palo tucked underneath his arm while taking a shot of Cocuy at the local pulpería, or walking down a country road sending pebbles flying with a quick twirl of the garrote, has disappeared over the last few years as the last generation of men brought up in this type of world are dying out. Accompanying the passing of this generation of men is a perception of the moral decline of today's youth by those old men who brandished and lay about with their palos in exuberant wild brawls or melees. Sixty-nine-year-old garrotero Ricardo Colmenares explained it to me this way:

Miguel: The men of your father's generation were different then the men of today?

Ricardo: Yes, they were a people who were very honorable, very sensitive.

Miguel: How so?

Ricardo: Very sensitive, very touchy, and for the least abuse of their trust this would cause them considerable discomfort.

Miguel: No?

Ricardo: Very sensitive and in raising a family, Oh my god! If a woman dishonored the family; this led to blows with the stick being laid about.

Miguel: They were more sensitive in the past?

Ricardo: Yes, they were much more.

Miguel: They were touchier in the past?

Ricardo: Yes, much more, much.

Miguel: Were they friendlier?

Ricardo: Yes, the men before are not like the men today, in that I would not tell a lie. I would sell you this house at this time, I would sell you this house for a million Bolivares, and suppose another man came along and said I will give you a million and a half, it would not matter to me, I would sell it to you for the million, and I would know that you will sell it to another for a million and a half.

Miguel: No?

Ricardo: My word is my contract.

Miguel: Is this true?

Ricardo: My word is a serious thing, I don't change my word for a million or a half a million Bolivares, because we already discussed a price of a million Bolivares and for any amount I would not change my word, this is certain.

Miguel: In the past did men carry sticks to the dance?

Ricardo: Yes, they carried them; yes, this was the weapon they carried.

Miguel: Why did they carry sticks?

Ricardo: They carried a _fusta_ to defend themselves.

Miguel: For what reason?

Ricardo: For whatever things would attack them out there.

Miguel: Snakes, jaguars?

Ricardo: Or whatever person.

Miguel: People too?

Ricardo: Ahhh! Then the people back in the past they would take offense at the smallest word, for any kind of word they would get mad.

Miguel: Why would the men fight in the old days?

Ricardo: Well it depended, because there is an individual that fights because he has to, because they will not let him alone, because of this they fight, the people and, ah, then I fight and you fight because they are going to rob you, they are not going to let you alone, to rob someone is very easy, you have stand bravely to defend oneself.

Miguel: Was it easy to get into a fight, to insult another man in the past, did people gossip a lot?

Ricardo: No, I tell you in those days the men, the men were very serious.

Miguel: Why were the men always joking around?

Ricardo: They always played with words.

Miguel: Yes?

Ricardo: Yes.

Miguel: But in the past no?

Ricardo: No, no not always, you used to have games and things but it was not a game taken seriously you understand.

Miguel: Taken seriously, yes.

Ricardo: But to look for an enemy, to provoke someone for no reason was to be a *Chalequando*, no Señor.

Miguel: In the past did men bring pistols sometimes?

Ricardo: Sometimes they would.

Miguel: Only a few times?

Ricardo: Yes, they used a revolver on occasion, because these men would not look to kill anyone, before the men fought with *palos y coñazos*.

Miguel: And sometimes knives?

Ricardo: They also used those, but it was not the intention to kill anyone no, no, no, no.[5]

Maestro Ricardo, much like Maestro José-Felipe, echoes a similar sentiment regarding the gravitas and moral uprightness of the men of their youth and the role of the garrote to minimize violence. It is obvious both men are relating an idealized normative view of the past. In addition to training, it is in the telling of stories and relating philosophical insights to younger eager students where ideas of proper comportment, ethics, and norms are transmitted. These stories and drills, which are eagerly sought after and practiced by many students, influence the ways young men talk and feel about garrote, themselves, and their relations with others through the active linking of themselves to a past through their practice with the garrote and their projecting of future imaginaries about how they would like to live life.

As hard working poor farmers, skilled craftsman, or landless laborers, men were supposed to face the vagaries of the world with nothing more than a hardwood, tapered walking stick and a pair of "balls" to survive his travails with honor and respect. The idea of a hard-won and ephemeral publicly bestowed honor assumes a natural hierarchy of honorable individualism and ties into other contradictory ideas and practices surrounding garrote, such as the need for secrecy, deception, and cunning as part of what the anthropologist Foster called the "idea of the limited good" (Foster 1965, 1972). What this meant is that is one's good luck or achievements should not be readily displayed to others as there is only a finite amount of good fortune and others will try to take it or somehow ruin it passively through sending bad luck with an envious or jealous gaze, or actively through seeking out sorcerers or other acts of sabotage. The high wire balancing act of remaining humble and respectful while at the same time trying to build and maintain one's own reputation is seen in the following stories recounted by José-Felipe. Reflecting on the virtue of humility, José-Felipe tells how he was always close to his teacher León Valera because he never displayed the full extent of his skills in front him. José-Felipe would tell me that León Valera would often, when talking about his student, say "José-Felipe is a good man, kind of slow and not too good with the stick, but a good man." This story was related in the context of a conversation about one of León Valera's first students, Domingo Escalona, and the falling out they had after participating in the 400th anniversary of the founding of El Tocuyo back in 1945. Exhibiting his Siete Lineas juego de garrote in front of a large hometown crowd, León Valera felt Domingo Escalona was trying to outshine him during the stick fighting demonstration, leading him to cut off all further contact with him until the day he died.

As an instrument to establish and maintain one's public reputation at a time when the idea of honor shaped all social interactions, every public act became an opportunity to display one's abilities, skills, or quick-wittedness, often at the expense of others highlighting the zero-sum stakes of honor. Speaking of a time when he desired to test his skills against others while at the same time seeking to remain within the good graces of his teacher León Valera and not cause trouble, José-Felipe reminisced about garroteros he knew in the past. He related a story about a duel between himself and José Sequera, the son of his teacher. Meeting in a recently harvested sugarcane field soon after daybreak, they met with their palos in their hands to see who was the better garrotero. Eagerly asking him what happened, José-Felipe merely smiled and said that he "gave him a little present of a strike behind the head, so as to give him something to remember me by." Soon after the subject then turned to local celebrations of the Tamunangue:

Miguel: Who was the Capitan?

José-Felipe: Leopoldo Aguilar, a very good Capitan, but he was not a jugador, all that he knew was two strikes, nothing more.

Miguel: I thought all Capitan's were good jugadores?

José-Felipe: No, no, no. I played many times and had to restrain myself.

Miguel: Why?

José-Felipe: Now, because I am a *Chueco*, but before I used to have to restrain myself, but before if there were hard strikes to be delivered, well then that is how the sticks would be done. (José-Felipe Alvarado interview with author, El Molino, March 15, 2005)

José-Felipe's stories shine a light on how he negotiated a position balancing the contradictory demands placed on him as a garrotero trained by the eminent León Valera. Showing restraint and humility around his teacher and other elders, José-Felipe displayed deference for his family and local community. Outside this circle, though, he claims he demonstrated a similar restraint but, if pushed, would gladly take advantage of the opportunity to test his skills and let the wider community know of his courage, prowess, and skills he had developed under the tutelage of his teacher from El Molino.

JOKING: TAKING IT TO THE LIMIT

Chaucer presciently observed that one can guild many an unpleasant truth in humor when he penned the line "there is many a truth between a jest and joke." Joking and an expansive sense of humor were another arena that allowed men to participate in high-risk public situations and push the boundaries of what a community would accept without resorting to violence, or other sanctions on the would-be comedian. I often use to see eighty-two-year-old Ismael Vásquez outside a bakery on my way to Saúl's school, just hanging out with other retired men. One day walking with Saúl with a pair of palos in my hand I had just bought at a little bodega, we met Maestro Ismael and stopped to say hello. Admiring my new purchase, Maestro Ismael grabbed the one I was then holding out of my hand. "This one feels nice, quick watch out!" he yelled, swinging the palo at the inside of my right knee. I retracted my leg out of the reach of the palo. "Watch out!" he yelled again as he swung a backhand blow at the inside of my left knee. Retracting that leg so my feet were parallel on a line and trying to keep my balance bending forward, Maestro Ismael lightly gave me a tap on the top of my head, leading everybody including myself to laugh at the impromptu garrote lesson. On another day, Maestro Ismael came by Saúl's school to socialize and let me interview him again. When it was time for us to break for lunch and we were packing up our stuff to go, Maestro Ismael unbuttoned his shirt and pulled out a big rubber dildo and showed it around, which provoked a lot of laughs.

These are examples of the more innocuous types of joking I was exposed to. On the other hand, a local chronicler from the hill town of Sanare recounted how in the past garroteros liked to get drunk and pull out their knives and sticks and fight, and as a joke liked to hang people by the neck for a while. He also tells of Don Sinforoso Goyo and his two sons Emisael and Manuel Lucena, describing them as "men of great spirituality, cordial jokers, musicians and notable as Tamunangeros and jugadores de palo (Peraza-Silva 1961, 161). Many times I witnessed or heard about other groups of acquaintances and friends who continued what I considered harsh running jokes, or inappropriate jokes, that went way past the point of acceptability in my opinion. Only a few of my friends drank alcohol, but I could imagine these types of situations where this type of joking behavior, occurring in a drinking environment, could easily lead to physical altercations. Asking about this propensity for hard joking, even with strangers, I was often told that this was a national characteristic among Venezuelans and was just part of the natural sociability and openness of spirit shared by all Venezuelan men. A spirit of open-handed generosity, repeated rounds of sharing drinks, and boisterous joking suddenly leading to bouts of bloodletting is often common throughout the world, where ideas of honor govern men's sense of self and their public reputation (Boschi 1998; Campbell 1965; Herzfeld 1985). One common element shared among these types of communities is a highly competitive masculinity characterized by regular acts of "Institutional Brinksmanship" (Paine 1989) or testing the boundaries of what is acceptable behavior, or achievable. Within this type of hypercompetitive environment, the refusal to acknowledge a display of courage, daring, or skill can be taken as an insult and lead to acts of violence to regain "face." In the early days of North America, for example, it was said the legendary Mississippi River keelboat man Mike Fink once began a fight with man for refusing to laugh at his jokes (Blair and Franklin 1933, 112–113). Declining to share a drink with another man, looking at another man's girl too hard, doubting another man's exploits, or in the past just carrying a palo down the street was enough of a reason to call a man out and test his mettle and at times are still valid reasons to begin a set-to today. For example, in the hill country above the Tocuyo Valley there is an agronomist who walks the fields conducting his work with two palos strapped to his back in a small bag, inviting those rumored to be garroteros themselves to a friendly exchange of the sticks.

As the process of conquest and colonization took on a distinctive trajectory in Venezuela, the civilian population developed a predilection for certain types of weapons and a marked way of using them in comparison to other areas of Latin America. In the Segovia Highlands, it was possible to identify the origins of the way a man swung his garrote based on the type of stick he used or the way he moved his body and handled his weapon. As a scholar though, it was usually better to talk to the person and asked where he came from and from whom he learned before making any claims to his origins or lineages. Any simple generalizations became much more difficult with the great deal of social mobility that has gone on since the 1950s and the idiosyncratic nature of martial artists, in general, to personalize their art. With this proviso in mind, the establishment of recognizable lineages of garrote is best seen as a collection of successful tactics or techniques that were passed down through family, friends, or neighbors that acted as proofs of a transmission or from a well-known fighter. Further militating against the desire to historically order garrote into a simple evolutionary scheme and as befitting the everyday, pragmatic nature of the art, the history of the lineage of a garrote-ro often goes back no more than three generations. In addition, compli-cating the use of the terms "lineages" or "styles" is the widely varying nature of the art overall. While some lineages are composed of a few basic principles or techniques required meet any exigency, other styles possess a sophisticated pedagogical progression of moves and drills to develop a well-rounded fighter. The wide array of moves within a line-age's repertoire calls attention to the differing interests that men have in perfecting, or transmitting, their skills. Not everybody sought out a repu-tation as a jugador. Other garroteros by contrast are fiercely proud of their abilities, often claiming to have created their own styles without any outside help. Still others are wary of potential treachery on the part of students using their knowledge against them and encourage students to develop their own styles to further their development, while in fact seek-ing to rid themselves of potential opponents. In spite of these provisos, during an intense private or semi-private disciplinary regime of training where local traditional knowledges are transformed into practical abil-ities, deep bonds are often formed between the teacher and the student, or between students, calling attention to the way subject-identities come into being and are linked to a community, a time, or a place.

In spite of the profound changes that have transformed the country over the last on hundred years, many garroteros still possess a strong sense of proprietorship and reticence when it comes to demonstrating their skill or even acknowledging their acquaintance with the art. One way this is seen is in the in the deep sense of responsibility that accompa-nies their teachings with a good dose of lectures, injunctions, stories, and aphorisms designed to instill in the students a strong ethical core. At present fists, belts, and revolvers are more common instruments of popu-lar violence in accordance with acceptable everyday dress of men today, while among the criminal element revolvers are increasingly easy to ob-tain. At the same time, ideas of honor have given way to a symmetrical ideology of dignity that is possessed by all. Accompanying these new ways of looking upon and judging others, the declining public accep-tance of rustic violent recreations and the settling of grudges or vendettas by violence has declined greatly, yet garrote continues to be trained and used in a number of different modalities, ranging from self-defense to passing the time and testing one's skill with a worthy opponent.

NOTES

1. This link was also made evident one afternoon for the Italian political philoso-pher, labor organizer, and member of Parliament Antonio Gramsci when he was im-prisoned by the order of Mussolini. As a way to entertain and show their respect for him on his birthday, prisoners in the jail he was being held put on a display of local knife fighting styles. Using spoons rubbed against the prison walls to leave a white-

wash mark on one's clothing to show successful strikes, Sicilians demonstrated against Apulians and Neapolitans against Calabrians to avoid facing traditional enemies. The champion though was a man who claimed to have no home (Gramsci 1975, 84).

2. Drawing upon the same attributes of the retina that capoeiraists called "looking sideways," this method of apprising the intentions of one's opponent or opponents takes advantage of the fact that the edge of the retina can detect movement more rapidly than the frontal part of the retina (Downey 2005, 186).

3. See Gallant (2000), on the cultural patterns of violence de-escalation among knife fighters in Greece and how the introduction of automatic rifle has changed intervillage stick dueling in Ethiopia and the Sudan, Abbink (1999) and Skedsmo et. al. (2003)

4. The state of Lara was carved out of the larger province of Barquisimeto in 1881.

5. Ricardo Colmenares, interview with author, Humacaro, May 29, 2005.

SIX

Forging the Warrior's Habitus

"Garrote is never taught for money, only friendship," José-Felipe explained to me one day as his other students listened and nodded gravely. This is not exactly accurate as there are accounts of schools of garrote in twentieth-century Venezuela, as I have shown. One element held in common among all those who decided to teach was in accepting someone as a student; a teacher keeps in mind the emotional stability of the student. At the very least, this is a self-aggrandizing attitude of self-preservation as the old medieval Persian adage warns "I taught him archer day by day/ but when his arm waxed strong t'was was me he shot" (Brodie 1967, 95). In line with this attitude, there is also a concern that the student reflects well on the teacher himself, who often lives in a small community where everybody knows each other's business and gossip can be endemic and vicious. In addition to finding someone of acceptable moral character, a teacher seeks a student who is not afraid of the stick or machete, who is already or who can be desensitized to the damage a weapon can inflict on the human body. From the process of screening potential students for a worthy student, I turn to examine what people have referred to as the "dark side," or the intense pleasure that comes with the physical domination of another. Mastering a set of technical skills is not seen as sufficient to be recognized as a jugador. Accounts of combat have shown there must be intent to close-in and engage with the opponent, to break his will and destroy his body. The determination to move in and the sense of excitement that often accompanies the engagement with an opponent plays a key role in those seeking mastery of the palo. Equally important among many elder garroteros I talked or trained with, is the acknowledgment of the humanity of the fallen opponent and the obligation laid upon one who has mastered the art to serve as a protector of his community rather than as a predator. Out of these concerns, I suggest the

97

development of a set of technical skills in conjunction with a material technology that serves to make up the repertoire of moves of a combative system is only one facet of the development of a combative exponent. Equally important is the ability to "turn off" the switch so to speak, to be able to reintegrate oneself into one's community as a respected and productive member of the community. The unique ways and challenges involved in teaching young men to fight, as well as the means or methods where they are taught to respect the sanctity of life, vary greatly through time and across cultures. The process of reintegrating individuals back into a community is fraught with grave difficulties that plague societies up through the present. The techniques, approaches, means, approaches, or practices to create such a warrior is what I call the "warrior's habitus."

VETTING A STUDENT

"What happened?" asked Uncle Manuel, believing that there was some scuffling going on outside amongst the cattle in the corral. I answered him, "It's nothing sir, just a dust-up with the boys. An old man has just arrived looking pitiful and down and out. The boys wanted to have some fun with him and hit him with a stick. The scuffling you heard is what is going on." He opened up some light in the corridor. In this way, he was able to see the old man put himself in an en-garde position and ready himself to fight: "Don't disrespect me Aguachinaos llaneros because I was a llanero long before you were born. Come to me one by one and I will teach you garrote."

After everybody had calmed down and retired to a nearby pulpería to have a drink and relax, the narrative continued:

> He had not finished talking when I made my way through a group of llaneros who were standing around him and, placing myself before him with my garrote in my hand, said, "I do not come to disrespect you sir, but I want to learn to defend myself from the attacks of those from in your grandfather's time."
>
> He looked me up and down and said, "And you, who are you my boy?"
>
> "Florentino Coronado, at your service"
>
> "Of the Coronados from Concepcion de Arauca?"
>
> "From the same sir."
>
> "Then you are worth teaching because I know of your family."

"Block this attack!"

"Blocked," I said. As he stood in front of me and gave me a gentle blow as to a young boy.

"And another?" he said.

"Won't touch me," I said. "Give me a strong blow."

"Ok, let's see if you can block it."

"Yes, that one got me," I had to tell him.

"Very hard?" he asked.

"Don't worry about it sir, that is how one learns." (Gallegos 1959, 22–24)

These passages from the novel *Cantaclaro* by the Venezuelan novelist and future president of Venezuela Rómulo Gallegos describes a young man seeking to learn, from the grandson of the famous llanero guerilla leader and first president of Venezuela José Antonio Paéz, how to handle a garrote. In addition to providing an evocative description of rural Venezuelan everyday life, what especially stands out in these passages is the constellation of memories, histories, and practices associated with the hardwood walking stick with the braided handle. Also reflected in the vignette are the everyday activities where stick fighting was often used as a rural pastime to break up the boredom of country life. Following the narrative, the act of making amends and retiring to a pulpería highlights the fact that the pulpería was the principal place of socialization for rural Venezuelan males. Here, a young man introduces himself to the older gentleman, asking to learn how to handle the palo like the men who fought in the wars of independence. The questioning that preceded the decision to teach the young man the art of the palo is seen as a valuable gift that takes place between two individuals of good birth and character and is not subject to commercial transaction. Finally, as it was said of the boy who was kicked by a mule, he was not as pretty as he used to be but was a whole lot wiser; the story foregrounds the role of the disciplined and socialized habitual body in conjunction with material technology in the development of practical skills, abilities, and ways of looking at the world still valued by many rural Venezuelans.

One afternoon after a hard session of training, Saúl Téran paid me a rare compliment, telling me I was a good student in that I was not afraid of palo. Asking him to explain, Saúl went on to say how difficult it has been to find someone who enjoys training garrote. Not only does a student need a good teacher to learn the art, but likewise, a teacher needs at least one good student to maintain his skills. A teacher will winnow through a number of individuals to find one good student. "Come on! Let's go home, my wife called and said lunch is ready!"

Once I learned a few of the basic two man drills or lineas that taught the fundamental characteristics of attack and defense and Saúl gained a level of trust in me, he began what he called an "accelerated program" in garrote. In what he described as developing my ability to *juego por la la vista,* or free-form sparring, Saúl would strike the same blow over and over, slowly increasing the speed, while I practiced parrying or evading the attack each time in a different way. Bypassing my reflective thought process by not giving me time to think, Saúl allowed my body to respond in ways that felt right and comfortable to avoid any attack, while adhering to the fundamental concepts of the Palo Sangriento. In what can be seen as a high level form of neuro-programming, Saúl was guiding me to, or evoking, an altered state of consciousness, where, while dealing with present challenges, I could simultaneously access the past through traditional responses while imagining the future through innovative yet technically efficient and effective counters to any attack. The emotional and psychological states evoked through this type of training are more fully explored below. Here, I want to emphasize how this two-man drill relies heavily on the teacher's intuitive understanding and trust in the student. The teacher becomes responsible for taking the student close to his breaking point, both physically, in terms of potential injuries as the blows come faster and harder as the student tires and the teacher must be careful of breaking or rupturing something, and psychologically, the teacher must be aware of the emotional resilience of the student and possess a level of confidence in the loyalty, or moral uprightness of the student to take him through this portal to a higher level of skill. In reality, drunken, sadistic, wary, or incompetent garroteros acting as teachers may distort, hide, or subvert this learning process, which brings attention to the relations of hierarchy among communities of garroteros where some have better access to good teachers or are better equipped to "steal" the information needed to excel from those unable or unwilling to teach.

The need for a good teacher in order to excel in garrote is key, as Félix García observed:

> It is a thing that must come from the heart, to learn to jugar garrote. Everyone does not learn to jugar garrote: one must like it a lot, you know. You must believe in yourself, there is no fear in the juego de garrote. Because the sticks come at you hard, and because of this, you must be liked by the person who is aiming a blow at you. If you are not liked by him, you are not going to learn anything. It is a very rough sport, you know that to jugar garrote with knives machetes, that is rough and one must be fearless (Félix García, interview with author, Barquisimeto, April 2, 2005).

Figure 6.1.   José-Felipe and Pasqual enjoy a friendly game

These words spoken by Maestro Félix reflect how a garrotero seeks to find a training partner he can trust to not turn his art against him or his community. There is the real worry that the new-found skills a man develops will turn him from a protector of one's community into a predator. Realizing the student does not measure up, there are a number of ways for the teacher to protect his art. Making oneself unavailable or inflating a student's ideas of his skills so as to encourage him to go his own way are a couple ways of protecting a treasured art. Other times, sloppy movements, awkward balancing, and weak offensive blow and defensive blocks by the student will not be corrected, leading to the development to a structurally inefficient repertoire of movements that will not work as intended when meeting a determined opponent. A man seeking to further develop his skills as a garrotero searches for a partner who he likes and trusts to respect and cherish his art. He also searches for a partner or student who shows or proves to have the requisite physical attributes and affective structures to withstand a brutal art. Not all who have access to and the trust of a good teacher achieve high levels of mastery, which demonstrates the highly contingent nature of imitative learning and the individual habitus.

THE INDIVIDUAL HABITUS

The range of variations among garroteros who share a common lineage and are less than fifty years old is most telling in the Siete Lineas system of garrote from El Tocuyo. Although to be fair, the Siete Lineas school shares a number of basic characteristics that I saw among garroteros from other lineages in the southern end of the Tocuyo Valley and the surrounding hill towns. The widespread pool of common movement within this region suggests a pool of traditional movements had a strong impact on the formation of this particular system. Notwithstanding, among the adherents of the Siete Lineas system, one element that stood out was the number of cuadras I was taught as representing the basic footwork defining the system. Altogether I was shown four different cuadras; two small squares, two small triangles, and what I call an "intuitive cuadra" where the development of footwork was felt to develop over time, intuitively by the student (table 5.1, B, D, E, F). The wide variation of footwork patterns evinced by practitioners suggests an open-ended dialectical relation between the stylistic predilections of individuals who have trained in the system in different times with different teachers, the amount of time and quality of teaching each student received, the willingness or ability of the student to incorporate the art, and the corpus of knowledge that makes up the repertoire of the art.[1]

Examining the role of individual variances in mastering a skill, Wacquant distinguished between the "primary habitus," as that which are the dispositions incorporated during one's childhood and youth, and those habits, dispositions, and other attributes an individual deliberately targets and works on, which are treated as a part of a "secondary habitus" (Wacquant 2013, 5). Here I focus on this secondary aspect of an individual's habitus, or those dispositions an individual actively seeks to incorporate through a disciplined regime of practice. Of all those older garroteros who had known León Valera and had met his students, they all acknowledged that his final student José-Felipe Alvarado reflected most accurately León Valera's way of doing garrote. Because of this general held consensus, one could assume everybody would assiduously seek to mimic José-Felipe's movements. Interestingly, even within José-Felipe's small group of students, relatives, and friends there were noticeable differences with those who had trained the Siete Lineas style with him or others over the years. Apart from the political and social relations that governed each person's learning experience, there were also a number of individual differences in the skill level and attitudes toward the art of garrote that shaped each individual's expression of the Siete Lineas. One occasional student, when jugando garrote, forgot everything he had learned, either reverting back to the hill-country style of garrote he had been exposed to as a youth or losing all sense of control, striking out wildly at any available target. A couple of students were content to learn the diluted versions they were taught without trying very hard to steal any of his knowledge and ways of moving. A couple of others had trained with a number of teachers at various times and played garrote with strong influences from other students of León Valera. These diverse levels of abilities and individual attitudes toward mastering garrote in the way it was taught by José-Felipe point to the fragility of the habitus to act as the driver of culture and socialization.

As for me, after a couple months of training I figured out I was being taught a purely performative version of the art, resulting in the inability to engage with garroteros from other styles in friendly matches—in other words, to recreate the moves I had learned with an uncooperative and resisting opponent. Only after training with teachers of other lineages who took the time to break the basics down for me until they became automatic reactions was I able to begin to see, retain, and imitate some aspects of the more antagonistically oriented moves of the Siete Lineas system. Through hard training under committed teachers who taught me how to jugar garrote, and when I began to be able to isolate and identify moves during the flow of a juego, I began to understand Lois Wacquant's observation about boxing—"Only when the eyes begin to recognize moves and combinations is when the apprenticeship process really begins" (Wacquant 2004, 117). Although my skill level improved, I did not automatically become a master of garrote during my stay as the story of a juego between myself and José-Felipe in the introduction recounts. I did begin to develop a greater understanding of the logical structures of the art in general and the Siete Lineas in particular and to be able to apply these moves against uncooperative or resisting opponents, which is the whole idea behind the art as a practically oriented set of skills. Returning to Venezuela in 2013, a number of my teachers took me deeper into their ways of playing garrote, giving me an appreciation of their specific ways of swinging the palo and understanding garrote in general. Nevertheless, there was a great deal of the Siete Lineas lineage that I have seen on occasion and never had the chance to record and have been unable to recreate.

The wide range of individual variations of schools or lineages of garrote in midwestern Venezuela and the varying level of skills evinced by those admitting to knowing the art calls into question the predominance, durability, and homogeneity of the habitus in the transmission of practical knowledge as a phenomena Mauss himself took note of in his article on body-techniques (Mauss 1979, 101). As it was repeatedly recounted to me and as I saw for myself, not all men learned garrote beyond the most basic skills, not all men sought to try their skills in impromptu duels in the past and even more so today. Nonetheless, there are a number of individuals who, in spite of the changes wrought by the latest wave of modernity, see the art of garrote or the practice of combative arts as relevant to their lives and an important cultural body of knowledge to be preserved, refined, and tested in varying types of contexts. The cynical and agonistic attitude toward the world that continues to shape one's training with the palo endures to shape and inform the ideas and practices of those who decide to pick up the palo today.

ENTERING THE DARK SIDE

Over the course of interviewing old garroteros I would always ask, "what is the most important characteristic a garrotero must possess." The second most popular response after pisada and vista was a predilection for the palo. Or as they would put it: "He must like it"; "It must be in the blood." What these responses share is an acknowledgment of the importance of the emotional commitment to endure the boredom and pain of training, and fear of being hit with a stick or cut by a blade, by those who would seek to become a master. The emotional excitement that comes from watching or participating in a good fight continues to be marginalized among scholars as something distasteful or deviant. Alternately, it is ignored or downplayed as a way to avoid giving the impression of a minority or subaltern community possessing an essential "blood-lust" or other aberrations that could be used to justify differential treatments for these members (Chacon et al. 2007). The enjoyment that comes with the physical domination of another or the thrill of a good fight has come to be known as the dark side among some practitioners of the martial arts.[2]

When speaking of the old days or meeting old garroteros, friends or informants would often refer to these men as *Guapos*, or speak of the *time of the guapos*. The term guapo refers to those quick-tempered, highly sensitive, fight-at-the drop-of a-hat men found throughout the folktales, songs, legends, and criminal proceedings throughout the world. Men like Mike Fink, "The King of the Mississippi River" keelboat men, Stagger Lee, the baddest man in St. Louis, The "Bad-Johns" of Trinidad, The Jagunços or Bambas of Brazil, the Bravi of the early-modern Italian city-states, the Loco-Vatos of East Los Angeles, or the Jawaras or Preman of Indonesia. Often times it is these sometimes cruel and violent men, and those who set themselves up against them, that a researcher must turn to to understand how close quarter combative practices were developed, used, refined, and transmitted.

During my time in Venezuela, I met a few older men who had gained a reputation as guapos in their youth. This term was used to identify old street fighters, as well as whose skill level never rose to the level of a "Maestro" by their peers. Often behind their back they were referred to as *guapos* or *zumbadores*. One character trait these men known as guapos all shared was an inordinate sense of pride in their skill combined with a dismissive attitude toward all other's abilities. Even into their eighties, these men still acted as if they were ready at a moment's notice to fight

Figure 6.2. Felipe Vásquez and his teacher training with knives. Courtesy of
Felipe Vásquez.

anyone who would doubt tales of their exploits. Often times they would
tell stories of fierce struggles where against all odds they came out on
top. Other times they would regale listeners about how they would visit a
neighboring village and the local garroteros would all feign sickness or
injury in these men's presence so as not to suffer a public beating. Listening to these stories helps us understand the ludic pleasure or enjoyment
that can arise out of a good brawl or melee. The enjoyment that comes out
of the total immersion in an adrenal-induced stressful event, such as
dropping someone with a well-placed blow or taking a terrible beating
only to come back from the brink of defeat to snatch victory, arises from
the cultivation of what has been called the dark side or the cultivated
callousness toward the suffering of others. Further listening to stories and
tales from these men or about these men reveal the dangers of going too
far to the dark side, where crippling injuries, death, imprisonment, or
alcoholism awaits those who can't turn back.

Up into the 1960s, Carlos Téran enjoyed a good party. When hearing
of a social gathering, he would saddle up his mule and amble over to
where a few friends or neighbors were gathering. Upon arriving and
tying up his mule, he would greet the host, grab a drink, and begin to

mingle. As the afternoon went on and men continued to drink and relax, tales turned to one's past exploits with the garrote. Listening respectively to a man tell of his abilities, Carlos would then politely ask the man if the man and himself might enjoy a "little game with the sticks." If the man tried to beg off, saying he would love nothing better than a good clash of sticks but unfortunately forgot to bring his palo, Carlos would go over to his mule, open up the saddlebags, and pull out two palos. If the man would then say that he was pretty good with the palo but really had an affinity for the machete, Carlos would return to his mule and pull out a couple machetes. Finally, if the man explained that while his skill with the machete was unparalleled, he had a special place in his heart for the knife. Once again Carlos would go to his saddlebags and pull out two razor sharp knives in order to oblige the man.

The excitement and pleasure Carlos took in a "hard game" of stick, machete, or knife fighting was not shared by all and culminated one night when on a deserted country road Carlos was met by six men armed with palos and knives intent on extracting revenge for past grievances. In the ensuing fight, Carlos struck one man across the ribs, rupturing his liver and mortally wounding the man. For this, Carlos spent six months in prison for involuntary manslaughter. During an interview with an older garrotero from the state of Guarico in north-central Venezuela, he lifted up his shirt and displayed a couple of thin pale lines that ran from his back around to his left side. Explaining how he received such a souvenir, he explained as a young man he loved to go to parties and, all too aware of the trouble that might break out where women and alcohol were involved, he would bring along his two-foot-long Vera wood garrote for protection. One night, paying too much attention to a woman from another village that another man thought of as his led to his being attacked by five men with sticks and knives and a woman with a lantern to provide illumination. First breaking the hand of the woman holding the lantern with his garrote and plunging the melee into darkness, he proceeded to deal with the others. Upon finishing one man with a blow to the back of his skull, another attacker took the opportunity to attempt to stab him in the heart from behind with a knife. Fighting his way free of the ambush, he tried to make his way back home but collapsed on the road. With some help from friends who went looking for him when he disappeared from the party, he was loaded on the back of a mule and taken back to their village and a neighboring doctor, and it took 110 stiches to close him up (Victor Ramirez interview with author San José de Guaribe, August 07, 2013).

In today's environment, there is much less public toleration for violent brawls in the streets, or at pulperías or parties, to test one's skills and enhance one's reputation, although there are still a number of garroteros eager to test their skills with worthy opponents. Not too long ago a man from another group of garroteros came to José-Felipe's farm to test his skills. Squaring off against Pasqual in a "friendly" exchange of techniques, the two men set-to with a beautiful, highly technical game of garrote. At one point during the exchange, pressing his attack, the visitor worked his way close to Pasqual and gave him a head butt in the face. Feeling his hospitality was being abused, Pasqual waited a bit and when the visitor swung a hard diagonal forehanded blow to Pasqual's neck, Pasqual ducked under and stepped to the outside of the visitor and then cut loose with a full power backhanded blow to the hipbone of the visitor dropping him to the ground like a bag of potatoes, where all he could utter was the mournful complaint "That hurts, that really hurts a lot!"

A reader might get the impression that Venezuela was a uniformly violent and dangerous place. What is deemphasized in many accounts of combat though are the highly asymmetrical levels of aggression or the will to close the distance and, regardless of the threat to one's own body, inflict even more damage to one's opponent so that he is unable or unwilling to continue to struggle. The attitude of leading one to close with and trade blow for blow is known as *palo por palo*, or stick for stick. It remains a highly valued attitude not only among garroteros, but among the local populace in other social situations as displaying an attitude of fearlessness and resilience. Many times I heard how in the past it was customary for two men with a disagreement to go to the outskirts of town, down by the riverbank, a recently harvested field, behind a house, or other "liminal" place and "have it out like men" without any interference from others trying to enforce a peaceful settlement. The ethos of two men settling things themselves is a common theme I have met with fighters I have come across around the world. In actuality, though, the level of actual physical violence in these types of encounters could vary widely from the bloody and brutal where one sought to inflict serious bodily harm on another. Or moving to the other end of the spectrum, there is the less violent but more emotionally charged verbal displays of rage, challenging, boasting, or some variation of chest pounding until mutual exhaustion overtook both of them. Ostensibly, the reason two men went off to settle things alone was to have it out without anybody stopping or hindering the fight. However, another very real reason not often discussed among fighters was to avoid the bloodlust of onlookers who took enjoyment in seeing a good fight and could often jeer, taunt, or physically push unwilling antagonists into each other in their efforts to witness an exciting brawl. As it relates to the general level of unwillingness of many individuals to risk their physical well-being in a fight, retiring to a secluded spot could allow both men to threaten posture and resolve the situation without recourse to fighting. Then both men could spin the story of what actually occurred in order to preserve their reputation as fearless honorable men (Falk 2004). While up until a few years ago most every man had to carry a garrote in public, not everybody who picked up a garrote became involved in melees and challenge matches with machetes and knives. Not everybody sought to cultivate a reputation as a dangerous man, and not everybody became seduced by the pleasures associated with the dark side. Much in the same way that there were a number of ways of swinging a palo and a highly uneven level in the technical skill of those who picked up a palo, those acts of self-selection or different temperaments of garroteros again highlights the highly uneven nature of the learning and transmission of cultural attitudes associated with the habitus as an overarching determining cause of culture.

I brought up the idea of the dark side earlier to discuss the emotional high that comes with swiftly or expertly dominating a combative encounter. There is an ever-present danger in going down this road that an individual will actively seek out or tend to refrain from backing out of combative encounters to recapture the feeling of immersing oneself totally in a high-risk situation. This can operate in two ways: the first is the way of the *zumbador* or *loco*, the second is the way of the *jugador*. One afternoon after practicing with José-Felipe, a few of us were standing around ready to disperse to our respective lunches when, in a rare exposition, Pasqual laid things out for me. A jugador actively stalks an opponent, looking for an opening. Closing in the jugador will deliver one to three committed blows and then back out to assess the situation, either to see if the opponent drops or if he is grievously injured.[3] Then, if necessary, the jugador will continue to stalk the opponent looking for another opening. A guapo or a loco by contrast is overcome by the emotion of the encounter, whether it be a friendly match or an outright antagonistic combat, and will flail away wildly at the opponent, seeking to hit something out of the sheer number of blows delivered.[4] While the loco is carried away by the emotional event of an encounter, a jugador harnesses his emotions, coldly analyzing the situation, watching in delight and satisfaction as he inflicts pain on the opponent, watching him flinch, bleed, grimace, bend over, keel over, grunt, scream, or whimper in pain. A sense of satisfaction emerges as the jugador notices the opponents' breath changing, becoming more labored as his stamina weakens or as the pain of a blow takes his breath away; he enjoys the sense of confusion, pain, and fear he sees in his opponent's eyes. The call to the dark side can be especially compelling when it comes to the blade.[5] In a bladed fight, the loss of blood from slashes or thrusts to the arms or legs reduces a man's reflexes as his organs begin to shut down, making it easier to inflict major debilitating blows. Finally, capitalizing on a tactical error or after wearing an opponent down, moving in and delivering a coup de grâce, thereby dominating the encounter, brings a deep sense of satisfaction as a craftsman contemplating the completion of a work of art.

Another aspect of the dark side is the need to desensitize themselves to the suffering of others. There is the understanding one must ruthlessly exploit any vulnerabilities perceived in one's opponent in order to eliminate the physical capacity or will of one's antagonist to continue through incapacitating injuries or pain. This desire to inflict pain on another is not just an aberrant or pathological attitude but a key attitude to surviving a combative encounter. The old motto from the battlefield "kill or be killed" reflects the hard-earned wisdom that any holding back of one's power or skills in a combative encounter, based upon the idea that one's own skills are so much more honed than one's opponent that one can adjust one's response to deter an enemy's aggression without unduly causing lasting injury, is pure folly. One possible origin of this misconception could arise from Hollywood movies where a gunfighter instead of killing a man outright would just shoot him in his gun hand, effectively ending the combat. As many have found out the hard way, street combat is short-lived, brutal, and unforgiving. Any type of holding back, any hesitation or mistake can lead to death or permanent crippling injuries, reminding the survivor of his errors.

From a variety of sources, those who have been involved or studied accounts of combat recognize the addictive element that comes about through the domination of another. An attachment to the dark side is felt to be even more powerful when it comes to armed combat, especially the blade, where the stakes are higher and the damage correspondingly more serious. Taking part in the university student dueling societies as a youth in Germany, Elias recognized in communities where honor was the key element in shaping male socialization practices that a certain number of men became quite adept at the communal weapon of choice in "honor contests," or impromptu, or what appeared to be spontaneous, duels. With their skills, they would actively seek out opponents and on the slightest pretext seek to vanquish them in a contest and take an inordinate pleasure in doing so (Elias 1969, 71). Going down this path addicted to the pleasure that comes from hurting others can be a path fraught with danger. Not all can come back from the overall effects of killing. The effect varies among individuals and contexts, but reading through a number of ethnographies where scholars have worked with or interviewed men who have killed often displayed show signs of what we in the United States would call post-traumatic stress disorder (PTSD) with nightmares, alcoholism, and insomnia bedeviling them. Or alternately, a person can become so besotted with killing that he transforms into a serial killer until he himself is killed or jailed. During my time in Venezuela, I heard stories and saw the scars of particularly feared or aggressive jugadores who were ganged up against with intent to kill them to put a halt to their terrorizing a family or a neighborhood or a village.

LEAVING THE DARK SIDE

The attraction to the dark side is regarded with great seriousness among garroteros today, even as the opportunities for men to engage in impromptu duels with sticks or knives has declined. The seriousness that garroteros today see as the power of combative arts to impose one's will on another or despoil them was made clear to me in a number or different contexts. After a few weeks living and training on José-Felipe's farm and after class had wound down, I would demonstrate a few moves from other combative systems in what I thought was a spirit of sharing, but was treated as a sign of disrespect or the threat of a potential challenger. Another time I had an interview with a local university professor in Coro. Gladly, he took some time out from his schedule to talk about the wonderful folk traditions of stick dances found in a number of festivals throughout Venezuela. Asking him about how garrote was used as a method of self-defense in his home village, his friendly demeanor suddenly switched, his eyes once flashing with friendliness narrowed and went cold and flat: "Why do you want to know about that?" he asked suspiciously. After explaining to him the interest many people have in different combative traditions around the world, I began to show him some Filipino and Pondo stick fighting moves I had picked up over the years to show what I had in mind. Changing tracks from defensive suspicion to flattery, he beamed, "Well, you are quite good already at stickfighting, you don't need to learn anything else." "Well," he continued, "this has been fun, but I am late for lunch with my wife. Come by some other time and we can talk some more. Good-bye and enjoy your stay," then he left.

   Training in many traditional armed combative systems teaches one to enter the dark side, to be able to call upon the emotional commitment to hurt and destroy those that threaten an individual, his social network, or his livelihood. Choosing this road can lead an individual down a path of the destruction of many others, eventually leading to one's own annihilation. Among the tribal communities of rural Montenegro where there was a tradition of blood feuds and vendettas and young men were brought up to embody a "warrior's virtue" there was the idea of *Čujisto* or manly virtue, or what was seen as the highest level of moral behavior where the demands of a "heroic warrior" are empowered by a sense of humanity extended to one's enemies (Boehn 1984, 73). As a number of garroteros have understood, the practice of garrote can be used to come back from this journey with a deeper more profound respect for life. There appears to be a number of possible avenues to come back from the dark side. One is through surviving a near-death experience or ageing-out of reckless behavior where one realizes the sanctity of human life. One afternoon, one of Saúl's old friends came to his school to say "hello." Taking a break from training, he began telling me how he was once in better shape and then recited the different arts he had once trained. I asked him why he stopped training, thinking that family commitments had led to this decision. Instead, he picked up his shirt and showed me some puckered up holes in his stomach. Holding his shirt up, he recounted how both Saúl and himself would go out on the weekend during the evening looking to try out the moves that they had been working on in the different combative arts they had practiced. This man did pretty well until he was stabbed repeatedly in the stomach with a screwdriver, resulting in his retirement. Even twenty years later as he showed me, he is still not healed properly, as he squeezed some fluid out of one the scars. Asking Saúl about this later, he admitted that he had took part in a number of armed street fights but had grown out of them over time. In these two examples, we can see how one man came to give up his art and develop a respect for the humanity of others through the serious injuries he himself had received, which plague him to this day. On the other hand, Saúl was able to escape fairly unscathed from these encounters and, through his continued practice of a number of combative arts, hone his skills to a high degree to where he felt he could protect himself or his family from any threat and matured out of the need to test his abilities in unrehearsed contexts. Furthermore, the hard training let him release any pent up emotional tension he had worked up during the day. Finally, he had turned to a deep study of East Asian healing arts and Buddhism for moral and spiritual support and as a way to support his family. Ever the philosopher José-Felipe had devoted lot of thought to the ways of the world and how to live honorably and productively as a man and a human being, as can be seen one night when sitting outside enjoying the nighttime quiet and fresh cool air:

> I need to teach you something, this, yes, before everything, I lay this down as the most important thing, the principal thing is that I am going to teach you, this I, what I have learned, what I know, it is not that you come to me and try on me what you already know, because I understand that a person who knows a martial art, it takes hold of one and you want to take off someone's head. You can take someone's head off, at times, you can take someone's head off, and you may even kill them, you can really get crazy. In an exchange with the sticks you can beat a person; you can beat another man badly, despoiling them. If one knows the attacks and the other does not know how to move, I will give another a light strike only. We are human beings, we have a responsibility that if one beats another in a match and from this he dies, in the long term, from the consequences of this strike that one knew how to do, but it is not right, as a human being, we did not have to do it, and this is my system and because of this until this moment, thanks to God, and this is the first time I have said it for whatever reasons that a person comes to me I tell them: Yes, why not, we can play, but like this, you with yours and I with mine, but first let's go and take it easy . . . Why, so that we don't go and give a blow that is intentional. But if another gives a strike and we make a brawl, we cross sticks, we beat each other, can this be right? It is not right. How is this being a human, this is not just. Today, much less, because I have many years, more knowledge, and furthermore from this I have this method here in

my head that is a sport and I found that if one begins to show a lack of
respect to a friend or to another then we go to him and we tell him to
take off and leave us alone. How are we going to make a demand on
him? We are the defiled ones first, the first of the disorderly ones,
lacking a sense of morality, (unintelligible) . . . are them, the master and
one moves, but that has passed. (José-Felipe Alvarado interview with
author, El Molino, March 15, 2005)

THE WARRIOR'S HABITUS

On a hot August day in 1900, the citizens of the town of Curaigua were
preparing a festival in honor of the patron saint of the town. The day
before a stranger was seen walking into town. Tall and well dressed in
a white liquilique with buttons of gold coins, and black and white
striped sandals on his feet. Tucked underneath his left arm was a
braided handled garrote of brilliant Vera wood. On his head he wore a
black hat of plush velvet. Walking straight ahead looking neither left
nor right eyes straight ahead he walked in to the first pulpería he saw
and asked the man behind the counter for a three fingered shot of
cocuy. Serving the stranger, the owner of the establishment asked him
from where he had come and answered he had come from El Tocuyo to
enjoy the festivities and meet a Gabriel Pastrán who it is said is very
skilled with a garrote. "Do you know of him?" "Yes," replied the pulpero. "Then do me a favor and tell him that at the Plaza Bolivar an
Isaías Garrán waits for him to show him that in El Tocuyo and everywhere else there is not a man that can beat me with a garrote in his
hand." "All right," responded the pulpero and sent his young son off to
deliver the message. Welcoming the young boy with a warm greeting,
Gabriel Pastrán listened to the message, thanked the boy and went
back to helping his wife prepare for tomorrows festival. (Escalona 1929,
43–45)

Thus began a short story by a local author about a particularly memor-
able duel between two men of high skill and renown. The rest of the story
revolves around Gabriel Pastrán waking up early the next morning,
dressing in his best clothes, and retrieving his favorite garrote from his
palm thatched roof of his house. Explaining to his wife he has a small
errand to run, he makes his way over to the pulpería where the message
came from and checks the veracity of the message. He then walks over to
the main square to awaken the challenger from a park bench and takes
him to a nearby pulpería for a glass of Cocuy to wake-up. Gabriel then
leads him to a more secluded area, where the challenger explains his
reason for meeting him and then attacks. After a couple minutes of a
highly technical display of garrote by both men, the challenger drops his
stick and admits the skill and chivalrous attitude of Gabriel, who must
have been greatly provoked to fight. He then asks for his forbearance and
friendship. Gabriel readily gives both, and after a handshake and an

embrace, the challenger turns around back to walk to El Tocuyo and Gabriel goes to meet his wife at church.

A couple of elements relevant to this discussion stand out in this story set among the sugar-cane plantations of the Segovia Highlands. What is most striking in this description of an honor duel among rural illiterate sugar cane workers are the restraint, the gentility, and the civility evinced by both men through their encounter, character traits once claimed to be an identifying characteristic of European elite. The restraint and politeness, which disappears in an instant when the dueling ground has been reached, and the way the aggression dissipates with equal alacrity when one man withdraws from the fight and offers his hand in friendship provide an example of the ideal behavior expected of a man trained in garrote. One who not only possesses a highly technical skill and the emotional commitment to close-in and seek to dominate an opponent, but the ability to turn right around and offer his friendship to a man of equal skill, who like him is a man of honor and who has cultivated a warrior's habitus.

The different ways men have organized systems to hone and perfect their bodies and minds for the stress of combat and then turn around and become a caring and respected member of a community is what I call the warrior's habitus. I find this a useful concept to explore how practitioners of different combative systems over time and through space have wrestled with and tried different solutions to deal with the realities of violence facing young men and the different strategies they have developed, the varied physiological skills, affective structures, and material technology to successfully dominate any combative act while instilling a sense for the sanctity of life.

From an analytical viewpoint, the warrior's habitus has three interrelated components that can be examined separated. First is the diverse number of technical skills or physiological attributes in conjunction with a material technology needed or allowed by the context of the encounter to dominate an opponent. Second are the diverse ways the proper affective intent needed to close-in and engage the opponent with the will to end the action quickly and efficiently is cultivated and manifested. Third are the varied ways that one is brought back from the dark side and reintegrated back into a community. The ways these elements are transmitted can vary widely across communities and through their history. Additionally, the success of the individual to incorporate these elements equally into their habitus can vary across the lifetime of an individual. One advantage to using these guideposts to investigate combative systems is that it becomes possible to examine cross-culturally the diverse way the physiological attributes, affectual structures, and culturally shaped moral guidelines that continue to be transmitted, wrestled with, negotiated, or resisted by those who must rely on their ability to cultivate a warrior's habitus to get through everyday life.

Far from being chaotic or acultural acts of deranged or enraged individuals, combat is a culturally organized meaningful act. The number of ways a combative act takes shape within a particular context and according to generally held understandings reveals that not only does combat have a practically oriented goal to dominate an opponent, but whose movements, material technology, and ways the act begins, progresses, and ends are suffused with meanings structured by competing sets of historical dispositions, norms, and mores. At the same time combat can also have a ludic or transgressive element, which delights in rule-breaking, that has no teleological end-point and is just done out of the pure pleasure of losing oneself in the act. Of course what one person calls "playing" might mean something much more serious and insidious to another. There is the danger in any recreational, friendly, or security-oriented combative act that individuals can get carried away in a sense of ecstais at the prospect of a fight, in the midst of a fight, or with the idea of going in and ending the clash with a well-placed blow, strike, or thrust to end the struggle as quick as possible. The ludic aspect of combat can upset all preconceptions of combat turning it into something more sinister or merely remaining as "hard-play" or "the use of necessary force." The sense of blurred genres inherent in any combative act imbues it with an ambiguity and ambivalence that can heighten the air of one's expectations, making it even more exciting and risky. Simultaneously, it can upset any strict classificatory organizational concepts. The adrenal-induced emotional commitment needed to close in quickly and take control of a combative encounter in order to end it can also be followed by an equally extreme let-down, or sense of guilt, leading individuals to have difficulties reintegrating back into a community as productive members. The differing strategies and tactics that developed across Venezuela over the last couple centuries to prepare young men for combat and its aftermath, as well as the uneven levels of mastery of the different components of combat, suggest the inability of the habitus to serve as a determining cause of culture and agency. As other scholars have suggested, the habitus is best seen as a complement of different physiological attributes, emotional structures, and cultural competencies operating at differing levels and at differing rates of success within individuals. The role of the habitus, influencing the ability of individuals to incorporate communal aspects movements, affects, and mores, in turn shapes the way communal norms are expressed. Out of this dialectical play of the individual and the world, individuals come to engage in practically oriented projects.

NOTES

1. By contrast, in the Palo Sangriento I learned two minor variations of how to position the body in relation to the opponent while working within the same cuadra. I hope other practitioners of the Palo Sangriento will come forward in the future, allowing us a deeper understanding of this garrote lineage.

2. In thinking about this aspect of martial arts, I was influenced by Marc Denny's blog post, "He Had His Art" (CDBInc), http://dogbrothers.com/phpBB2/index.php?topic=1971.0. (accessed 04/10/2016), and the writings of the students of Sonny Umpad in the 2012 book *Sonny Umpad's Escrima: The Life and Teachings of a Filipino Martial Arts Master*, George Yore (ed.). Berkeley: Blue Snake Books.

3. When mortally injured, it has been observed, an opponent will often flail away out of pain and fear for 10–20 seconds before dropping to the ground.

4. In the old Irish warrior epics some men underwent a battle fury or "warp-spasm" so severe while waiting to engage they fell on the ground in a type of epileptic fit and died. Before some of his major battles, even Julius Caesar, it was recorded, had been stricken by fits.

5. See the discussion with Benjamin Rittner on how the blade can call out the dark side of one's self in the DBMMA Podcast 2016-06-08 podcast with Benjamin Rittner, Mark Houston "Mark O'Dell," and Ryan Gruhn. Recorded at Central PA Mixed Martial Arts. State College, PA. June 18, 2016.

SEVEN

The Creation of a National Patrimony

Since the first conquistadores stepped onto the land to be known as Vene-zuela, indigenous communities and other non-elitist groups have contin-ued to struggle to retain and renegotiate threats to their autonomy. As part of this struggle, garrote as a foreign prestige item was co-opted as one tool or tactic allowing lower status Venezuelans to maintain or re-negotiate their autonomy and agency within a dominant and asymmetri-cal political-economic structure. With the rise and consolidation of a modern centralized state power able to legitimize their use of power, there has the concomitant decreasing toleration for self-help strategies of violence and other types of violent activities. By the early 2000s, the in-creased interest in garrote as a uniquely Venezuelan combative art al-lowed some local practitioners to reconfigure the use and display of gar-rote to negotiate new forms of relationships with the state. In this account of an exhibition showcasing the cultural heritage of garrote, the way that some garroteros draw on their existing cultural capital as garroteros to forge new relationships to the state is described and explored. At the same time as one group seeks to link their art to the nation in order to promote their art as a unique cultural heritage of the Venezuelan people, they deceive and mislead the organizers and participants by passing on an invented "public" garrote to protect their art and their status from outsiders reinforcing the gulf between the pueblo and the state.

The role of new forms of media allowing elite individuals to imagine nation-states into existence highlighted an important aspect of the emer-gence of these entities in the nineteenth century (Anderson 1991).[1] No less important to the nascent state's development was its harnessing of and dependence on a cadre of men willing to physically close in on, engage with, and eliminate its opponents. Traditionally, these were men whose principal loyalties were not to the idea of a community of like-

117

minded thinkers but to what were perceived by the wider society as localized, feared, disreputable, or otherwise marginal castes, occupation guilds, or families (Amos 1997; Boretz 2011; Douglas 2002). Official histories have often honored these men as defenders of the nation and paragons of its strengths, virtues, and values. Ironically, however, these same groups or their spiritual heirs often regularly threaten the nation as they seek to restore or redefine what they perceive as the proper relationship between the state and the citizen. Recent history, for example, reveals how the discipline and motivation of the Kronstadt sailors of St. Petersburg and the Wahhabi sect of Arabia proved to be key elements in ensuring the existence of the early USSR and Saudi Arabia, respectively, only to be directed later toward challenging the state apparatus (Algar 2002; Getzler 2002). Likewise, once-stalwart supporters of the Algerian revolutionary movement (FLN), the Berber communities of the Kabyle (made famous through the works of sociologist Pierre Bourdieu) had, by the 1980s, begun to openly resist the Arabization policies of the Algerian government (Colonna 2009). Even today, the spiritual heirs of Emiliano Zapata continue to fight against the corruption and violence of the Mexican revolutionary government that Zapata and his followers helped to create (Brunk 2008). The innumerable skirmishes, actions, and battles of motivated, trained fighters, alternately protecting and threatening the state, highlight the uneasy relationship that exists between the institution of the nation-state and local communities. Paralleling this phenomenon, some among these local groups of fighters also sought to modernize, rationalize, clean up, or make respectable the ways they had learned to punch, kick, grapple, fence with, cudgel, and stab others. Oftentimes, they promoted local combative practices as conferring the ability to counter the debilitating effects of modernity, colonialism, or globalization while creating healthy, loyal citizens fit for combat (Abe 2000; Assunção 2005; Gainty 2007; Morris 2004).

Nevertheless, as subsequent events have shown, advancing local combative specialists or other marginal individuals as ideal citizens of a modern nation-state often elides the restricted or local nature of these men and their practices. All too often, such individuals perceive alternative or more local forms of identity to be more relevant to their everyday lives than more inclusive or abstract ways of belonging. A type of commitment to local ways of belonging often results in the disruption, subversion, or embarrassment of the state and its representatives, a phenomenon anthropologist Michael Herzfeld and other scholars have referred to as "cultural intimacy" (2005). The persistence of transgressive or subversive behaviors among practitioners of traditional fighting arts, in particular, has manifested itself in a particular unique way in the Tocuyo Valley. Here the articulation of global and local forms of subject formation and belonging are being contested, subverted, and redefined in the popularization and transmission of a set of local combative practices as a "traditional" martial art of the Venezuelan people. The preservation and transmission of the expressions of popular culture has been an important aspect of the Bolívarian Revolution of Hugo Chávez (Instituto del Patrimonio Cultural 2010). The late president's efforts to support these popular practices can be seen as part of a larger process to empower the popular classes, a sector of the Venezuelan population that has regularly been excluded from the economic benefits and political processes of the nation (Dineen 2001). Supporting Chávez's attempts to create a more inclusive Venezuelan nation is a group of combative experts who champion their local form of stick fighting as a traditional martial art of the Venezuelan people. This group claims that the history, rituals, and combat efficacy of Venezuelan stick fighting are as rich and deep as those of any East Asian martial art. Moreover, stick fighting, group members declare, can be practiced by all citizens for self-defense, to increase one's health, or as a pastime. What makes this group's activities unique in the emerging global popularization of combative practices is the way members have organized and promoted their art. To meet the needs of a modernizing public, combative practitioners in other parts of the world have modified their art to make it safe or fun to practice, or, alternatively, they have retired from public view to teach the art as it was originally intended.

One group of Venezuelan stick fighters has created a third alternative: inventing histories, rituals, and techniques with no combative value to gain state and transnational patronage for its art as a collective manifestation of the Venezuelan people. Drawing on local strategies of deception and feelings of localism associated with the art, one group takes advantage of the lack of familiarity with armed combat among many people today to promote a simulated version of fighting with the stick, machete, and knife. Through these tactical moves vis-à-vis the state and the public, the group is able to tap into the patronage of state and transnational networks interested in the popularization of vernacular traditions while preserving its local culture against what many group members feel are the corrupt and exploitative intentions of outsiders. In addition to making some money and gaining a little national and international recognition, these men earn a grudging respect among many of their peers for their ability to manipulate and exploit both the state's and foreigners' naiveté and curiosity while maintaining the integrity of their art.

Focusing on the cultural politics of nationalism and tradition among a group of stick fighters points both to the persistence and the growing popularity of local combative arts and their intimate association with nation-building projects. Moreover, it casts light on the excesses of the rough, pragmatic, or rustic aspects of combative practices and other forms of popular culture that are often left out of or marginalized in officially sanctioned popular practices, including those associated with sites at which elites seek to represent themselves to both local and global audiences as civilized, modern, or in possession of historically authentic traditions.

NATIONALISM AND COMBAT ARTS

The manner in which combat practices or combative pastimes articulate with processes of nation building indexes the importance that many different institutions attach to cultivating specific physical and effectual attributes that root individuals to specific political and social worlds (Abe 2003; Brownell 1997; Morris 2004). Far from being a wild, uncontrolled act of acultural behavior, combat has always possessed a set of generally understood rules, although they have varied through time and space, showing how culturally transmitted ideas of right and proper behavior shape the way muscles, reflexes, and overall bodily comportments are trained and molded to respond in morally and practically recognizable ways. To put this in a broader context, with the rise of the modern state as understood by Norbert Elias, certain areas have, over the years, experienced a civilizing process, with an ever-widening set of public emotional displays or physical acts increasingly segregated from public space as communities developed sets of progressively interdependent ties. Such a process of state formation has contributed to the decline of stick fighting in Venezuela, Curaçao, Trinidad, Brazil, and Ireland, as well as foot fighting in Brazil and East Timor or fist fighting traditions among the Ga, Quechua, and Aymara-speaking communities.[2] Paying particular attention to struggles over the training and representation of the body can shed light on how contemporary or global cultural values and practices associated with modernity and nationalism are co-opted, reconfigured, and subverted while being made familiar through the matrix of a local community's practices and values (Armbrust 2004; Collins 2004; Ozyürek 2004). Central to my understanding of the relationship between acts of cultural intimacy and nationalism is the role of the habitus in association with a material technology in shaping how an individual moves through, judges, and is rooted to a community.

FUNDACÍON ESCUELA DE GARROTE TOCUYANO

The Fundacíon Escuela de Garrote Tocuyano (School of Tocuyano Stick Fighting Foundation) is a small group of one full-time and four to five part-time members, who are predominantly involved, in varying degrees, in promoting and coaching Chinese wushu, the communist-approved, nonviolent, sporting version of the Chinese martial arts. The group was founded in 1993 by a self-ranked former wushu instructor who, in promoting the art of garrote, sought to "cultivate a spirit of introducing one's culture within the academic curriculum, to recuperate our indigenous sports as a way to instill proper behavior . . . to cultivate virtues such as justice, obedience, responsibility, honesty, friendship, cooperation, courage as a firm base to contribute to the community" (González 2003, 27–28). The school at the time this research was conducted was the only organization dedicated to investigating and promoting the existence of combative arts as they developed in Venezuela after the semiretirement of master garrotero Eduardo Sanoja. This group has given demonstrations, both nationally and internationally, and its members act as guides to foreign or local scholars during short-term stays. Every couple of months, the group travels around the local area to give a series of short workshops and lectures on Venezuelan cultural practices for schools and folkloric groups. Most seminars are devoted to teaching how to weave the handle that once adorned the walking stick. Once a year, the state office of the culture ministry pays the leader a lump sum for the group's efforts, which he distributes as he sees fit among its members. In addition to educational seminars and workshops as a means of preserving its local heritage, the group has identified and interviewed many local stick fighters who still live around the Tocuyo Valley and neighboring hill country. In accordance with the mission of the foundation to promote garrote as a Venezuelan martial art and to disseminate it as it developed from the Tocuyo Valley, it has produced three booklets and an instructional book, all published by the former Ministry of Culture (CONAC), and now known as Con Cultura. The group has also been successful in having the two fighting sticks belonging to the late garrotero León Valera categorized as national treasures of the Venezuelan people (IPIC 2010).

One of the booklets produced by this group, recounting the history of garrote, provides a very disconnected narrative that draws uncritically from sources all around Venezuela to promote the idea that garrote originated in the Tocuyo Valley as a result of the admixture of indigenous groups, maroon colonies, and European immigrants. The second half of the booklet is dedicated to laying out the levels of learning that a student advances through as he masters the Siete Lineas style of garrote. The instructional book on garrote shows the would-be garrotero some basic moves in mastering the art. Drawing on European physical education drills, it encourages students to swing their arms, to rotate their necks, and to breathe through the nose and out through the mouth as they warm up their bodies. From this point, readers are taught how to salute, step, and move, as well as some basic attacks and defenses. At the end of the book, an appendix lays out the different types of moves that are taught according to one's rank in the art. I found the inclusion of Western physical education drills interesting, as such exercise has its roots in nineteenth-century nationalist movements that sought to embody a spirit of patriotism in young men and prepare them for wars of liberation (Pfister 2003). A disingenuous aspect of this training is the teaching of numerous stepping patterns. In a previous chapter, I described how one principal characteristic that distinguishes the different garrote lineages in an area is footwork, how one holds and moves the body to maintain the proper distancing necessary to attack or defend oneself. Of the basic footwork patterns described in the book, I was taught one that I never saw any other garrotero use and whose purpose I still do not understand. A second pattern was taken from the Riña con Palo lineage of garrote that originates from outside the Tocuyo Valley in the town of La Piedad. A third stepping pattern comes from the Palo Sangriento lineage, from the city of Barquisimeto, again, outside the Tocuyo Valley. A fourth stepping pattern of Tocuyano footwork strongly resembles garrote from the Andes, where the leader of the Fundacíon Escuela de Garrote Tocuyano was raised and I later studied. Training with Maestro José-Felipe, I learned a fifth basic pattern of Tocuyano footwork that everybody in the group had me practice. When I asked members of the group about these different patterns, I was told that the ordering and organizing of moves was a way of making the people at Con Cultura happy and allowing the Tocuyano group to teach seminars. I was also told not to worry too much about the book material but to follow the training I was receiving from Maestro José-Felipe. Overall, what made this group's curriculum unique is not the inventing of histories, rituals, ethics, or a pedagogical progression of moves but that no one I interviewed from the Siete Lineas system was ever taught in the way shown in the books. Nor did anyone that I met who practiced the Siete Lineas system ever teach according to the book, outside of the short-term instruction of foreigners or young people in public workshops. The result was, as I had written earlier, the confusion why the teachings of both myself and the few other students with José-Felipe looked completely different than how I saw other practitioners of the Siete Lineas lineage move, as well as a complete inability to engage in a stick fencing matches with individuals from other schools of garrote.

COMMEMORATING THE MARTIAL ART OF GARROTE DE LARA

One event that showcased the local fighting practices of the Venezuelan pueblos and their transformation into a martial art accessible to all took place during the 460th anniversary of the founding of El Tocuyo. With the support of the local office of Con Cultura and the beverage company Polar, the Fundacíon Escuela de Garrote Tocuyano presented a commemorative event–workshop. This event was a rare occasion when Garrote de Lara was taught in a public setting. Having left the area two months before it took place, I relied on still photos, videotape, and web interviews with members of the group and other garroteros who witnessed it for information. It occurred on a Saturday afternoon near the main plaza of downtown El Tocuyo at the old Franciscan nunnery that serves as the office and workshop rooms of Con Cultura. Gathering in the inner courtyard, local officials from Con Cultura made introductory speeches, reminding everybody of the importance of honoring and transmitting all aspects of the local culture developed by the people of the Tocuyo Valley. As part of this project, the head of the local Con Cultura office handed out medallions to a select older generation of garroteros from the Tocuyo Valley and the surrounding hill towns of Sanare, Guarico, and Los Humacaros. The recipients included the local centenarian, ex-guerrillero, herbalist, and non-garrotero Bérnebeis Quíntero. These older men form a pool of men that the leader of the stick-fighting group calls on when needed for special occasions.

From this point, the event moved outside to a space facing the street that is often used as a performing area during celebrations. Garrote demonstrations were performed by many of the men who had just been honored, thus providing an opportunity for observers to see the unique variations of attack, defense, and counter that distinguish lineages from each other. Afterward, rows of schoolchildren, both boys and girls aged eight to sixteen, were lined up in a grid formation fifteen wide, seven deep, and one arm's length apart. The grade level of these children was easily distinguishable owing to the school uniforms that they all wore to commemorate this special occasion. Three instructors associated with the school of Tocuyano stick fighting passed out *varas,* or thin wooden training sticks, to all the children. They were then ordered to come to attention and taught how to salute. The students followed the examples of the teachers, who alternately stood in front of them demonstrating the proper form and walked along the rows correcting them. After learning how to salute, the students were taught a series of basic solo and two-person routines aimed at showing the public and instilling in the students the unique martial heritage of the Tocuyo Valley. Ostensibly honoring the Tocuyo Valley, many of these routines originated outside the valley. After about one hour spent teaching and practicing moves, the event came to a close. Restricting the focus of this event to the drilling and training of the student body in a public performance space calls attention to the way garrote is being promoted as a martial art today. Where once individuals or small groups were taught to fight in out-of-the-way sites by a relative or close friend, garrote is now taught in public spaces by paid coaches as a local form of self-defense. The effects of this shift in the ethos and cultivation of attributes accompanying these practices can be seen in movements as basic as how a garrotero approaches an opponent, in this case, the salute. In this public event, students are placed in grid formation and taught to move in a situation that highlights the open, agonistic nature of a martial art. This sportive setting is a site in which two individuals fairly and openly pit their physical skills against one another for the greater glory of the Venezuelan nation. Beginning in a type of ready position, students stood at attention with their feet on a horizontal line, giving them no firm base to repel a strong frontal rush. In addition, when standing at attention, the students expose their entire body to their opponent. One arm is left to dangle uselessly at the side while the other holds the stick raised parallel to the ground, elbow locked out at shoulder height. This was the first move taught to me in El Tocuyo, and I was told disingenuously the move demonstrated to your opponent that you would engage in a clean fight and that your palo did not have a blade or spike hidden in the butt end.³ From this point, the students were taught to step forward and lower their palo in an en garde stance, crossing it with the palo of their partner. I recognized this move from old swashbuckling and martial-art movies, when two fighters cross their arms or weapons before a duel as a signal of readiness. From a combat perspective, this move makes no sense, as each individual then has to withdraw and chamber his stick to attack, thereby telegraphing his intentions clearly. Overall, however, these opening gestures reinforce the nature of the upcoming encounter as a fair match between two equal and willing individuals. From a number of garroteros where I learned how to begin a traditional juego de garrote, I began to understand the ambivalence inherent in the meeting of two armed men. Alternately circling clockwise and counterclockwise, I learned to present myself in profile to my opponent, minimizing exposure of vulnerable points. I held my palo in my rear hand and twirled it, enabling a much more powerful attack at the same time partially concealing the palo from the view of the opponent, who is kept guessing how the attack will come. Slowly circling the other man, they size each other up, mentally and physiologically preparing themselves for the clash of sticks and trying to outflank each other so as to get a clean hit while avoiding one in return. The act of circling, moreover, allows each man to take in a 360-degree view of the surrounding environment, scouting for malevolent intentions in his opponent's friends or relatives that might precede their ganging up on him. As the two men slowly tighten the space between them, one man will usually sense an opening in his opponent's attitude or posture and launch an attack during which the sticks will clash in bouts ranging from five to twenty-five seconds before the men separate or one of them drops to the ground unable to continue. Depending on the context of the encounter, a participant may pull out a knife to get in a quick stab to the stomach or the kidneys or he might grab the other's stick to keep him from striking with it or using it to block an attack. Other options include spitting in another man's eye to distract him from a powerful attack or as a way to keep him occupied as a friend prepares to hit him from behind. From the practical and useful strategies enabling fighters to emerge successfully from the chaos of combat, habitual ways of holding and moving the body have been retained by many garroteros today, highlighting the more tolerable acts of an older violence that have shaped the current practice and distribution of garrote. The manner in which two men approach a contest also highlights the contingent nature of using the body in association with material technology, how, depending on the circumstances, little-used physiological attributes become available to individuals willing to put in the necessary effort to cultivate them to a high degree. The wealth of information accessible to a fighter able to perceive and evaluate the most minute gestures and comportment of an opponent can be seen in a Japanese anecdote from the Meiji era, in which sword master Yamoka Tesshu interviewed a renowned Tokyo street fighter who had recently been released from prison after having remained undefeated in over thirty sword fights. Asked how he won so many fights, he was said to have replied that he maneuvered close enough to touch his sword against the opponent. "If the [opponent's] sword was held stiffly, he knew he could cut him down with one blow. However, if the man's grip on his sword was flexible and firm flowing with *ch'i,* he took no chances; he just threw his sword at him and ran away" (Stevens 1984).

Among the students in the commemoration ceremony, the coaches stressed the ability to stand and move in synchronous fashion while repeating a number of prearranged sequences of waving and clashing sticks at and against each other in a martial fashion. What was important for these coaches was to give the students a heightened sense of confidence in their skill by teaching moves that resemble how garrote is actually instantiated. Even more important in this public event, however, was the popularizing of the local combative art as a way to instill a sense of collective belonging to a nation through the synchronous repetition of movements (Browenll 1995; McDonald 2007; Pfister 2003). Synchronized drills, as a disciplinary technique, have been identified as "the most powerful way to create and sustain a community that we have at our command" (McNeill 1995). In a similar fashion, those students in the semiprivate setting who do not possess a familial or close relationship with José-Felipe or his senior student, and who are aware that much of the art is being withheld from them, are able to learn some basic moves and engage in controlled free-fighting matches with the maestro and his visitors who come to socialize and have a friendly match. Through attendance in the informal classes and the socializing that occurs during visits, as well as through taking part in seminars and workshops, these men develop a heightened sense of belonging to a place and of being part of a living tradition. Through this feeling, they come to see themselves as part of a local tradition of fighters, just as their grandfathers or granduncles once were. During a public event, one group of garroteros ostensibly honors the old traditions of garrote and promotes the benefits of the art to the public. At the same time, they promote garrote as an authentic martial art able to improve one's self-defense abilities and health. At these events, they also publicly display their cunning and ability to manipulate the state and the unaware public to impress fellow garroteros. They behave much like the cell-phone users in Italy who conduct private business in a voice loud enough for others to overhear them; cell phones and fire-hardened walking sticks are not merely instruments to preserve an individual's privacy or honor but, as material technology, are used to increase an individual's cultural capital while maintaining a claim of privacy or honor in a public setting (Herzfeld 2009, 156). In this way, this group's proclivity to mislead and deceive students and the state draws on stigmatized local ways of moving through and judging the world to resituate themselves to take advantage of a renewed global popularity of combative arts and their historical links with nationalist projects. In this way, group members are able to link their project of promoting their version of garrote to the nationalistic projects of a state that portrays itself as a champion of the people and as a modern civilized nation at the same time; they subvert and resist what they see as just one more attempt by outsiders to exploit the resources or destroy autonomy of the pueblo.

Driven into exile by the same group of diverse men that he wielded into a fighting force to create a Gran Colombia, Simón Bolívar was reported to have said of his work to create a unified independent Latin America, "I have plowed the sea" (Chavez 2009). This lament by the liberator of much of Spanish-speaking South America points to a regularly occurring tendency in the life of nation-states: Dependence on or valorization of local marginal groups to maintain the integrity of the state often leads to group members, their descendants, or their spiritual heirs resisting or subverting the increased centralizing or disciplinary policies of state institutions. Examining how the corporeal body of the citizen can act as the site of these processes, I have looked at the combative practices of a civilian population and the way these practices have been deployed to understand, make familiar, and reconfigure the cultural domination of North Atlantic ideologies, practices, and policies. In the process of creating a modern Venezuelan state, which began in the mid-nineteenth century, elites set themselves against older forms of sociality based on patron-client relations, a racially based caste system, and the role of honor. These were elements that succeeding governments both drew on and were, in turn, threatened by in their attempts to create a modern state.

By the early twentieth century, the countryside had been largely pacified through the co-optation or neutralization of local strongmen and the final destruction of free rural farmers. A few years later, a domesticated folkloric version of the stick and machete fighting arts under the rubric of the religious ritual dance known as the Tamunangue gained a national following as part of an attempt to instill a feeling of national solidarity. By the 1980s, a global revitalization of martial arts, spurred by the popularity of martial-arts movies, led to the resurgence of many local combative styles. These arts were often linked to nationalist aspirations by ethnic minorities or postcolonial populations who sought to legitimize their presence on the national stage by reference to the existence of an indigenous martial art. Similar attempts occurring in the Tocuyo Valley are felt by many garroteros to be the latest in a long line of attempts by elites to steal and exploit the lands, labor, and knowledge of the pueblos or local communities. In the Tocuyo Valley, one group of garroteros draws on a once popular and largely stigmatized or unknown local knowledge and its associated identities to take advantage of a renewed global interest in local combat arts and President Chávez's interest in promoting the once-denigrated popular culture of the pueblos as a basis to solidify his Bolivarian revolution. Resituating their traditional mode of practicing and transmitting garrote from the semi-obscured, recently harvested fields at dawn to the Saturday afternoon public stage, schoolyards, and police training academies, one group promotes a combatively worthless yet visually exciting repertoire of moves and rituals to accrue both financial gain and public acclaim. Nonetheless, at the same time, its members maintain the integrity of the art among themselves and a select few others. Simultaneously, as this group claims to reconfigure an aggressive, honor-bound type of masculine practice to meet the needs of the state, it subverts and resists the cultural and political attempts of the state and global forces to turn this local practice into another forum for cultivating a docile and loyal citizen-body. Through these tactical moves, which are exercised through the body and the inculcation of bodily habits, these men gain the grudging respect of other garroteros as fierce and cunning men while also reinforcing their marginal status as insubordinate and rebellious men and demonstrating to their peers the value of the old Venezuelan aphorism that good is always repaid by evil.

NOTES

1. A partial list of popularizers of native combative systems includes adherents Kano Jigoro in Japan; Agenor "Sinozinho" Sampaio, Annibal Burlamaqui, and Manoel dos Reis Machado in Brazil; and V. Narayanan Nair and Kottakal Karnaran Gurukkalin in Kerala, India. Institutions include the Ikatan Pencak Silat (IPSI) in Indonesia, the Ching Wu Athletic Association in Nationalist China and Southeast Asia, and the Dainippon Butokukai in Japan.

2. For Venezuela, see Assunção (1999) and Ryan (2015). For Trinidad, Cowley (1996), and Ireland, Conley (1999) and Hurely (2007). Foot fighting traditions have been looked at in Brazil and East Timor. See Assunção (2005) and Hicks (2006). Fist fighting traditions have been noted among the Ga, (Akyeampong 2002), the Quechua, (Chacon et al. 2007; Wibbelsman 2009), and Aymara-speaking communities (Zorn 2002).

3. Looking over footage of an impromptu bout between friends at a Tamunangue festival in the hill country, I saw that one man had presented his palo to his friend and opponent in such a way as a challenge him, provoking him to respond. In future trips, I will go back and ask about this gesture and the traditions and meanings behind it. But outside this episode, I have never seen any other garrotero make this move or mention this move until I met up with this group from El Tocuyo.

EIGHT

Concluding Thoughts

One afternoon, a neighbor ran up to José's-Felipe's little plot of land to warn him a group of young men were roughing up his grandson. At this time in his seventies and his joints wreaked with arthritis, he nevertheless reached for his hat and garrote and hobbled off best as he could out of his house, out of the front gate, and down the dirt road where he had heard the beating was occurring. Arriving at the scene and seeing what was going on, José-Felipe did not hesitate but rushed right into the middle of the maelstrom, swinging his garrote right and left at the inside of the knees of the bullies, knocking down five young men one after the other, all at least fifty years younger than him. Having laid them out where they writhed in pain in the dust, he helped his grandson up and brought him back home without a word to anybody. Just another story told about the old man that added to his reputation as a fearsome garrotero, such as they had back in the old days, and that it was best for him to be treated with respect.

The main question driving this research project was why people continue to train and fight with sticks, machetes, and knives in rural Venezuela. Similar to attitudes among upper and middle-class people I have come across elsewhere in the world, violence among Venezuelans is perceived to be an atavistic or pathological condition or as a blend of a personal defect of the individual and a societal failing. Among a number of working-class people in these same countries, violence is likewise often condemned, but more honestly, often recognized and treated as a pragmatic exertion of physical force to attain one's goals or to dominate another person, or sometimes as a pleasant recreational activity—and sometimes as a combination of all three. In other words, one reason garrote has persisted in Venezuela is, as the story beginning this chapter shows, that it is still seen to be an extremely practical form of-self-defense originating out of the Venezuelan pueblos.

After training me for a while, Saúl would accompany me on my trips around the area to locate and interview other garroteros. Every time, Saúl would strike up a conversation with the cab driver we hired and tell him about me and what I was doing in Venezuela. Almost always, the driver would respond he had a grandfather or great-uncle who had a reputation among the family as a hard-drinking, crazy, or feared garrotero and had since died without passing on his art to anybody. After a few months of traveling with me and helping me interview people, Saúl estimated that in Barquisimeto with a population of approximately 500,000 people, there must be about fifty active garroteros, or a ratio of 1/10,000 people. In contrast to Barquisimeto a day's ride by bus and taxi north into the mountains of Falcón where I only spent a few days and interviewed one garrotero and heard about one other, the number of active garroteros there seemed even less. Then moving east into Guárico and Miranda states for one week, I received a mixed impression of not only an overall decline of active garroteros but also a reconfiguring of the art among a number of still active practitioners. One afternoon, speaking with an elder garrotero in Guárico, I asked him and his middle-aged son when men quit carrying their palos in public. Discussing the answer with each other, a contractor who was part of a group reworking another part of the house walked through their kitchen where we were talking and laughingly interjected, "We all still carry palos—now we just carry them in our car trunks now, ha ha ha!" leading the father and son to laugh and nod their head knowingly, "That's right! He right!" the son told me. "That's what they do now." This exchange, as well as other fragments of information I have been collecting for months, led me to see the accuracy of one individuals summing up of the state of garrote in his youth that seems to characterize the status of garrote today in Venezuela. Growing up, he explained, in every neighborhood there was an individual or a family that people would only talk about in whispers, that everybody knew had a reputation as a garrotero, and that one should not needlessly antagonize them. While it may have disappeared or is close to disappearing in many areas of Venezuela, in a number of rural areas there are still strong pockets where garrote as an art of self-defense has declined but persists through the efforts of a dedicated minority of people, kept from the gaze of the curious, the idlers, and potential enemies of the pueblo. In previous chapters, I showed how the saber, machete, and the garrote have long been an intimate part of everyday life in Venezuela. It is fair to say by the early nineteenth century, after the wars of independence, a wide spectrum of the male Venezuelan population had some knowledge of fencing with single-edge bladed or percussive weapons, deriving from a range of civilian and battlefield disciplines and sometimes a mixture of both. This period also saw the first written accounts of local Venezuelan stick-fighting styles whose immediate roots lay in a civilizing process occurring in Western Europe around the same period. One result of this civilizing process was the substitution of the public display and use of bladed weapons with less lethal hardwood walking sticks and sword canes. Bringing to their new homes their own traditions of combat, waves of immigrants and slaves continuously influenced the way men fought with sabers, machetes, knives, and walking sticks. Supporting this idea of garrote as a continuously changing, practically oriented form of armed combat is the biographies of two men from the Segovia Highlands, the nineteenth-century politician José Espiritusanto Gil and the turn of the century merchant León Valera. The two men, it was said, trained in some combination of Spanish military saber, English thrusting swords, Canary Island and local Venezuelan stick-fighting systems to increase their skills. Closer to the present, two garroteros from mid-century Barquisimeto, the policeman Ishmael Colmenares and the laborer Baudillio Ortiz, in addition to learning local styles of stick fighting, also took advantage of any opportunity to broaden their skills. For example, while both men claimed to have studied European fencing manuals, Baudillio Ortiz claimed to have learned some stick and machete tactics from afrodescendente laborers when working in the port towns of Puerto Cabello and Tucare in the 1930s. I should add at the time Ishmael Colmenares was a policeman in Barquisimeto, policemen were issued machetes to enforce the law, increasing one's motivation to gain any advantages when closing with one or more lawbreakers. In addition to the archival evidence or the seemingly minor differences in the length or the gripping of the stick, there is a wealth of evidence pointing to a mix of a wide range of influences mediated by individual preferences. Then, in addition, if one takes into consideration the number of stick and machete fighting styles in nearby Colombia, it only reinforces my belief of the heterogeneous, fragmented, and localistic nature of garrote. Garrote is an example of a living traditional art composed of a blend of traditional yet ever-changing local methods of self-defense that are still seen as extremely efficient, effective, and morally right where the use of guns are difficult to acquire or shunned as unmanly, uncivilized, or evidence of an unsound mind.

The idea that a number of local people still feel the proper way to meet an intracommunal threat is through a less violent and more honorable means than recourse to a firearm is one reason I feel that contributes the persistence of garrote in Venezuela. The iconic aspect of the garrote and its connection to an older generation of men, who fought with honor during a perceived rougher yet simpler time, also exerts a great emotional pull toward the past by those who feel an attachment to the art of garrote when facing the uncertainty of the present or new challenges of the present. There is the idea that as recent as a generation or two ago, their fathers, grandfathers, or granduncles, with little in the world besides a "pair of balls" and a hardwood stick, were able to not only survive but thrive with honor. The powerful pull of garrote as symbolizing an older yet more noble and heroic way of facing the world was brought home to me one day when I was up among the coffee farms of the Andes. I had accompanied Argimiro González, Pasqual, Julio, and a couple local members of a folkloric group on a walk around the area. Walking through the dirt roads separating the fields, we came across a lone small country store where we stopped to seek some shade from the sun and quench our thirst. Buying a Coca-Cola, I went outside and stood on the veranda, looking out on the valley and surrounding hills. There I saw an old man dressed in work clothes walking along the same road we had just taken. In his right hand, he carried a garrote. I told the group inside what I had seen and asked them if they knew who he was. Waiting to get a closer look at the man, he continued his stroll toward the store, stepped on the veranda, greeted us, and went to the owner and requested some coffee, soap, and Chimú. The local men introduced themselves and the rest of us to the old man then complimented him on the quality of the old, weathered garrote he was carrying. I introduced myself and asked the man why he carried a garrote out here in the country? Responding in a calm quiet voice he said, "you never know when you are going to run across snakes or wild animals around here." "Oh, are there are a lot of wild animals still around here?" I asked. "Oh yes," he replied. "You never know when you will run into a wild animal," he said, his eyes shining with a particular glint. Members of my group and the owner all lifted their eyebrows at each other and their eyes glinted in return as they nodded gravely, acknowledging the humor of a traditional veiled response for carrying a garrote. "Now would you please excuse me," he said. "I have to get back home. It was a pleasure meeting you all, and I wish you good luck on your endeavors. I hope you have a safe trip back home. Good-bye." He walked out the store and back down the dirt road from whence he came. We all came out to watch him leave. When he was about fifty feet away from us, he gave a sudden twirl to his garrote and sent the head of a blossoming flower across the road. Murmurs of acknowledgment and nods of the head from the group of men followed this display. A few seconds later, he repeated his trick. Then they all went back inside, where one of the locals told me,

> Did you see that? That is one of the old-time men that used to be around here. Did you notice how polite he was and the way he deflected any acknowledgment of the garrote as a fearsome weapon. Then when he walked off a bit too far for us to easily catch up to him, he twirled his garrote and knocked off the heads of a couple flowers. He was telling us that he knew what we were really driving at by asking him questions and that he wanted us to know that he was indeed a skilled garrotero. That is the way men used to be.

The owner of the bodega nodded in agreement and then the group broke up into a big laugh and begin jabbering excitedly at witnessing such a traditional scene that must have been repeated many more times in their youth.

Sometime in the early nineteenth century in the frontier lands of the Segovia Highlands, non-elite men of differing backgrounds co-opted the garrote as a prestige item to proclaim to the world they, too, were men — that they, too, were willing to settle any disagreement in a way that elite, European men of honor would deem right and effective, and in a way that acknowledged the status of his opponent: a white man of means and good breeding. I do not possess any evidence that the sight of racially marked men carrying a palo incited any outbursts of rage or assault when this first began to occur, but can confidently assume there were a lot of conflicts that may have been exacerbated by the sight of a man claiming to be of a status it was felt he was not entitled to before it became an unmarked fashion accessory in the region. By the early twentieth century, along with the garrote, a wide-brimmed straw hat, a big moustache, long sideburns, a gob of tobacco lodged behind the lower lip, and a pair of alpargatas sandals on the feet was an accepted manner of adorning the body, of inhabiting and moving through space in a way proclaiming that here was a man among men. Not only a man of honor equal to another, but perhaps even a bit superior to any other man. Carrying a garrote, a man claimed here was someone who could grow a bigger moustache, tell a better joke, laugh louder, drink more, sing better, fight harder, spend more money on friends and strangers than any other men around. Here was someone who knew how to swing a garrote backed by an indomitable aggressiveness, but was also full of a cunning charm that could trick a rattlesnake out of his skin or make a nun leave her orders. Carrying a hardwood walking stick also calls attention to the way the way space is shaped with racial, class, and gender norms that inform how people occupy and move through space. In his ethnography on Bahian capoeira, Greg Downy looked at how students of Capoeira Angola are taught to squat low to the ground, invert themselves upside down, or flow in seemingly awkward or older, racially marked forms of body-techniques. One point Downey was trying to make was how learning how to occupy or move through space in different ways can act as a conduit to open up individual's usual ways of looking upon and acting in the world. After loosening up the body and getting used to move in unfamiliar ways, one's own set of attitudes and physiological dispositions of one's "primary habitus" could be decentered to take advantage of new possibilities of moving through, looking upon, and judging the world, in a type of corporeal political activism (Downey 2005, 200–202). In a similar condition of a harsh racial and class-based castes system enduring through the colonial and post-independence era, and shaping the current social realm, racially or class-marked men were expected to minimize their occupation of space by moving to the side of the road when meeting their betters, to avoid eye contact, to passively accept insults and humiliations, to hold themselves ready for the call of their patrons or masters or by those who saw themselves as their betters. It was such a meeting between a group of merchants and laborers meeting in the middle of the road outside Barquisimeto in 1825, soon after the wars of liberation, each refusing to make way for the other, that led to one of the first mentions of fighting with a garrote (Assunção 1999, 69–72). The connection between the garrote and the on-going resistance of non-elite communities to the demands and repressive policies of hacenderos, wealthy merchants, and a series of government officials can be seen as one of a variety of tactics that has continued to serve as part of a continual struggle of resistance and accommodation to the forces that have tried to curtail or subdue the autonomy of the pueblos of Venezuela. Men such as León Valera, Sandalio Linnares, and José-Felipe Alvarado once acted as labor-organizers, militia leaders, and shock troops in support of more sympathetic regional caudillos, struggling against the oppression of other powerful caudillos hacenderos and politicians. These men from a previous generation, who strode through the back roads and dusty trails of rural Venezuela with a straight back, eyes forward, and swinging a garrote in their hand, are the men whose memories are cherished by those who pick up the garrote today, as well as by a number of other local village people who remember or were told stories about them. Stopping random people on the street of Caracas, Valencia, or Maracaibo today and asking them about garrote will lead to shoulder shrugs or quick but polite exits. In the working-class neighborhoods and villages in the Segovia Highlands and a few other places, the garrote still acts as a powerful symbol of courage, fortitude, honor, and resistance. Hearing stories from older relatives, seeing these men in action while growing up, or, alternately, seeking out these men to train garrote and actively listening to their stories is understood as a way to instill valued character traits, a moral compass, and a number of physical skills that prepare a young man to face the trials, tribulations, and contradictions a man must negotiate in everyday life with honor and pride. Of course, as other stories and anecdotes have shown, not all men sought to be feared garroteros, and not all men who sought to master garrote or idolized the men of old became masters of garrote. Not all men who mastered garrote acted in a restrained, humanitarian way through their whole life. In this contingent and incomplete process of transmission ideas such as subjectivity, intersubjectivity, the role of materiality, and the varied ways and innumerable ways of using the body to face to the challenges of the world grouped under the term of the habitus is foregrounded

As a teenager in El Tocuyo coming home from school one day, Pasqual happened to see a Tamunangue ritual where the garrotero Juan Yépez was taking part in the la batalla. Enthralled by what he saw, he went home and asked his father to ask Maestro Juan to teach him garrote. Demurring and putting him off for a time, his father finally agreed to ask him on the behalf of his son. Finding Maestro Juan, his father asked the maestro to have a cup of coffee with him to discuss a matter of some importance. After drinking a couple cups of coffee and discussing the weather, the health of family members, and how work was going, Pasqual's father requested Juan accept his son as student of garrote. In response, Maestro Juan asked him if Pasqual was a good and dutiful son and if he did well in school. Responding in the affirmative, Maestro Juan agreed to teach Pasqual if he kept doing his chores at home, treated his parents with respect, and continued to do well in school. He would be required to come to his house every day after school to practice, no excuses and no stopping to hang out with friends. Both his father and Pasqual agreed. For four years, Pasqual trained diligently, perfecting his skills while developing a deep attachment with the old man. Feeling sick and recognizing he had little time left on this earth, Maestro Juan went up to El Molino to ask his old friend José-Felipe Alvarado if he would take on the responsibility of looking after Pasqual's development after he had gone. Soon afterward, he died. For a long time, Pasqual was inconsolable and wanted nothing to do with garrote. Finally, after some time had passed, Pasqual made up his way to El Molino to begin training with José-Felipe, watching over the old man and his wife, driving them to doctors' appointments and such. He also befriended another old garrotero form the hill town of Sanare, Ramón Mateo Goyo. Likewise, he trained with the Maestro Goyo and looked after him as his health declined and he finally died. Then, when the health of José-Felipe turned and it was time to die, Pasqual was there during this time, trying to provide what support he could for the old man.

In Pasqual's story, a number of elements stand out that show how garrote can take hold of one, how embodied knowledge is transmitted, and why it continues to persist through the generations. I have claimed throughout this work that it is through the body, in conjunction with material technology, that we come to have knowledge of and are able to successfully engage in projects and face the challenges of the world. Making these claims, I drew on the idea of the habitus. Since revived in the twentieth century, the idea of the habitus and other similar terms have been used in a number of specific ways by a number of social scientists and philosopher to elucidate certain aspects of the way people think, move, and interact with the larger world in a way that relies on past successful responses, yet remain malleable to change depending on the call of the situation. One element that stands out in this study is that the persistence of armed combat calls attention to the durability of the habitus. Or as Elias put it, "changing the habitus is not as easy as changing one's clothes" (Elias 1991, 224–225). At the same time, practically oriented, embodied knowledges, often associated with material technologies, are subject to deliberate and unintentional change both on a macro-historical as well as on an individual level, calling attention to the incomplete transformative nature of the habitus on the individual and highlighting non-habitual forms of agency in the formation of subject identities. I have looked upon the habitus both on the communal and individual level to account for the persistence of armed combat in Venezuela. Pasqual's journey of learning garrote is a unique journey that lends itself to elucidating the complexity of the habitus. The family of Pasqual moved to Venezuela as part of the larger post WWII immigration of Western Europeans into Venezuela, as the government officials hoped to "whiten the country" and raise its standards of civilization. Bringing over their own sets of ideas, practices, and imaginaries, they further marginalized older ideas and practices that were currently being decentered with the emergence of a growing middle class reaping the rewards of an increasing global demand for oil. One aspect of the conservative nature of the habitus is seen in how a number of rural people still see the garrote as a culturally appropriate manner to settle any intercommunal conflicts. At the same time, pointing toward the innovative nature of the habitus, people who carry garrotes do so now in a more discreet manner, pointing to a negotiated acceptance of modern norms relating to acceptable norms of sociality and violence. The blend of the old and the new, as it relates to Pasqual's development as a garrotero, was seen in how Pasqual never carried a palo in public; however, every day for a period of time, he did wear a T-shirt promoting a Canary Island stick-fighting group. In this way, he was able to proclaim his acquaintance with stick fighting without admitting to anybody that he was a skilled stick fighter himself. He also performed his garrote at a number of festivals and had a couple of students; however, he never taught them anything of value. At present, it is impossible to know if a man carries a garrote in his trunk unless he says something. Getting on a city bus in Barquisimeto, sometimes you will see the driver is holding a pile of paperwork on his dashboard with a guapo-manso in easy reach. Walking through the fields of the Segovia Highlands, one can come across a farmer riding along the road to or from work with a dark lustrous garrote of Guayaba Negro, or the gleaming yellow of a Vera wood garrote, strapped underneath the top horizontal bar of his bicycle or moped. Invited into a man's house to partake of their well-known hospitality, one can often find a beautiful light brown garrote of Jebe wood stood up behind the door, in much the same way people here in North America keep a baseball bat behind their front door—something that they are familiar swinging and can pack a powerful wallop. This idea of the familiar reconfigured to meet changing attitudes demonstrates an adherence to local practices of dealing with life's challenges and was also examined in terms of how a social or communal habitus or ways of moving the body, in conjunction with material technology, can anchor or emotionally anchor an individual to a place, a situation, or lineage, fundamentally reshaping the way they move, look upon, and feel about the world.

Examining the diverse ways individuals become invested in responding in specific ways deemed culturally right and meaningful is seen in the way Pasqual went about learning garrote, relying on the social network of his family to create a link to another social network coalescing around the fact of having been taught the Siete Lineas lineage of garrote by León Valera. Drawing on the key role that social networks play in the transmission of embodied knowledge is seen in the gravity in which the request to accept Pasqual as an apprentice is presented. There is still a great sense of responsibility a teacher feels in taking on an apprentice who may waste his time, turn the art against him, or bring shame upon him in front of his family and community. In the first meeting with Maestro Juan, Pasqual conducted himself in such a way as to demonstrate to the elder Juan Yépez that he had been brought up right, he knew how to act, and recognized the great favor he had requested and would treat it with the respect it deserves. Through a number of years of training every day, Pasqual developed his physiological skills to a high degree in specific ways that showed one skilled in garrote that he was trained by a man of high skill from the Tocuyo Valley. Within the community, he became known first as a student of Juan Yépez and then José-Felipe Alvarado, sharing some of the respect, fear, and admiration that was attached to the two old men. Pasqual also continuously acted in a way that recognized the importance of older ways of sociality, such as the need for secrecy or cunning at times in order to protect his art and other times to let loose with everything he had in order to protect himself or his reputation as a student of two well-regraded Tocuyano garroteros—but at all times acting in an honorable and ethically right fashion. Over the years, his skills and comportment were noticed by his teachers and the elder generation of garroteros, who responded with care regarding his continued well-being and development, which was reciprocated as Pasqual consciously strived to imitate these men he admired. By the time I began my dissertation in the area, other garroteros all began to recognize and agree amongst themselves that Pasqual had indeed become a master of the garrote.

Learning a new way of interacting with the world not only requires a social network but is often surrounded with a set of material technologies that becomes intertwined with an individual's sense of identity and how he fits in with the world. The old Anglo-Saxon word for weapon, *Wæpond*, illustrates the close link that can form between objects and individuals or groups as symbolizing group belonging or some other type of status or identity marker. The term *Wæpond*, literally meaning all humans or warm-blooded mammals, was also used to refer to a restricted class of men of wealth and social status who were permitted to carry a weapon (Bosworth 2013).[1] Over time, in Venezuela the carrying of a garrote in public meant that one was claiming to be an honorable man equal to any elite European male. Sometime later, most all men carried garrotes as a public sign of their manhood and sense of honor. During this time, rural men would regularly gather where, in addition to bonding over drinking or gambling, engaging in games of skill, or telling stories, they would also seek to distinguish themselves through these same activities, as well as dueling with sticks, machetes, knives, and revolvers. In this way they could proclaim and prove their humanity to the world in wild, risky contests where death was not often the primary goal, but was always a distinct possibility. These extreme forms of masculinity had been tamped down by the early twentieth century along the coasts and urban areas by an expanding middle class and had spread into the interior over the decades. However, the stories of the skills, character, and attitudes of these men still strike a responsive chord among a strong minority of peoples. As a local form of self-defense, it is seen and felt to be one of the unique cultural treasures that originated with the common people of Venezuela and still has relevance for today.

Going up into the hill-country, I went to the town of Los Humacaros to see the Fiesta de San Antonio. The morning of the festival people began wandering down to the central area of the village around 7:30 to hear mass. After mass had concluded and people began to leave the church, a float of San Antonio was brought out on the shoulders of four men, accompanied by the pealing of church bells and the setting off of fireworks, to herald the beginning of the Tamunangue. With an ever-revolving number of men carrying the float, Saint Anthony was paraded around the block where the church was built about 15–20 times over the next couple hours. Leading the procession was a well-known garrotero in his finest, freshly pressed liquilique and a garrote in his hand, guiding the ever-revolving procession of men playing garrote to honor the saint. Also preceding this crowd was the village priest. A newcomer from Peru, I was told he did not approve of all these superstitious activities and had to be alternately persuaded and informed by an elder garrotero that this was a very old and special part of village life that must be respected. The procession was very colorful and lively, with a group of musicians playing, with many in their Sunday best and others in colorful traditional costumes, highlighting their indigenous and or colonial heritage. I saw two good brief exchanges of garrote by the leading family of garroteros in the village, and overall, a very pleasant time was had by all. Afterward, Saint Anthony was placed by the front doors of the church in the front of the Plaza Bolívar. From here, the musicians gathered in front of the float and began to play the series of sones in honor of Saint Anthony for promises received or for the granting of future promises. Beginning with La Salve for a few minutes, I worked my way closer to the circle of musicians to witness those who would take part in la batalla. Disappointed, I saw many of the same people I had seen earlier do the same performance-oriented type of garrote. The crowd, too, was impatient at this spectacle of people swinging garrotes at each other. After about ten minutes of la batalla, the musicians switched to playing the series of other sones over and over. The music and dances were beautiful; I watched for a while then got bored and wandered off. Up the hill, I saw my garrote teacher Wencio, Manuelito who was a garrotero I had met previously a number of times, and a couple of other men sitting on the curb passing around a liter bottle of Cocuy. I told them they missed la batalla, to which they responded not to worry, it would roll around again. I was offered a swig of Cocuy, and in spite of the early hour and the heat from the sun, I took a long, deep, and manly swig and felt it burn a line right down my body into my stomach, which turned into a lake of fire. "Ahhhh smoooooth!" I croaked. I then asked about the garrotes I saw the men carrying. Manuelito put his garrote in my hand. It was longer, thicker, and heavier than the majority of garrotes I had seen up to then. Then Manuelito introduced me to his cousin Damaso, who showed me a big, thick, heavy garrote with finger grips carved into the base of the garrote for a better hold. His cousin was at least six feet tall with a barrel chest and thick arms and legs, smiling and friendly, then looking over at Manuelito, a shorter version of his cousin about of about five feet and nine inches, who shared the same barrel chest and thick arms and legs with his cousin. I thought, "Boy! I would really hate to get involved in a feud with that family back in the past." Offering me another swig, I took another long draught that made my whole body feel like it was on fire and then wandered off, wondering if I could make a quick dash up the hill to the river and dive in and cool down a bit. Feeling a scholarly obligation to stay in the village and witness the entire event, I took a few laps around the plaza and then the block, saying hello to familiar faces and pretending to be an attentive, curious, and serious anthropologist. Working my way back to the Plaza Bolívar, the crowd had tightened up around the musicians and people who were enjoying dancing and watching others dance. Then, off to the right of the crowd I saw Damaso point his garrote at Manuelito, saying something, while Manuelito in a defensive stance held his garrote in a ready position in his rear hand, looking at Damaso and taking an occasional sip from his beer with his lead hand. One friend suddenly took the can of beer from Manuelito, and the two men began to circle each other, smiling the whole time and then swinging a few halfhearted pechero and barriguero blows at each other, which crashed against each other creating a loud and familiar clacking noise. Breaking contact with each other, Wencio took the opportunity to take the garrote from Manuelito, who turned to face Damaso with the garrote down by his waist, holding it with both hands on each side. After a few seconds of talking, Damaso advanced on Wencio, leading Wencio to raise the garrote high above his shoulders, step out to the left, let go of the garrote with his left hand, strike the right bicep of Damaso with a de-

scending blow, striking Damaso's right bicep, and then back up awkwardly as Damaso attacked halfheartedly with forehand and backhand
diagonal blows until Wencio gestured that he could not defend himself
anymore. Seeing this, Manuelito took back his garrote, and the two men,
Damaso and Manuelito, began to circle each other warily. Suddenly, as
Damaso stepped toward him and came within range of a strike, Manuelito swung his garrote in a big arc over his head while taking a step back-
ward with his right leg in a ready stance, causing Damaso to halt his
advance. Then cocking his garrote and laying it back along his upper
arm, Manuelito advanced and, stepping out with a right step, swung a
forehanded barriguero that Damaso tried to block but hit his hand. Manuelito swung a backhanded and then another forehanded pechero strike
that Damaso blocked, but slid up and hit his hand. The familiar clack of
sticks drew a few more men's attention, who began to watch with a little
more interest. Manuelito halted his attack and leaned back out of range,
gripping his garrote with both hands hanging down by his waist, waiting
to see what will happen next. Damaso shuffled back a bit and lifted his
stick arm high and rearranged his rolled-up sleeve to ensure freedom of
movement. Gathering themselves together for the next bout, Manuelito,
letting go of his garrote with his left hand, brought it back on his right
shoulder and suddenly stepped forward with his lead right leg and, leaning forward, swung another three-strike combination of a forehand barriguero, a backhanded pechero strike, finishing with a forehand barriguro
strike connecting with Damaso's bicep. Once again, Manuelito stepped
back to assess the situation. Safely out of each other's range, both men
urged each other to advance again and try conclusions. Now, about a
dozen men were watching the action intently, while about seventy people no more than twenty feet away remained oblivious and uncaring
about this impromptu juego. Manuelito was resting his garrote on top of
his right lead shoulder, the garrote of Damaso was also in his lead right
hand, his elbow sticking out and whose tip was pointed at the ground at
a 45-degree angle in a type of defensive guard. Again, Manuelito, with a
quick movement, aimed a strike at Damaso's hand, hitting it. In return,
Damaso struck the back of Manuelito's arm. Continuing the momentum
of the attack, Manuelito stepped out with his left leg, took another step
with his right leg, and then spun 360 degrees, in a full circle, counterclockwise, leading Damaso to step back. Finished spinning in a complete
circle, Manuelito cut loose with another forehand barriguero, hitting Damaso's hand and causing him to drop his garrote. This mistake was
greeted with cheers and catcalls by the few men watching. As he shuffled
back out of range again with a little grin on his face, Manuelito struck and
missed with another snapping forehanded barriguero before withdrawing back about 15–20 feet, allowing Damaso to retrieve his garrote. Thus,
both armed again, they began circling each other. Approaching each other again, with Damaso having raised his stick high above his head,

threatening to strike, suddenly a young woman casually strolled right between the two men, oblivious or uncaring about what was going on. Pausing like gentleman for the unintended interruption, they began to circle each other once she passed by. Suddenly, Manuelito attacked once again with a forehand barriguero before bringing his garrote back to rest in both hands by his waist, his right side facing Damaso. Once again, Damaso raised his garrote high. Manuelito, holding his garrote in his left hand, swung his empty right hand out in a fake backhanded barriguero to make Damaso react, then, bringing his arm back, he grabbed his palo with his right hand and swung a real backhanded barriguero at the upper arm of Damaso, causing his garrote to slide out of his hand and out on the ground to a chorus of hoots and hollers of derision. Damaso then stepped forward and brought his stick down in a vertical strike well to the left of Manuelito's head and stepped back. Manuelito followed, parried the strike downward with his left hand, stepped in, and, with his right hand, tried to grab Damaso's garrote. Damaso pushed him off and away with his left hand. Manuelito put himself in a boxer's crouch as Damaso advanced. Manuelito attacked first with a low-scraping kick to the shin that fell short and then moved in, trying to grab Damaso's stick. Damaso pushed him off again with his left hand, keeping his stick raised high in his rear hand. Threatening to strike and holding his stick up one second longer while Manuelito circles, he dropped the stick to his waist, moved it to his left hand, and extended his right hand to Manuelito. They shook hands and began smiling, laughing, and jabbering at each other. By this time, the Jefe Civil who had been watching retrieved Manuelito's palo. Manuelito almost immediately took back his palo. Then with both men properly equipped with their palos to mark such a special day, they wrapped their arms around each other's shoulders, and one friend handed them their beer and they wandered off into the crowd.[2] Maybe this was not a stellar example of highly formal and technical garrote encounter, but there are a number of elements that make this minor impromptu juego a good example that explains the persistence of garrote and the role of a warrior's habitus in a modern, ever-changing world.

Within the greater struggle of local people to preserve their traditional festival from cosmopolitan global forces represented by disapproving foreign priests, there is the what I see as an increasing embarrassment or unconcern by a number of locals toward the rough wild traditional ways of men, as seen in the perfunctory space given over to la batalla. I was told by Manuelito that more opportunities to engage in la batalla would roll around again. After the first cycle of sones had been played in the early afternoon, I stayed downtown until 11:00 p.m., wandering around, and only saw a few brief rounds of la batalla, with people demanding a chance to dance in the circle instead after a few minutes of la batalla before it disappeared entirely from the ritual. During the impromptu juego, I witnessed only around a dozen men paid any attention to what was going on maybe twenty feet away from the main activities. The unconcern or embarrassment in the display of this juego de garrote, resulting in a number of deep contusions and smashed knuckles, was made particularly clear to me when the young woman casually strolled through the middle of the two men armed with garrotes. Only a small committed number of people took an interest in the development and outcome of the juego, a type of occurrence that used to be a lot more common with a lot more serious consequences than what I saw that day, as I was told numerous times by those who sought to educate me about garrote. What I saw that day was an increasing marginalization of older masculine pastimes; at the same time, though, there remained a dedicated few men of all ages who still took a great interest in the art and what it had to offer, as I saw in the number of young men who participated in the la batalla as the devout circled the church. These young men from a number of families around the area came down from the hills specifically to show off their family's knowledge of garrote to the village, while dedicating their performances as an offering to Saint Anthony. A number of older garroteros responded similarly when I asked if they were worried about the disappearance of garrote. They answered "no," because the children or grandchildren will carry it on or there will always be a small number of the younger generation who will love the art and carry it on.

Looking more closely at the juego just described, the claims made that the practice of garrote can transform one's way of moving through, looking at, and judging the world can be examined. In what I called the warrior's habitus as a set of local embodied practical knowledges, affects, and moral understanding regarding one's involvement with combative arts, the technical skills evinced by the two men in the juego, although compromised by alcohol, was still very high. It is difficult for people not used to fighting to tell what is going on because the action occurs at such a high rate of speed. What I saw and described were a number of subtle feints, the use of stepping to control the space between the two men, and the delivering of well-executed and targeted blows to non-vital areas of the body. In other words, they showed an understanding of vista, or visual awareness, and pisada, or footwork. Following this line, the way that the men attacked in combinations of one to three strikes reflects a calm, cool, deliberate mind of a man who steps in and attacks and then withdraws to assess the situation. Finally, there was the humanity of both men seen in the primary need to not hurt others, even when they wander through the space where men are having serious "fun." Their humanity can also be seen in the kind of attacks launched. Both men were swinging blows aimed at a level of the chest and stomach avoiding the head and bony areas of the leg. The majority of shots that landed that I saw landed on the hands and arms of both men, resulting in some deep bruises and a couple broken knuckles but nothing too serious. In addition to no thrusts employed, there was only one attack aimed at the head that was deliberately targeted wide of the other man's head just to be sure of the other man's safety. Finally, showing an understanding that was just all just "good rough fun" between friends, when each man in turn lost their garrote, the other backed off to allow the opponent to retrieve his weapon. The second time that Manuelito lost his palo, Damaso raised his garrote a little higher, as to threaten Manuelito, then immediately lowered it, switched it to his left hand, and extended his hand in friendship as a type of rough joke. Then, putting their arms around each other's shoulders and holding their garrotes in their other hands, they laughed and strolled off with beers in their hands ready for more good times. In these actions a young man begins to see the technical skills, the moral compass, the joy of living on the edge, and the importance of compassion among garroteros, an exemplary example of a local warrior's habitus as developed among his home, as something uniquely Venezuelan. While ignored or dismissed by many, the art of garrote still captures the hearts and minds of a few who ensures its relevance and transmission to Venezuelans in the future.

NOTES

1. Bosworth, Joseph. 2013. *An Anglo-Saxon Dictionary.* Accessed 04/14/2016. www.bosworthtoller.com/034339.

2. My vantage point made me unable to see if Damaso had landed more strikes than I was able to see. When I saw Manuelito later that day, he showed me a number of contusions up and down his arm and mentioned he had more on his ribs. I don't know if I missed more juegos or if I missed seeing the strikes during the juego described.

Glossary

Afincar: Picking up and stamping of the foot on the ground. A type of footwork used in the Palo Sangriento.

Afrodescendente(s): a term that stresses the African origin of former slaves in Venezuela. The Venezuelan author Juan Pablo Sojo coined the term "Afro-Venezolano" in the 1940s. By the 2000s, Afrodescendente has become preferred over Afro-Venezolano by local political activists.

Aguachinaos: A term of insult.

Alpargatas: A type of outdoor slipper or sandal that rural men used to commonly wear.

Barrecampo: A signature attack among garroteros. It is an upward strike aimed at the inside of the lower shin, the inside of the knee, or the groin. Also called a Palo Arriba, Baseado, and Barrejuste.

Barriguero: A forehand strike aimed at the gall bladder, liver, or the spleen. A backhanded barriguero would be called a *revês barriguero*.

Baseado: Another term for the Barrecampo used by those who practice la riña con palo.

Barrejuste: Another term for the Barrecampo. A term used by many garroteros living in the Andes.

Batalla, La: This refers to the mock duel that accompanies the Fiesta de San Antonio.

Bolivar or *Bolivares*: Unit of currency used in Venezuela at the time of the research.

Boton: A woven stop that is used in weaving handles for palos. Sometimes, only one boton is used toward the butt end of the palo. Other times, two are used, which sandwich the hand between them. Maestro Ismael preferred six of them on his palos. In this way, he could get a good, hard grip around the palo with his fingers.

Capitan-Mayor (a): The Capitan-Mayor and the Capitan-Mayora are in charge of the promessas dedicated to Saint Anthony. They keep things moving along smoothly. The Capitan–Mayor should also be a good garrotero able to break up fights and discipline outbreaks of violence if it arises. The Capitan–Mayora is in charge of the female dancers.

Carajo: An expletive "fuck!"

Caserio: A hamlet.

Caudillo: A type of regional or national strongman who ruled through a threat of force and his ability to convince men to fight for him. This type

3

46 Glossary

of governing was common throughout much of South America up through the early twentieth century.

Chalequando: A person who causes trouble for pleasure or to cause some excitement.

Chueco: A clubfoot or having a crippled leg or foot. José-Felipe was feeling the effects of arthritis pretty bad, and at times, he referred to himself this way.

Chimú: Chímu is a tobacco paste product resulting from tobacco being soaked for a time in a solution of water, bicarbonate of soda, and salt, as well as some aromatic substances. This is left to soak until it attains the consistency of a paste and then is sold in small flat pocket-size trays. Uzcátegui (1941, 495).

Čujisto: A term used in rural Montenegro referring to manly virtue or the highest level of moral behavior, where the demands of a heroic warrior are empowered by a sense of humanity extended to one's enemies.

Coñazos: Slang for a pair of balls or being audacious or courageous.

Cocuy: An alcoholic drink made from the native cactus *Agave cocui*. Often it is flavored with local fruits.

Cuadra: Refers to a number of geometric patterns many garroteros used to develop one's footwork in garrote.

Cuerpo Limpio: This refers to the predilection of some garroteros to not rely on blocks but through the judicious use of body movements to avoid an opponent's attack. See *negava*.

Dejarretadera: A cattle goad.

Doble y Cruzado: A lineage of garrote developed by Napoleon Zapata.

En Perfil: A way of standing so one is profile to the opponent, minimizing one's exposure.

Espada y Daga: Refers to using a palo and knife in combination. So far I have only seen the practioners of Palo Sangriento and a student of Ismael Colmenares's, Mario Echegrerrai, use this combination of weapons.

Espitualista: The term is used for devotees of Maria Lionza. Devotees will allow the spirit of Maria Lionza enter them in return for favors received.

Fusta: A little coachman's whip or stick.

Garrote: A hardwood walking stick. A term also used to characterize a number of fighting practices around Venezuela that rely on a walking stick for their primary weapon. Also called los juegos de palos.

Garrote de Lara: A general term recently invented to refer to a number of armed combative traditions practiced around the Tocuyo Valley.

Garrote Venezolano: A general term recently invented to refer to the innumerable number of armed combative methods practiced in Venezuela.

Garrotero: One who knows how to swing the palo.

Godos (or Goths): A nineteenth-century term used to portray those Venezuelans who hewed to the centralized policy of administration, whose polices were enforced by local oligarchies of landowners, merchants, and businessmen.

Guapo: manso: A "bully-tamer." A short (twenty to twenty-six inch), thick, hardwood stick used as a weapon of self-defense, similar to a small truncheon.

Isleño(s): A person from the Canary Islands.

Jefe Civil: Equivalent to the mayor of a US town.

Juego Duro: A stick fight with hard contact, but short of an outright fight or riña.

Juego de Oscuridad: A lineage of garrote taught in the early twentieth century by Raphael Peraza (1898–1986).

Juego de Garrote: Refers to the sparring of two men. Alternately, it can refer to a basic body of techniques that belong to a lineage.

Juego Pachuquero: A lineage of garrote from El Tocuyo that claims roots from an immigrant from the Canary Islands. It also refers to a specific modality of garrote done among a few Tocuyano garroteros where both men hold their sticks in the middle, trying to strike each other.

Juego por la Vista: Literally "playing by sight." The ability to engage in a free-flow stick bout, ranging from a recreational match between friends to an all-out battle with multiple opponents and any number of weapons.

Juego Trancado y Tenido: A lineage of garrote developed by the Colmenares family and taught in the villages around their homes in Los Humacaros.

Jugador (pl). *Jugadores*: There are a number of meanings to this term, depending on the context in which it is used. For example, among garroteros it is used to refer to those who do garrote. The term jugador can be used to differentiate an individual who is learning to jugar in that a jugador can competently engage in a free-flow match. Alternately, it can refer to one who has attained a high skill in the art. Popularly used to refer to a "gambler."

La Riña con Palo: A lineage of garrote from La Riconanda and brought to La Piedad in the early twentieth century and taught outside Cabudare and brought to the areas by Clarencio Flores. In turn, he taught Gualberto Castillo, who taught, among others, Mercedes Pérez (1918–2003) and Ramón Aguilar. Maestro Mercedes, in turn, taught Eduardo Sanoja, who has spent his whole life researching and popularizing this art. Both Umberto Burgos and Ramón Aguilar, in turn, taught Danys Burgos, who along with William Liscano, is the foremost exponent of this lineage in the village.

Linea: Refers to a sequence of moves.

Liquilique: A formal type of suit worn by older rural Venezuelans.

Llamadas: These are static challenge postures where a man will deliberately leave himself open, daring an opponent to take advantage of his weakness if he has the courage to do so.

Llanos, Llaneros: The term Llanero refers to somebody from the savannahs of southwest Venezuela that stretch over the states of Apure, Barinas, Guárico, Portuguesa, Cojedes Anzoátegui, and Monágas and into Colombia. For Venezuelans, the llanos hold the same type of history and mythmaking as the old West does for the reader in the United States.

Loco: Crazy. Also see *zumbador* or *guapo*.

Mandador: A leather whip about six to eight feet long, attached to a handle about eighteen to thirty-two inches long. Often used by muleteers. Maestro Adrían Pérez drew on memories as child to include the mandador as a weapon. Maestro Adrían teaches it alone and in conjunction with a knife.

Mañoso: This is an ambivalent term that refers to a sneaky, tricky guy who cannot be trusted. Other times, it is used in an admiringly way to refer to a particularly dangerous garrotero.

Mansa: An act of slyness.

Mestizaje: Refers to the mix of the Indian, African, and Europeans that make up the Venezuelan people today. Many Venezuelans use this idea to claim there is no racism in Venezuela today, as they are all the same.

Negava: A way of avoiding an attack. Usually by withdrawing or moving your arm out of the trajectory of the counterattack. Also a type of cuerpo limpio

Palo: A hardwood walking stick. Or it can refer to a specific attack.

Palo Arriba: See Barrecampo.

Palo Chico: A now extinct style of small stick fighting from the Canary Islands thought to have persisted in some form in Cuba, Venezuela, or Louisiana.

Palo por Palo: Literally to exchange blow for blow and is often the rejoinder when somebody suffers a slight, insult, or attack and the recipient is dealt one in kind right back. This resilience to take a blow and deal one right back at someone is still a valued attitude among rural Venezuelans and admired in garrote encounters.

Palo Sangriento: A lineage of garrote developed in Los Boros in the Tocuyo Valley and brought to Barquisimeto, where Félix García learned it and taught it in his shoe shop for forty years. The lineage has a wide array of weapons taught, including the garrote, espada y daga, daga, and machete.

Pico e' Loro: Literally a parrot's beak knife. A pocket knife used by many laborers in Venezuela. It's approximately eight inches long when open. It has a curved tip, much like a carpet knife or a parrot's beak. Serves well as an agricultural tool. It was also often used by garroteros.

Pisada: Footwork.

Promessa: A religious act where one asks a favor from a saint or repays a favor granted by a saint.

Pueblo: Referred in the past to a poor peasant village, but now has a sense more of the common people.

Pueblo de Doctrinas: These were developed by the Spanish crown, whose governors designated specific indigenous villages as protected sites where all indigenous people in the area must relocate. Nearby Spanish landowners were required to make sure that they received a good Christian education, and in exchange, the indigenous communities were required to provide them with a number of days of free labor and other forms of tribute.

Riña: A fight. This also refers to a number of finishing techniques.

Saint Anthony of Padua: A twelfth century Portuguese Franciscan monk. He preached in Morocco and died near Padua, Italy. In Venezuela, he was one of the patron saints among African slaves in the Tocuyo Valley.

Siete Lineas: A lineage of garrote developed by León Valera of El Molino in the late nineteenth century.

Son: Refers to a dance that is accompanied by a specific type of song.

Sones de Negros: This is how the older Venezuelans remember what the Tamunangue festival was called when first interviewed about it in the 1940s.

Sprezzatura: The Oxford dictionary defines it a "studied carelessness."

Tamunangue: This is how the festival dedicated to St. Anthony of Padua is known. It also refers to the log drum that accompanies the musicians during this event.

Tuura: The garrotero Félix Pérez explained to me a Tuura was a pouch that contained special or blessed objects to obtain supernatural protection. *Tura* is also an Ayaman indigenous word, referring to an annual harvest dance where the ancestral ancestors of the corn are honored.

Velorio: See *Promessa*.

References

Abbink, Jon G. 1999. "Violence, Ritual, and Reproduction: Culture and Context in Surma Dueling." *Ethnology* 38: 227–242.

Abe, Ikuo, Yasuharu Kiyohara, and Ken Nakajima. 2000. "Sport and Physical Education under Fascistization in Japan." *InYo: The Journal of Alternative Perspectives on the Martial Arts and Sciences.* Accessed September 19, 2009. http://ejmas.com/jalt/jaltart_abe_0600.htm.

Akyeampong, Emmanuel. 2002. "Bukom and the Social History of Boxing in Accra: Warfare and Citizenship in Precolonial Ga Society." *International Journal of African Historical Studies* 35: 35–60.

Algar, Hamid. 2002. *Wahabism: A Critical Essay.* Oneonta, NY: Islamic Publications International.

Almeida, Ubijara. 1982. *Capoeira: A Brazilian Art Form.* Richmond: North Atlantic Books.

Alter, Joseph S. 1994. "The Body of One Color: Indian Wrestling, the Indian State, and Utopian Somatics." *Cultural Anthropology* 8: 49–72.

———. 1992. *The Wrestlers Body: Identity and Ideology in North India.* Berkley: University of California Press.

Amberger, Christopher J. 1999. *The Secret History of the Sword: Adventures in Ancient Martial Arts.* Burbank, CA: Unique Publications.

Amos, Daniel M. 1997. "A Hong Kong Southern Praying Mantis Cult." *Journal of Asian Martial Arts* 6: 30–61.

Anderson, Benedict. 1991. *Imagined Communities: Reflections on the Origin and Spread of Nationalism.* New York: Verso.

Anglo, Sydney. 2000. *The Martial Arts of Renaissance Europe.* Hartford, CT: Yale University Press.

Aquilino, Ribiero. 1987. "O Malhadinhas" In *Obras Completa de Ribiero Aquilino.* Lisboa: Bertrand Editora.

Armbrust, Walter. 2004. "Egyptian Cinema On Stage and Off." In *Off Stage/On Display: Intimacy and Ethnography in the Age of Public Culture,* edited by Andrew Shryock, 69–100. Stanford: Stanford University Press.

Arvelo, Lilliam. 2000. "Change and Persistence in Aboriginal Settlement Patterns in the Quíbor Valley, Northwestern Venezuela (Sixteenth to Nineteenth Centuries)." *Ethnohistory* 7: 669–704.

Assunção, Matthias Röhrig. 2014. "Stanzas and Sticks: Poetic and Physical Challenges in the Afro-Brazilian Culture of the Paraíba Valley, Rio de Janeiro." *History Workshop Journal.* History Workshop Journal Advance Access. Accessed 24 February 2014. https://muse.jhu.edu/view_citations?type=article&id=542896.

———. 2005. *Capoeira: The History of an Afro-Brazilian Art.* New York: Routledge.

———. 1999. "Juegos de Palo en Lara: Elementos para la Historia Social de un Arte Marcial Venezolano." *Revistas de Indias* LIX: 55–89.

Baños, José de Oviedo Y. 1987. *The Conquest and Settlement of Venezuela.* Translated by J. J. Varner. Berkley: University of California Press.

Baroja, Julio C. 1965. "Honor and Shame : A Historical Account of Several Conflicts" In *Honour and Shame: The Values of Mediterranean,* edited J. Peristiany, 113–140. Chicago: University of Chicago Press.

Berry, Herbert. 1991. *The Noble Science: A Study and Transcription of Sloane Ms. 2530, Papers of the Maisters of Defence of London, Temp Henry VIII to 1590.* London and Toronto: Associated University Press.

Bishko, Charles Julian. 1953. "The Peninsular Background of Latin American Cattle Rounding." *Hispanic American Historical Review* 32: 419–515.

Blair, Walter, and Franklin J. Meine. 1933. *Mike Fink: King of the Mississippi Keelboatmen.* New York: Henry Holt and Company.

Boehn, Christopher. 1984. *Blood Revenge: The Enactment and Management of Conflict in Montenegro and Other Tribal Societies.* Philadelphia: University of Pennsylvania Press.

Boretz, Avron. 2011. *Gods, Ghosts and Gangsters: Ritual Violence, Martial Arts and Masculinity on the Margins of Chinese Society.* Honolulu: University of Hawai'i Press.

Boschi, Daniele. 1998. "Homicide and Knife Fighting in Rome." In *Men and Violence: Gender, Honor and Ritual in Modern Europe,* edited by Peter Spierenberg, 128–158. Athens: Ohio State University Press.

Bosworth, Joseph. 2013. *An Anglo-Saxon Dictionary.* Accessed 04/14/2016. www.bosworthtoller.com/034339.

Bourdieu, Pierre. 1977. *Outline of a Theory of Practice.* translated by R. Nice. New York: Cambridge University Press.

———. 1965. "The Sentiment of Honour in Kabyle Society." In *Honor and Shame: The Values of Mediterranean Society,* edited by J. G. Peristany, 193–241. London: Weidenfeld and Nicolson.

———. 1962. *The Algerians,* translated by A. C. M. Ross. Boston: Beacon Press.

Bourdieu, Pierre, and Loïc J. D. Wacquant. 1992. *An Invitation to Reflexive Sociology.* Chicago: The University of Chicago Press.

Brodie, Fawn M. 1967. *The Devil Drives: A Life of Sir Richard Burton.* New York: W. W. Norton & Company, Inc.

Brownell, Susan. 1995. *Training the Body for China: Sports in the Moral Order of the People's Republic.* Chicago: University of Chicago Press.

Brunk, Samuel. 2008. *The Posthumous Career of Emiliano Zapata: Myth, Memory, and Mexico's Twentieth Century.* Austin: University of Texas Press.

Bujanda-Yépez, Carlos. 1969. *Crónicas de la Ciudad Madre.* El Tocuyo: El Colegio de Abogados del Estado Lara.

Caçador, Antonio. 1963. *Jogo de Pau Esgrima Nacional.* Lisboa.

Campbell, J. K. 1965. "Honour and the Devil." In *Honor and Shame: The Values of Mediterranean Society,* edited by J. G. Peristiany, 141–170. London: Weidenfeld & Nicolson.

Canada, Geoffrey. 1995. *Fist, Stick, Knife, Gun.* Boston: Beacon Press.

Canelón, Jesús. 1994. "El Juego de Garrote." *Fermentum. Revista Venezolano de Sociología y Antropología* 4: 10.

Cañizales-Verde, Francisco. 1992. *Diputación Provincial de Barquisimeto: Ordenas, Resoluciones, Decretos, Acuerdos y Comunicaciones (1833–1957) Vol. II.* Barquisimeto: Publicaciones del Centro de Historia Larense.

Capoeira, Nestor. 2002. *Roots of the Dance-Fight-Game.* Berkeley: Blue Snake Books.

Carneiro, Robert. 2003. *Evolution in Cultural Anthropology: A Critical History.* Boulder, CO: Westview Press.

Carruthers, Donald. 1998. "Kung-Fu Fighting: The Cultural Pedagogy of the Body in the Vovinam Overseas Vietnamese Martial Arts School." *The Australian Journal of Anthropology* 9: 45–67.

Castiglione, Baldassare. 1967. *The Book of the Courtier.* London: Penguin.

Castillo, Luís Rafael. 1908. *San Antonio de Boro: Son y Danza de Negro.* Barquisimeto: Impresora Graficolor C.a.

Century, Doug. 2000. *Street Kingdom: Five Years Inside the Franklin Avenue Posse.* New York: Warner Books.

Chacon, Richard and Rubén Mendoza. 2007. *Latin American Indigenous Warfare and Ritual Violence*, edited by Richard Chacon and Rubén Mendoza. Tucson: University of Arizona Press.

Chacon, Richard Y. Chacon and Angel Guandinango. 2007. "The Inti Raymi Festival among the Cotacachi and Otavalo of Highland Ecuador: Blood for Earth." In *Latin American Indigenous Warfare and Ritual Violence*, edited by Richard Chacon and Reubén Mendoza, 116–141. Tucson: University of Arizona Press.

Chávez, Hugo. 2009. "Introduction." In *Hugo Chávez Presents Simón Bolívar: The Bolívarian Revolution, vii–xvi*, edited by Matthew Brown. London: Verso.

Chavier, Miguel-Ángel. 2015. "Co-Construcción de Sentidos sobre el juego de palos como herramienta para Educar en valoers: Una perspectiva socio construccionista." *Compendium* 35.

———. 2009. "Aproximación a la Pelea de Palos o Juego de Palos." *Fermentum* 19: 184–198.

Childe, Gordon V. 1941. "War in Prehistoric Societies." *Sociological Review* 33: 126–138.

Colonna, Fanny.2009. "The Phantom of Dispossession: From *The Uprooting* to *The Weight of the World*." In *Bourdieu in Algeria: Colonial Politics, Ethnographic Practices, Theoretical Developments*, edited by Jane E. Goodman and Paul A. Silverstein, 63–93. Lincoln: University of Nebraska Press.

Conley, Carolyn. 1999. "The Agreeable Recreation of Fighting." *Journal of Social History* 33: 57–73.

Cooley, Charles H. 1956. *Human Nature and Social Order*. New York: Schocken Books.

Cowley, John. 1996. *Carnival, Canboulay and Calypso: Traditions in the Making*. Cambridge: Cambridge University Press.

Crossley, Nick. 2001. *The Social Body: Habit, Identity and Desire*. London: SAGE Publications.

Curtin, Phillip. 1969. *The Atlantic Slave Trade: A Census*. Madison, WI: University of Wisconsin Press.

Davies, Andrew. 1998. "Youth Gangs, Masculinity and Violence in Late Victorian Manchester and Salford." *Journal of Social History* 32: 349–369.

Davis, Robert C. 2004. "The Language of Rock-Throwing in Early Modern Italy." *Ludica* 10: 113–128.

Davis, Robert C. 1994. *The War of the Fists: Popular Culture and Public Violence in Late Renaissance Venice*. New York: Oxford University Press.

Desch Obi, T. J. 2008. *Fighting for Honor: The History of African Martial Art Traditions in the Atlantic World*. Columbia: University of South Carolina Press.

———. 2009. "Peinillas and Popular Participation: Machete Fighting in Haiti, Cuba, and Colombia." *Memories. Revista Digital de Historia y Arqueología desde el Caribe* 11. Accessed 02 February 2011. http://rcientifcas.uninorte.edu.co/co/index.php/memorias/article/vieArticle/517.

Dineen, Mark. 2001. *Customs and Cultures of Venezuela*. Westport, CT: Greenwood Press.

Downey, Greg. 2012. "Neuroanthropology and the Encultured Brain." In *The Encultured Brain: An Introduction to Neuroanthropology*, edited by Greg Downey and Daniel Lende, 23–66. Cambridge, MA: MIT Press.

———. 2010. "'Practice without Theory': A Neuroanthropological Perspective on Embodied Learning." *Journal of the Royal Anthropological Institute* (N.S.): S22–S40.

———. 2008. "Scaffolding Imitation in Capoeira: Physical Education and Enculturation in an Afro-Brazilian Art." *The American Anthropologist* 110: 204–213.

———. 2007. "Producing Pain: Techniques and Technologies in No-Holds-Barred Fighting." *Social Studies of Science*. 37: 201–226.

———. 2005. *Learning Capoeira: Lessons in Cunning from an Afro-Brazilian Art*. Oxford: Oxford University Press.

Dunning, Eric and Norbert Elias. 1986. *The Quest for Excitement: Sport and Leisure in the Civilizing Process*, edited by Eric Dunning and Norbert Elias. Dublin: Oxford: Blackwell.

Earthtrends. 2010. pp.1. Accessed April 19, 2016. http.//earthtrends.wri.org.

Eastwick, Edward Backhouse. 2013. *Venezuela or Sketches of Life in a South-American Republic; With the History of the Loan of 1864.* (1868 Reprint) London: Forgotten Books.

Elias, Norbert. 2000. *The Civilizing Process: Sociogenetic and Psychogenetic Investigations*, translated by E. Jephcott. Oxford: Blackwell.

———. 1991. *The Society of Individuals*, edited by Robert van Krieken, translated by Edward Jephcott. Oxford: Basil Blackwell.

Emsley, Clive. 2005. *Hard Men: The English and Violence since 1750.* London: Hambledon & London.

Escalona, Arturo. 1929. *Cuentas de Curaigua.* Barquisimeto: Biblioteca de Autores Larense Fundalara- Fundacultura.

Ewell, Judith. 1984. *Venezuela: A Century of Change.* Stanford: Stanford University Press.

Falk, Oren. 2004. "Bystanders and Hearsayers: Reassessing the Role of the Audience in Dueling." In *A Great Effusion of Blood?: Interpreting Medieval Violence*, edited by Mark D. Meyerson, 98–130. Toronto: University of Toronto Press.

Farrer, D. S. 2009. *Shadows of the Prophet: Martial Arts and Sufi Mysticism.* New York: Springer.

Farrer, D. S. and John Whalen-Bridge. 2012. *Martial Arts as Embodied Knowledge: Asian Traditions in a Transnational World*, edited by D. S. Farrer and John Whalen-Bridge. New York: SUNY Press.

Fletcher, Jonathan. 1997. *Violence and Civilization: An Introduction to the Works of Norbert Elias.* New York: Polity Press.

Fontana, Bernard L. 1997. *Where the Night Is the Day of the Moon.* Tucson: University of Arizona Press.

Foster, George M. 1972. "A Second Look at Limited Good." *Anthropological Quarterly* 45: 57–64.

———. 1965. "Peasant Society and the Image of Limited Good." *American Anthropologist* 67: 293–315.

Foote, Nicola. 2010. "Monteneros and Macheteros: Afro-Ecuadorian and Indigenous Experiences of Military Struggle in Liberal Ecuador, 1895–1930." In *Military Struggle and Identity Formation in Latin America: Race, Nation and Community during the Liberal Period*, edited by Nicola Foote and Renée D. Harder Horst, 85–98. Gainesville, FL: University of Florida Press.

Foucault, Michel. 1988. "Technologies of the Self." In *Technologies of the Self: A Seminar with Michel Foucault*, edited by L. Martin and P. Hutton, 16–49. Amherst: University of Massachusetts.

Gainty, Dennis. 2007. "Martialing the National Body: Structure, Agency and the Dainippon Butokukai in Modern Japan." Ph.D. diss. University of Pennsylvania.

Gallant, Thomas W. 2000. "Honor, Masculinity and Ritual Knife Fighting in Nineteenth Century Greece." *American Historical Review* 105: 359–382.

Gallegos, Rómulo. 1959. "Cantaclaro". In *Obras Completas. Vol. 1.* Madrid: Aguilar.

García, Raúl Sánchez and Dale Spencer. 2013. *Fighting Scholars: Habitus and Ethnographies of Martial Arts and Combat Sports*, edited by Raúl Sánchez García and Dale Spencer. London: Anthem Press.

Getzler, Israel. 2002. *Kronstadt 1917–1921: The Fate of a Soviet Democracy.* Cambridge: Cambridge University Press.

Gilbey, John F, and Robert W. Smith. 1992. *Western Boxing and World Wrestling; Story and Practice.* Berkley: North Atlantic Press.

Gilmore, David D. 1987. "Introduction: The Shame of Dishonor." In *Honor and Shame and the Unity of the Mediterranean*, edited by D. Gilmore. Washington DC: American Anthropological Association.

Gilmore, Robert L. 1964. *Caudillism and Militarism in Venezuela, 1810–1910.* Athens: Ohio University Press.

Goffman, Erving. 1971. *Relations in Public: Microstudies of the Public Order*. New York: Basic Books, Inc. Publishers.

———. 1963. *Behavior in Public Places: Notes on the Social Organization of Gatherings*. London: Free Press of Glencoe.

———. 1956. *The Presentation of Self in Everyday Life*. Garden City: Doubleday.

González, Argimiro. 2004. *El Juego del Garrote: Arte Tradicional Venezolano. El Tocuyo, Venezuela*. El Tocuyo, Venezuela: Consejo Nacional de la Cultura (CONAC).

———. 2003. *Regreso del Palo Chico*. El Tocuyo: Consejo Nacional de la Cultura (CONAC).

———. 2003. *Historia—El Juego del Garrote*. El Tocuyo, Venezuela: Consejo Nacional de la Cultura (CONAC).

Gorn, Elliot. 1985. "Gouge and Bite, Pull Hair and Scratch: The Social Significance of Fighting in the Southern Backcountry." *The American Historical Review* 90: 18–43.

Gramsci, Antonio. 1975. *Letters from Prison*, edited by Lynne Lawner. New York: Harper Colophon Books.

Green, Thomas. 2012. "Sick Hands and Sweet Moves: Aesthetic Dimensions of a Vernacular Martial Art." *Journal of American Folklore* 125: 286–303.

Green, Thomas and Joseph Svinth. 2010. *Martial Arts of the World: An Encyclopedia of History and Innovation*. 2 volumes, edited by Thomas Green and Joseph R. Svinth, Santa Barbara: ABC-CLIO, LLC.

———. 2003. *Martial Arts in the Modern World*. eds. Thomas A. Green and Joseph R. Svinth, Westport, CT: Praeger.

Grub, W. B. 1904. *Among the Indians of the Paraguayan Chaco: A Story of Missionary Work in South America*. London: Charles Murray & Co.

Guss, David M. 2000. *The Festive State: Race, Ethnicity and Nationalism as Cultural Performance*. Berkley: University of California Press.

Haas, Jonathan. 1990. "Warfare and the Evolution of Tribal Politics in the Prehistoric Southwest." In *The Anthropology of War*, edited by J. Haas, 171–189. Cambridge: Cambridge University Press.

Harvey, David. 1990. *The Condition of Post Modernity*. Oxford: Blackwell.

Hellinger, Daniel. 1991. *Venezuela: A Tarnished Democracy*. Boulder, CO: Westview Press.

Heredia, A. Cipriano. 1974. *El Año 29: Recuento de la Lucha Armada*. Caracas: Avilarte.

Hernandez, Cacoy "Boy." 1985. *Balisong: Iron Butterfly*. Tiptree, UK: Anchor Brendon.

Herrera, Jesús María. 2003. *El Negro Miguel y la primera revolución venezolana. La cultura del poder y el poder de la cultura*. Caracas: Vadell Hermanos.

Herzfeld, Michael. 2009. "The Performance of Secrecy: Domesticity and Privacy in Public Spaces." *Semiotica* 1: 135–162.

———. 2005. *Cultural Intimacy: Social Poetics in the Nation-State*. 2nd edition. New York: Routledge.

———. 1985. *Poetics of Manhood: Contest and Identity in a Cretan Mountain Village*. Princeton: Princeton University Press.

Hicks, David. 2006. "Blood, Violence, and Gender Alignment: Cockfighting and Kick Fighting in East Timor." *Cambridge Anthropology* 26: 1–20.

Huggins, Mike. 2001. "The Regular Re-Invention of Sporting Tradition and Identity of Cumberland and Westmoreland Wrestling. 1800–2001." *The Sports Historian* 21: 35–55.

Hurley, John. 2007. *Shillelagh: The Irish Fighting Stick*. Pipersville, PA: Carvat Press.

Ikegami, Eiko. 1995. *The Taming of the Samurai: Honorific Individualism and the Making of Modern Japan*. Cambridge: Harvard University Press.

Ingold, Thomas. 2000. *The Perception of the Environment: Essays in Livelihood, Dwelling and Skill*. London: Routledge.

Instituto del Patrimonio Cultural (IPC). 2010. Poder cultural poder popular, aquí se están aplicando las3R. Accessed January 21, 2010. http://www.ipc.gob.ve.

Jingoes, Stimela Jason. 1975. *A Chief Is a Chief by the People: The Autobiography of Stimela Jason Jingoes*, translated by J. Perry and C. Perry. London: Oxford University Press.

Johnson, Paul Christopher. 2002. *Secrets, Gossip and Gods*. Oxford: Oxford University Press.

Jones, David E. 2002. *Combat Ritual and Performance: Anthropology of the Martial Arts*, edited by David E. Jones. Westport, CT: Praeger.

Judkins, Benajimin, N. and Jon Nielson. 2015. *The Creation of Wing Chun: A Social History of the Southern Chinese Martial Arts*. Albany: State University of New York Press.

Khozali, Malim K. 2010. *Memories of Paramaribo*. Kuala Lampur: Institut Terjemahan Negara, Malaysia Berhad.

Kritz, Mary M. 1975. "The Impact of International Migration on Venezuelan Demographic and Social Structure." *The International Migration Review* 9: 513–543.

Línarez. Pedro Pablo. 2004. *La Lucha Armada En Los Montanas De Lara*. El Tocuyo: Editorial Gayon Colección.

———. 2003. *Sones de Negro, La religión de los afrodescendientes en el valle de El Tocuyo Curarigua y el culto a San Antonio*, edited by Gayón. Barquisimeto: Fundación Museo de las Riberas del Tocuyo.

———. 1990. *Sones de Negroes*. Caracas: Universidad Central de Venezuela.

Liscano, Juan. 1951. *Folklore del Estado Lara: "El Tamunangue"*. Caracas: Tópicos Shell.

Lombardy, John V. 1982. *Venezuela: The Search for Order/the Dream for Progress*. New York: Oxford University Press.

López, José Eliseo. 1999. *La Emigracíon Desde La España Peninsular a Venezuela: En Los siglos xvi, xvii, xviii Tomo I, II*. Caracas: Impresores Unidos.

Lopez, Rafael Mariá Rodrigues. 1945. *La Leyenda de Pelón Gil*. Caracas: Impresores Unidos.

McDonald, Ian. 2007. "Bodily Practice, Performance Art, Competitive Sport: A Critique of Kalarippayattu, the Martial Art of Kerala." *Contributions to Indian Sociology* 41:143–168.

Mahmoud, Saba. 2005. *The Politics of Piety: The Islamic Revival and the Feminist Subject*. New Jersey: Princeton University Press.

Marchand, Trevor H. J. 2010. "Making Knowledge: Explorations of the Indissoluble Relation between Minds Bodies and Environments." *Journal of the Royal Anthropological Institute* 16: 1–s21.

———. 2001. *Minaret Building and Apprenticeship in Yemen*. Surrey: Curzon.

Markoff, John. 2005. "Civilization and Barbarism: Cattle Frontiers in Latin America." In *States of Violence*, edited by F. Coronil and J. Skurski, 33–73. Ann Arbor: University of Michigan Press.

Marsland, William D., and Amy L. Marsland. 1954. *Venezuela through Its History*. New York: Thomas Y. Crowell Company.

Martínez, Iveris Luz. 2002. "Danzas Nacionalistas: The Representation of History through Folkloric Dance in Venezuela." *Critique of Anthropology* 22: 257–282.

Matta, Roberto. 1991. *Carnivals, Rouges and Heroes: An Interpretation of the Brazilian Dilemma*. Notre Dame: University of Notre Dame Press.

Mauss, Marcel. 1979. *Sociology and Psychology: Essays*, translated by B. Brewster. London: Routledge and Kegan Paul.

McNeill, William H. 1995. *Keeping Together in Time: Dance and Drill in Human History*. Cambridge: Cambridge University Press.

Mead, George Herbert. 1967. *Mind, Self and Society*. Chicago: Chicago University Press.

Merleau-Ponty, Maurice. 1973. *Adventures in the Dialectic*. Evanston, IL: Northwestern University Press.

———. 1962. *The Phenomenology of Perception*. London: RKP.

Miller, Daniel. 2005. *Materiality*. Durham, NC: North Carolina University Press.

Morris, Andrew D. 2004. "From Martial Arts to National Skills: The Construction of a Modern Indigenous Physical Culture, 1912–1937." In *Marrow of a Nation: A History of Sport and Physical Culture in Republican China*, edited by Andrew D. Morris, 185–229, Berkeley: University of California Press.

Naím, Moisés. 2001. "The Real Story Behind Venezuela's Woes." *Journal of Democracy* 12: 17–31.

Oliveira, Josivaldo Pires de. 2005. *No Tempo Dos Valentes: Os Capoeiras na Cidade da Bahia*. Salvador: Quarteto.

Osornio, Mario A. López. 1995. *Esgrima Criolla*. Buenos Aires: Ediciones Nuevo Siglo.

Ozyürek Esra. 2004. "Wedded to the Republic: Public Intellectuals and Intimacy-Oriented Publics in Turkey." In *Off Stage/On Display: Intimacy and Ethnography in the Age of Public Culture*, edited by Andrew Shryock, 101–130. Stanford: Stanford University Press.

Paine, Robert. 1989. "High-Wire Culture: Comparing Two Agonistic Systems of Self-Esteem." *Man* 24: 657–672.

Parsons, James J. 1983. "The Migration of the Canary Islanders; An Unbroken Current Since Columbus." *The Americas* 39: 447–448.

Perozo, A., and B. Pérez. 2001. "La cara oculta de la pluriculturalidad: el caso de los Afrovenezolanos". *Memorias II Encuentro para la promoción y difusión del Patrimonio folklórico de países andinos. Influencias africanas en las culturas tradicionales*. 111–122. Santa Ana de Coro.

Perry, Mary Elizabeth. 1980. *Crime and Society in Early Modern Seville*. Dartmouth, NH: University of New Hampshire Press.

Pfister, Gertru. 2003. "Cultural Confrontation: German *Turnen*, Swedish Gymnastics and English Sport—European Diversity in Physical Activities from a Historical Perspective." *Sport in Society* 6: 61–91.

Piccato, Pablo. 2001. *City of Suspects: Crime and Violence in Mexico City, 1901–1930*. Durham: Duke University Press.

Piot, Charles D. 1993. "Secrecy, Ambiguity and the Everyday in Kabré Culture." *American Anthropologist* 95(2): 353–370.

Pitt-Rivers, Julian. 1977. *The Fate of the Shechem or the Politics of Sex: Essays in the Anthropology of the Mediterranean*. London: Cambridge University Press.

———. 1965. "Honor and Social Status". In *Honor and Shame: The Values of Mediterranean Society*, edited by J. G. Peristiany, 21–77. London: Weidenfeld & Nicolson.

Querales, Ramón. 1997. *Resistencia Indígena en Barquisimeto Contra la Ocupación Española (1530–1572)*. Barquisimeto: Centro de Historia Larense.

Rasmussen, Wayne D. 1947. "Agricultural Colonization and Immigration in Venezuela 1810–1860." *Agricultural History* 21: 155–162.

Restall, Matthews. 2000. "Black Conquistadors: Armed Africans in Early Spanish America." *The Americas* 57: 171–205.

Rodríguez, F. A., and Ossorio Cárdenas. 1987. *Tradiciones Canarias Juego del Palo, Peleas de Gallo*, edited by F. A. Rodríguez and Ossorio Cárdenas. Las Palmas: Gran Canaria.

Rojas Rodríguez, Pedro. 2009. "80 Años de la Gabaldonada. Communicaion Popular para la Construcción del Socialismo del Siglo XXI." Aporrea.org. Accessed on 21 November 2014. http://www.aporrea.org/actualidad/a76934.html.

Rojas, Reinaldo. 2002. *De Variquecmeto a Barquisimeto*. Barquisimeto: Italgrafica.

———. 1996. *La Economía de Lara en Cinco Siglos*. Barquisimeto: Asociación Pro-Venezuela. Seccional Lara. Asemblea Del Estado Lara.

Rojas, González Sorraya. 2010. *San José de Guaribe una historia que contar*. San José de Guaribe. Publisher unknown

Rojas, Tibaire R. 2010. *Hacia la Contextualización de la Bandola Cordillerana y sus especies musicales*. Ateneo de Guaribe. Centro de Investigación "Guaribe de los Palenques." San José de Guaribe–Edo. Guárico.

Rourke, Thomas. 1969. *Gómez: Tyrant of the Andes*. New York: Greeenwood Press.

Ruette, Krisna. 2011. "The Left-Turn of Multiculturalism: Indigenous and Afrodescendant Social Movements in Northwestern Venezuela." Ph.D. Diss., The University of Arizona.

Ryan, Michael J. 2015. "'Does Anybody Here Want to Fight' . . . 'No, Not Really, but if You Care to Take a Swing at Me . . .': The Cultivation of a Warrior's Habitus in a

Venezuelan Combative Art." *Ido Movement for Culture. Journal of Martial Arts Anthropology* 15: 1–7.

———. 2011. "Pueblo Street-Fighting to National Martial Art: The Politics of Tradition and the Nationalization of a Venezuelan Civilian Combative Practice." *American Ethnologist* 39: 531–547.

———. 2011. "I Did Not Return a Master, but Well Cudgeled Was I: The Transmission of Embodied Knowledge in Venezuelan Stick and Machete Fighting." *Journal of Latin American and Caribbean Anthropology* 16: 1–24.

———. 2011. "Garrote de Lara: The Development of a Creole Armed Combat from the Pueblos of Venezuela." *The Latin Americanist* 55: 67–92.

Salas Herrea Jesús, María. 2005. "Ethnicity and Revolution: The Political Economy of Racism in Venezuela." *Latin American Perspectives* 32: 32–92.

Sanoja, Eduardo. 1996. *Juego de Palos o Juego de Garrote: Guía Bibliohermografica para sus Estudió.* Caracas: Miguel Ángel García y Hijo.

———. 1984. *Juego de Garrote Larense: El Métodos Venezolano Defensa Personal.* Caracas: Miguel Ángel García e Hijo.

Santos, Martha S. 2007. "On The Importance of Being Honorable: masculinity, Survival, and Conflict in the Backlands of Northeast Brazil, Ceará, and 1840s–1890*." *The Americas* 64: 35–57.

Sartre, Jean-Paul. 1960. *Anti-Semite and Jew*, translated by G. J. Becker. New York: Grove Press.

Service, Elman. 1975. *Origins of the State and Civilization: The Process of Cultural Evolution.* New York.

Sharar, Meir. 2008. *The Shaolin Monastery: History, Religion and the Chinese Martial Arts.* Honolulu: University of Hawai'i Press.

Shoemaker, Robert. 2001. "Male Honour and the Decline of Public Violence in Eighteenth-Century London." *Social History* 26: 190–208.

Shryock, Andrew. 2004. *Off Stage/On Display: Intimacy and Ethnography in the Age of Public Culture*, edited by Andrew Shyrock. Stanford: Stanford University Press.

Skedsmo Arlid, Kwong Danhier, and Hoth Gor Luak. 2003. "The Changing Meaning of Small Arms in Nuer Society." *African Security Review* 12: 57–67.

Silva, Gerardo P. 1993. *De Yacambú a Sanare.* Sanare (Edo. Lara).

Simmel, George. 1906. "The Sociology of Secrecy and Secret Societies." *The American Journal of Sociology* 11: 441–498.

Spencer, Dale. 2012. *Ultimate Fighting and Embodiment: Violence, Gender and Mixed Martial Arts.* New York: Routledge.

Spierenberg, Peter. 1998. *Men and Violence: Gender, Honor, and Rituals in Modern Europe and America*, edited by Peter Spierenberg. Athens: Ohio State University Press.

Stevens, John. 1984. *The Sword of No-Sword: The Life of Master Warrior Yamoka Tesshu.* Boston: Shambhala.

Tapía, José Leon. 2010. *El Tigre de Guaitó.* Caracas: Ediciones Centauro.

Tardieu, Jean–Pierre. 2013. *Resistencia de los Negros en la Venezuela Colonial.* Madrid: Iberoamericana

Thomas, Hugh. 2005. *Rivers of Gold: The Rise of the Spanish Empire from Columbus to Magellan.* New York: Random House.

Thompson, Robert F. 1992. "Forward." In *Ring of Liberation: Deceptive Discourse in Brazilian Capoeira.* xi–xiv. Chicago: University of Chicago Press.

Tilley, Charles. 2006. "Objectification." In *Handbook of Material Culture*, edited by C. Tilley, W. Keane, S. Küchler, M. Rowlands, P. Spyer, 60–74. London: SAGE.

Todd, Fredrick F. 1938. "The Knife and Club in Trench Warfare 1914–1918." *The Journal of American Military History Foundation* 2: 139–153.

Turney-High, Harry H. 1971. *Primitive War: Its Practice and Concepts.* Colombia: University of South Carolina Press.

Urban, Hugh B. 1997. The Torment of Secrecy: Ethical and Epistemological Problems in the Study of Esoteric Traditions. *History of Religions* 37(3): 209–240.

Uzcátegui, Silva Rafael Domingo. 1959. *Barquisimeto: Historia Privada, Alma y Fisonomía del Barquisimeto de Ayer*. Caracas.

————. 1941. *Enciclopédia Larense . Tomo II*. España: Escuela Prof. "Sagrado Corazón de Jesús."

Venezuelan Violence Observatory. Accessed 23 May, 2016. http://observatoriodeviolencia.org.ve/.

Wagley, Charles. 1977. *Welcome of Tears the Tapirapé Indians of Central Brasil*. Oxford: Oxford University Press.

Wacquant, Löic J. 2013. *"Homines In Extremis*: What Fighting Scholars Teach Us about Habitus*."* In *Fighting Scholars: Habitus and Ethnographies of Martial Arts and Combat Sports*, edited by S. Raúl Sánchez García and Dale Spencer, 193–200. London: Anthem Press.

————. 2004. *Body and Soul: Notebooks of an Apprentice Boxer*. New York: Oxford University Press.

————. 1995. "The Pugilistic Point of View: How Boxers Think and Feel about Their Trade." *Theory and Society* 24: 489–535.

Warnier Jean-Pierre. 2011. "Body/Material Culture and the Fighters Subjectivity." *Journal of Material Culture* 16: 359–375.

————. 2007. *The Pot-King: The Body and Technologies of Power*. Leiden, Netherlands: Brill.

Wibbelsman, Michelle. 2009. *Ritual Encounters: Otavalan Modern and Mythic Community*. Urbana: University of Illinois Press.

Wilson, Ian Douglas. 2002. "The Politics of Inner Power: The Practice of Pencak Silat in West Java." Ph.D. diss. Murdoch University.

Wilson, Lee. 2015. *Martial Arts and the Body Politic in Indonesia*. Leiden, Netherlands: Brill.

————. 2009. "Jurus, Jazz Riffs and the Constitution of a National Martial Art in Indonesia." *Body & Society* 5: 93–119.

Wolf, Daniel R. 2000. *The Rebels: A Brotherhood of Outlaw Bikers*. Toronto: University of Toronto Press.

Wolf, Eric, and Edward C. Hansen. 1967. "Caudillo Politics: A Structural Analysis." *Comparative Studies in Society and History* 9: 168–179.

Wolf, Tony. 2002. "Singlestick Fencing: 1787–1923." *The Journal of Manly Arts*. Accessed 06 February 2007. http://ejmas.com/jmanly/jmanlyframe.html.

Wright, Winthrop R. 1990. *Cafe con Leche: Race, Class and National Image in Venezuela*. Austin: University of Texas Press.

Yarrington, Doug. 1997. *A Coffee Frontier: Land, Society and Politics in Duaca, Venezuela, 1830–1936*. Pittsburgh, PA: University of Pennsylvania Press.

Yilkangas, Heikki. 2001. *Five Centuries of Violence: In Finland and the Baltic Area*. Columbus: Ohio State University Press.

Zarilli, Phillip B. 1998. *When the Body Becomes All Eyes: Paradigms, Discourses, and Practices of Power in Keralapayattu, A South Indian Martial Art*. Delhi: Oxford University Press.

Zorn, Elayne. 2002. "Dangerous Encounters: Ritual Battles in Andean Bolivia." In *Combat Ritual and Performance: Anthropology of the Martial Arts*, edited by David E. Jones, 119–152. Westport, CT: Praeger.

Index

About the Author

Michael J. Ryan is a Research Associate with the Department of Anthropology at Binghamton University. His interest is in embodiment, modernity and violence, martial studies, Venezuela, and the Amazon. The author has pursued the formal study of martial art traditions since 1977. During this time, he has undergone long-term formal studies in studying Korean, Chinese, Brazilian, Filipino, and Indonesian systems. In furtherance of his studies, he continues to study and train in traditional combative systems in Venezuela and Italy.